The Reverend Richard Coles is the presenter of *Saturday Live* on BBC Radio 4. He is also the only vicar in Britain to have had a number 1 hit single. He read Theology at King's College London, and after ordination worked as a curate in Lincolnshire and subsequently at St Paul's, Knightsbridge, in London. He is also the author of *Lives of the Improbable Saints* and *Fathomless Riches*, the bestselling first volume of his memoirs.

@RevRichardColes   www.richardcoles.com

BRINGING IN THE SHEAVES

Wheat and Chaff From My Years as a Priest

RICHARD COLES

WEIDENFELD & NICOLSON

A W&N Paperback
First published in Great Britain in 2016
by Weidenfeld & Nicolson
This paperback edition published in 2017
by Weidenfeld & Nicolson,
an imprint of Orion Books Ltd

5 7 9 10 8 6

A CIP catalogue record for this book
is available from the British Library.

ISBN 978 1474 60086 6

Typeset by Input Data Services Ltd, Somerset
Printed and bound in Great Britain by Clays Ltd, Elcograf S.p.A.

Weidenfeld & Nicolson

The Orion Publishing Group Ltd
Carmelite House
50 Victoria Embankment
London EC4Y 0DZ

An Hachette UK Company

www.orionbooks.co.uk

IM

Nigel Coles

1932–2016

Contents

Acknowledgements

I would like to thank my publisher Alan Samson and everyone at Weidenfeld & Nicolson, my agent Robert Caskie and everyone at PFD, and especially my editor Gillian Stern for her skilful husbandry.

Thanks too to my parishioners in Finedon.

And thanks always to David.

Sowing in the sunshine, sowing in the shadows,
Fearing neither clouds nor winter's chilling breeze,
By and by the harvest and the labour ended,
We shall come rejoicing, bringing in the sheaves.

Knowles Shaw, 1874

FOREWORD

I'm sitting at my desk in my study looking at the hypericum crowding in at the window. Rose of Sharon, as it is known, an indefatigable bloomer, twice a year, but not now in the early spring. I think of the passage from Song of Songs in which the bride is compared with its bloom. It cannot be what we call Rose of Sharon, I think, or the lover would be quite the wrong colour and cast with a sickly hue, so I decide to Google it. Suddenly there's a commotion and I see a long-tailed tit has arrived, perching right in front of me. Perhaps the pane of glass between us makes me invisible, but then the phone rings and I move and he flies away. Someone has called to tell me a parishioner, long unwell, is dying and would I go to see him.

I take the necessary kit – a stole and an oil stock and a prayer book – and when I get there he's with a nurse. I ask how he is and she says comfortable, but on a morphine driver which delivers a regular dose to anaesthetise him from the pain, which I can see is taking its toll, and he is in and out of lucidity. She leaves, and I talk to him but I am not sure if he understands much or anything of what I say. I anoint him with holy oil and he seems to respond to that, to stir a little, so I sit beside him and read to him from the Psalms, which I know he prefers in the Book of Common Prayer version. 'I will lift up mine eyes unto the hills from whence cometh my help.' After a while he seems to wake almost, and taking this as encouragement I carry on through the Songs of Ascents, as they are known, until we reach the great Psalm 130, De Profundis: 'Out of the deep have I called unto thee, O Lord; Lord, hear my voice.' He stirs again and tries, I think, to say something, so I pull my chair closer. He looks at me and with a great effort says, 'Shut up, you stupid twat.'

PETERTIDE

In my church, St Mary the Virgin, Finedon, Northamptonshire, I look towards the altar and to our great east window. It is a Victorian effort to recreate the glory of Medieval stained glass, smashed up by the reformers in the seventeenth century, reimagined by the High Church revival two hundred years later. It shows the Ascension – I don't know why, in a church dedicated to the Virgin Mary and which celebrates its patronal festival on the Feast of the Holy Cross – that episode when after the Resurrection Jesus goes with his disciples (eleven, not twelve, since the departure of Judas) to Bethany and there he ascends to heaven. The figure of Jesus rising appears in the centre, hand raised in a posture of blessing, while beneath his feet the disciples watch as he passes through the ranks of angels and archangels, past John the Baptist and the Old Testament priest Aaron, swinging his smoky censer, Joshua the warrior with spear and shield, and David the king playing his harp, past Moses with the Ten Commandments, and Elijah the prophet, towards the Godhead. The latter is clumsily indicated by a cross from whose arms hang the Greek letters alpha and omega, the beginning and the end, and just beneath it, squashed in its individual pane, is the Holy Spirit in the form of a dove – the only things descending in this window of ascents.

'I will not leave you alone,' Jesus says, but you cannot help wondering if the disciples are entirely reassured by this. Peter stands directly beneath him, identifiable by the two keys he holds, to unlock the doors to salvation or damnation. He looks tense, straining, unable to follow; Peter, appointed by Jesus, not without irony, as the rock on which he will build the Church; Peter, the pattern of all those called to Christ's ministry; Peter, who is recalled too in a window in the south wall of the chancel – installed in memory of one of my predecessors, Canon Paul, who was vicar for sixty-one years, following his father, between them notching up one hundred and one years in the office I now occupy. 'Feed my sheep' runs the text beneath a pane showing a priest baptising a baby in the font which stands by the south door of the church, in which I too baptise babies nearly a thousand years after a nameless predecessor did the same. Feed my sheep, says Jesus to Peter and to all who have followed him as pastors and shepherds.

Peter, in whose season of Petertide ordinations by tradition take place. For the newly ordained, taking our first steps – and for the communities we serve, no less unsure – it is the honeymoon. Ordination is for most of us a two-fold process: first deacon, then priest.

When I was made a deacon I was given the title 'the Reverend', put in a dog collar, and set to work in a parish under the supervision of my training incumbent, Fr Robin Whitehead, Team Rector of St Botolph, Boston, the biggest parish church in England, depending on how you measure it. Training incumbents are charged with ensuring their curates are fit for purpose, both in general terms – settling into the day-to-day life of a parish – and in the specifics of the duties of deacons and priests.

My first public appearance was at the early Holy Communion on Sunday; unable to fly solo yet, but assisting the priest in the deacon's traditional role. I stood on his right at the altar and sat on his right to the side, and had small but precisely defined things to do: elevate the chalice, announce the exchange of a sign of peace, and at the end pronounce the dismissal. The deacon's most important job in the Communion service is to read the Gospel, the passage from the stories of Christ's life recorded in the accounts we know as Matthew's, Mark's, Luke's and John's. This is done formally, with ceremony, with processions and puffs of incense and singing.

Presented thus, the familiar words sound fresh again; sometimes it is like hearing them for the first time, a drama enacted in speech at the centre of the gathered community.

As I was reading there was an unaccustomed shout at the back of the aisles, slightly strangled with embarrassment, for shouting is not much done in church. Someone had snatched a handbag and made a dash for the north door, but had been caught by a sidesman and wrestled to the ground. The service must go on and the priest signalled for me to finish the Gospel and ascend the pulpit to preach. Let us not shirk our duty to the poor and the marginalised, I intoned, as the cops came and took away the poor marginalised person who nicked the handbag and handed him over to the jailer.

I went to the police station after the service and asked if I could see the person they arrested, to ask if he was OK, but he didn't want to see me.

In the summer of 1374 one of the worst outbreaks of dancing mania of the Middle Ages took place. Known also as St Vitus's Dance or St John's Dance, it is a very peculiar condition which produces in those it afflicts an irresistible impulse to dance. This particular outbreak began in Aachen, Germany, and soon spread to neighbouring villages and towns. People appeared in the streets, dancing maniacally, jumping, and hopping, screaming, laughing and crying. They danced without ceasing, hyperventilating, falling into fits, and hallucinating, some even suffering broken ribs before eventually dropping down dead of exhaustion. Others appeared dressed in garlands of flowers, or undressed, some made obscene gestures, others coupled in the street. The mania spread to Cologne, to Metz, Strasbourg, to Flanders and Utrecht, where it was observed some participants evidenced a violent dislike of pointy shoes and a dread of the colour red. The authorities responded by exorcising the afflicted, by playing soothing music to calm them down, and by praying to St Vitus, whose intercession was believed to be particularly efficacious in these cases. Nevertheless, it spread to Luxembourg and even as far as Italy before abating; but it re-curred in 1375, 1381, 1418 and 1428, when a group of normally rather staid Swiss ladies danced themselves to death in Zurich. There are a number of explanations, including mass hallucinations due to ergot poisoning, 'shared stress' caused by plagues and floods, mis-understood quasi-religious devotion, or just playing the giddy goat. In my view, based on experience, aspects of it recurred in the rave culture of the eighties and nineties, including the hallucinatory ef-fects of psychoactive agents, copycat cultural contagion, and chill tracks played at going-home time.

I was licensed and installed as Vicar of Finedon just in time for Holy Week 2011. Canon Beaumont, my predecessor but one, was there, walking around courteously, trying not to look like the incumbent (I couldn't help but notice). He was vicar for twenty-six years; a mere flash in the pan compared with the Pauls. Tradition has it that the number of rings the new incumbent gives on the bell, signifying arrival, will be the number of years served. I carefully pulled sixteen times, which should take me to retirement.

My friend Martin Henry, who played an important part in me getting this far, had come down from Scotland for the service. Afterwards, he held court at the back of church, surrounded by an admiring crowd of my new parishioners. 'Does he drink?' they asked him, meaning me. 'Yes, he does,' he replied, 'whisky – lots of it.'

My father sat in his wheelchair, slumped in it, dropping his ser-vice paper, which was courteously returned to him by the members of the Parochial Church Council sitting at the front. The church was full of friends of mine who hadn't seen him in years and if they were taken aback at his condition they didn't show it; and, perhaps worse, by former employees of his who used to work for Coles Boot. My partner David, also a priest, was by my side, with his parents, Irene and Vinny, and his Auntie Jean in the pews too – and there was a meeting of in-laws at the vicarage which I missed. It is not unusual for priests to be absent from events at which presence is normally required because of parish responsibilities.

These days, I am absent from the parish on Saturday mornings, for I belong to the BBC that day. I am the fifty-ninth Vicar of Finedon – priest-in-charge, actually – but the parish's first half-time incumbent, in so far as a vicar can be said to be half-time. That half-time, half-stipend status enables me to pursue my other career as a broadcaster with more freedom than when I was working full-time as a priest at Boston and then in London.

Since 2011, I've been co-presenting *Saturday Live* on Radio Four. On Friday nights I stay in a hotel round the corner from New Broadcasting House, leaving at half past six for work – 'Good morning, Mr Reverend.' When I arrive, I go straight to the canteen in the basement. It is an in-between time, the night shift not quite gone, the day shift not quite on, and some people are having their supper while others have breakfast. I like routine on a programme day, an unconscious gesture to the gods, I guess. If I go in the front entrance I have to touch the toe of Eric Gill's *The Sower* by the lifts, a slightly less scandalous sculpture than Prospero and Ariel over the doors. In the canteen, I always have the same thing: a cappuccino out of the machine, which is not a cappuccino, and a croissant with butter and honey. Sometimes it is Joanna on the tills, who always greets me in the name of Jesus, and we discuss matters like the salvation of souls and the indelible stain of Adam's sin, which would be taxing at my peak, but this early rather defeats me. In the office, seven floors above, we sign off the scripts, gossip, and then at half past eight Aasmah Mir, my co-presenter, and I go to the *Today* studio on the third floor. They are approaching the end of their programme and there is usually a demob-happy atmosphere, which suits the tone of our brief visit to trail what's coming up in half an hour. Care must be taken not to sound too breezy if the news is especially bad that day, or if there is a big interview following. Several times I have alerted listeners to a lady from a bat protection league, or a man dressed up as Henry VIII, or a soap star's live confessions, while the Chancellor of the Exchequer, sitting next to me, pores over a page of scribbled calculations.

Towards the end of my first year in orders, I and my peers, also completing their first year as a deacon, were invited back to our theological college at Mirfield in Yorkshire for Deacons' Week, a seven-day rehearsal for priesthood, the ontological alteration that lay ahead for us. Not all of us; for Luke in Africa, with whom we had trained, such a trip was not possible, stuck in Zimbabwe with a currency worth less than confetti, and under a madman's rule. Nevertheless, it was a reunion, and perhaps we were apprehensive about that, for our experience of college had been so mixed. It was an odd feeling to return to a place which once had such a claim on you, but now, you realised, had a claim on others too, especially those currently resident, who looked at us old boys with a sort of proprietorial hauteur.

The week began with the community in Upper Church where we joined them for Evensong. A year away and yet it felt like no time at all as we fell in rhythm with the chant and the ultra-soft, ultra-slow delivery that is the house style. Fr Peter, the Precentor, responsible for worship, always said that praying the monastic liturgy is like getting the bus. It goes round and round and we step on and step off; another way of saying what T. S. Eliot said in *Four Quartets*.

There was some novelty, a few unfamiliar faces in the grey scapular (a sort of big bib worn over a cassock); brethren from South Africa, returned to the mother house after the closure of the house there, looking a little at odds after decades in Sophiatown where they'd played such a prominent part in the fight against apartheid. There was one awful absence, Brother Jonathan, that most permanent of people, whose impermanence came as a surprise to everyone; I saw another monk get teary talking about him, and that doesn't often happen between people who've lived in a community for forty years. After supper in college we all went to the pub and had a jolly evening. We got back after midnight and sat up telling horror stories, of a psychopathic training incumbent, of wheels coming off, of fear and loathing and odium theologicum.

A day of glorious weather dawned, and I got up early with it and went to Lower Church half an hour before Matins and sat, uncomposed, in front of the Blessed Sacrament, adjusting I suppose to a life lived around it. Breakfast – merciful austerity and in silence – was followed by a workshop with a professional storyteller who gave us the techniques of his craft to get the gospel across. It wasn't the kind of thing we boys went for, and for the rest of the week we were mimicking him (in the beginning . . . was the WORD . . . and the WORD . . . was with . . . GOD), but something happened, something opened, because we began to talk properly to one another, to have the conversation we all needed to have but hadn't, because only a group who'd been through what we'd been through together could talk in that way. I realised there was a security in continuing a relationship with a group of people you didn't choose to be with, with whom you disagreed, and who have seen your best and your worst, yet who choose to come back to one another. It was as if the friendships too difficult to sustain when we were there could at last flourish. And unfinished business could be finally addressed.

A liturgist on the staff at Mirfield gave us a session on Eucharistic presidency, which sounds like a generous model of political leadership but really means how to say Mass. We were talked through it, although we knew it intimately, and then did a dummy run, and I found I had to stop. It was unnerving to suddenly find yourself at the centre of the altar, knowing that you had to make it happen. I'd watched other people doing it countless times, I'd stood beside people doing it countless times, but I discovered it was very different when you did it yourself. It's as if one moment you're sitting at the back of an aircraft, then a stewardess runs out of the cockpit saying, 'The captain's passed out, can anyone fly a plane?' Having admitted that I once read a book on the subject, I'd been thrust into the pilot's seat, where I found myself wrestling with the controls in complete panic.

During that Deacons' Week, I sought out one of my peers, someone I liked but with whom friendship had become impossible in the close and febrile world of the cloister. He sought me out too and we arrived at the same thought simultaneously: we didn't want our relationship to be defined by the shared problem of having lived and worked together in college.

There was goodwill all round, and as a group we resolved to make it a regular event and form a cell. The Cell of St Jude, co-patron of the college, was proposed.

We never met again.

After Boston, I went to be curate at St Paul's, Knightsbridge, no longer formally in training but not yet in charge. One Petertide during my time there I attended the ordination of priests at an equally smart neighbouring parish. Most of the church had actually burned down a few years before – oh, cleansing fire – and had been rebuilt to the then vicar's spec, which meant that behind its severe classical façade, light and space opened up with a fanfare from its lovely new organ. And behind that there was accommodation, including a duplex flat for the curate, which made my mean basement on the other side of Belgrave Square seem all the meaner.

The Bishop of London, the last grandee, presided. His presence, his personality, his very voice, seemed barely contained within the comprehensive splendour of St Paul's Cathedral, so to see him at work in some of the less noble spaces in his diocese was like coming across Kiri Te Kanawa in Poundstretcher. One of the deacons being priested was serving in one of the least formal evangelical churches around and rejoiced in the name Gaz, not as a nickname but as the only one he wished to be known by. The Bishop obliged, and if he spoke through gritted teeth it was hard to tell. 'Confirm thy servant . . . Gaz . . . in the office and duty of a priest,' he beseeched, and the Holy Spirit, unconcerned by such things, obliged – or I hope it did.

*

Discussing the diocesan selection procedures with a potential, very promising, candidate, I asked him what he thought were the three most important things in the process of discernment. 'Vocation, vocation, vocation,' he replied. Recommended.

Usually a priest is ordained after a year spent serving in the parish as a deacon. My second ordination took place in a bumper year for Lincoln Diocese, which meant there was not enough room in the old Bishop's Palace for all the ordinands to stay for the three-day retreat preceding it. With my contemporary Patrick Morrow, with whom I was ordained deacon at Boston Stump, I was farmed out to the Cantilupe Chantry in the Close, medieval home of the Cathedral Precentor and his adorable dog. After Compline in Bishop King's medieval chapel and the Great Silence that followed, Patrick and I crept away. The rival claims of society and solitude contended, and society on this occasion prevailed; we sat up with the Precentor's dinner guests: the chairman of the Cathedral Council, a former commander in the Parachute Regiment, and a dowager countess, who was splendidly convivial and came over like Bette Davis doing a Lady Grantham.

I had told the Precentor that I liked to rise at six and get to church before the rush to say my prayers – pious face – but this did not happen on the morning of my ordination. I crawled out of bed at eight and found the Precentor already downstairs, raising an eyebrow at my late arrival. I said a miserere as a penance in the old Bishop's Chapel, but there was more penance to come for it was a hot summer's day, the hottest of the year, which had I been in a T-shirt and shorts I would have enjoyed, but it is the curse of those ordained at Petertide to endure July temperatures wearing several layers.

To preside at the Eucharist, in the traditional form, the priest wears a vest (always a vest or T-shirt lest sweat-marks cause scandal); a shirt with a linen dog collar fastened with studs; a cassock, in black worsted; an amice, which is a linen cloth tied round the shoulders; an alb, a head-to-toe white robe of cotton; a stole like a long scarf round the neck; a maniple, a type of short scarf worn tied round the right forearm; and a chasuble, a thick, heavy-lined poncho garment, with braid and orphreys and embroidery over all. There are ways of lightening this load, though traditionalists like the Precentor wince at the thought; the one I opted for was a cassock-alb, which combines both cassock and alb in a single white garment. My concession to traditional form was to have a bit of decoration at the wrists and at the hem, a rather butcher nod to lace than the wildly lacy albs and cottas (a sort of negligee-style alb used when the priest and other clergy are not at the altar during a Mass) the ultra-traditionalists prefer. I'd washed mine at the precentory and left it on the line to dry, but it was so hot it wrinkled rigidly on the line. I asked the Precentor for an iron, but made such a pathetic job of it that Patrick took over and did the whole thing while the Precentor showed me his feriola, a sort of clerical evening gown, and his musetta, a fur-trimmed cape worn by canons, and other finery from his ecclesiastical wardrobe. Only afterwards did it occur to me that Patrick had done an impeccably diaconal thing on the eve of his priesting by ironing my alb while I played at dressing-up.

The morning of my ordination to the priesthood dawned. After Morning Prayer, Patrick and I went into the garden at the old Bishop's Palace, a lovely terraced garden looking out over the city, and practised our moves for our first Masses, much to the amusement of our peers, who watched from the library window. Kay, the house manager, had found an old Communards CD and, bizarrely, we went through the manual actions, adopting the *orans* position and so forth, to the sound of 'Don't Leave Me This Way'.

Then to the cathedral, and the laying on of hands, the bishops joined by attending priests, so the candidate kneeling there was rather buried in a huddle of strangers and friends, and one rose from it ontologically altered, we'd been told. Braced for bathos, I expected to feel exactly the same as before; but I didn't.

On leaving the cathedral, I called in at the precentory. The Precentor was in the kitchen and when I went in to say hello, he dropped to his knees and said, 'Pray, Father, a blessing.' For a moment I thought he was joking; but of course he wasn't, this was the traditional way in which the newly priested are greeted by the faithful. So I collected myself, mumbled something that I made up, invoked the Holy Spirit upon him, wished him peace, and he kissed the palms of my hands, as custom dictates.

After this, my ordination to the sacred order of priests, we celebrated with a picnic on the lawn of Edward King House, looking across the city to the Waddington airbase, where big jets with what look like giant mushrooms stuck on the fuselage – actually AWACS radar dishes – clustered around the hangars like cattle at their shed.

And then to Boston for my first Mass, my first time presiding at the Eucharist, my first flight as captain. This is traditionally a big do, but it need not be. A friend, ordained in the fifties, told me his first Mass was at seven the morning, with only his training incumbent and his mum in attendance. But these days they are like weddings, with invitations sent out, solemn invitations, issued to a preacher and a deacon and readers, and guests in Sunday best arriving in charabancs. The Mass itself is complicated and preserves particular customs; some I like – the blessing given by the new priest to the faithful, who queue up for it – and some I dislike, like the one in which the priest and his mother lay a posy at the feet of the statue of Our Lady as a sort of bachelorish gesture to the fake wedding contracted between nuns and Jesus when they are admitted to their convents. We did not do that; indeed, I especially asked that my first Mass mark the Feast of St Thomas the Apostle, Doubting Thomas, whom we prevailed upon to bless a new red altar frontal, created by the church's team of embroiderers. In acknowledgement of this we sang to the rather pompous Welsh tune 'Ton-y-Botel', 'Who Is This with Garments Gory?' (red being the colour of vestments and hangings for apostles and martyrs, Thomas doubly qualified). The choir sang a full repertoire of my desert island anthems, we sang my favourite hymns, and Leslie Houlden, who taught me New Testament at King's College London, preached. Before we set off in procession, the clergy all met in the Cotton Chapel and sang the 'Veni Creator Spiritus' – 'Come, Holy Ghost, our souls inspire and lighten with celestial fire' – and then in we went.

The first reader didn't show up for the first reading, I got the greeting wrong, Leslie's sermon was loved by some, disliked by others, and I blessed a long queue of people, from family, to friends, to former BBC colleagues, to new parishioners; only afterwards did I realise it had been wonderful. A priest for ever after the order of Melchizedek ended the day with a chicken tikka at the Masala Zone.

Do you feel any different now you are priested? I was perhaps expecting to answer, No. But it was different, in at least two ways. On my first full day on priestly duty four people unburdened themselves to me; and when I'd presided at the Eucharist, it felt like the day was done.

A friend was completing his deacon's year at a parish not far from Boston, where he was curate, and his first Mass was being celebrated at the spikiest highest church in his diocese. The altar was crowded with relics, the vestments clanking with bullion and jewels, the liturgy as refined as a Japanese tea ceremony. Outside, it was the first day of the new smoking ban. Inside, we were keeping the Feast of St Peter and St Paul and in a typically contra mundum gesture, the incense rose even more thickly than usual. Through its haze I caught sight of a young man, handsome, in the congregation, looking at me with something more than curiosity.

I preached the sermon. 'In a few minutes,' I said, 'you will hold in your hands the body of Jesus Christ, in its wholeness and perfection, and you will break it in half and separate those two halves; and you will look at the space that opens up between them. Uncertain, unstable, uneasy, like the space which separates us, divided in the Church, divided in the world, divided within ourselves; yet that division is in itself a sign of – a hope for – the restoration of wholeness. I have a Romanian icon of Saints Peter and Paul, those early ecclesiastical controversialists, kissing one another in an unlikely embrace – more than unlikely, impossible, save in Christ. The Christ who chose Peter to be his rock and Paul to spread his word and who has chosen you to follow them and to make your own unlikely embraces . . .'

The handsome young man moved across the pew to get into my queue for Communion. Afterwards, as the altar was being cleared by a relay of servers of its relics, he introduced himself as David, a member of the Parochial Church Council. On an impulse, I asked if he had a fag – he did – and in a gesture of courteous hospitality gave me his last one. We stood outside, me in a cassock, smoking on a roastingly hot day, and then he took me to the Tesco Local to buy another pack. Back in church, clerical eyebrows were raised, a comment was passed, but when he said he would like to discuss his vocation with me and asked for my phone number, I gave it to him and headed for home.

He called, a week later, and said he was passing through Boston – like anyone ever just 'passed through' Boston! – and he came to lunch on Sunday. I baked some cod and tomatoes, Greek style, but it didn't really work and we chewed our way through it, making polite conversation. I was reserved, quite properly, but he was so very handsome and very charming, and perhaps a bit flirtatious – but I couldn't go there. We talked all afternoon and then I had to leave for Evensong. He said he would like to come and see me again; I said OK, and offered a Sunday a month or so ahead. He seemed a little disappointed, and we said goodbye and he left. Then, as I was walking to church, a text arrived: *Don't you get it?*

Four years later David and I were living together in Wymond-ham, me in the gap between leaving Knightsbridge and arriving at

Finedon, he in his first post as a training curate at the abbey there. It was his turn now to be ordained to the priesthood, at the cathedral in Norwich, and then to preside at his first Mass at the abbey.

We had people staying and while David was on his pre-ordination retreat I was in charge, which I slightly resented because I was not yet properly in gear with the change in his life. On the way to the retreat, at the local convent, we had a bit of a row. I dropped him off and said hello to the others (and discovered that the nun on duty was called Sister Calamity). I headed for home with a list of jobs to do, leaving David to the ministrations of the retreat leader and his brother and sister ordinands.

Calamity indeed struck the convent. A couple of days later, David called to say that they'd all come down with a terrible virus and were dropping one by one – or rather, running out of chapel and classroom and refectory, the effects so sudden and calamitous. They were not sure if the ordinations would take place, so I cancelled our guests and took the dogs for a long walk down a bridle-way in deep, deep Norfolk, where I came across a farmhouse which looked as though it had not changed in at least two hundred years: red pantile roof, massive central chimney, and an orchard and a barn and a pond. I thought: this is the part of Norfolk I love most; not the glamorous Gold Coast between Hunstanton and Cromer – where we had a cottage when I was boy and where we spent every holiday – where today only the super-rich can afford to live, buying up every fisherman's cottage within a ten-mile radius of Brancaster golf club.

The ordination did go ahead, in spite of the whey faces of ordinands and the restricted diet they were obliged to follow. I was glad we didn't have a houseful after all. When I thought of my own ordination and the knees-up afterwards, it seemed wrong to me that it should have been marked with a celebration in that way, as if being ordained were a personal accomplishment. It's not really that at all. I went to the consecration of a bishop in St Paul's Cathedral and the preacher, an old friend of his, ascended the enormous pulpit in that enormous space and began by saying, 'Well, who would have thought we'd have ended up here?' in a slightly laboured way, as if it were a turn-up for the books that the likes of them should be centre stage and on so grand a stage. It struck exactly the wrong note. The crowding round and laying on of hands by (back then) brother bishops effecting the ontological alteration by apostolical means I still found moving, though whenever I see it now I remember an ordination where one of the newly ordained priests, after the bishop raised his hands from his head, turned to family and friends and did a thumbs up.

Conversation with a stranger in McDonald's. He was playing golf one day and on the fourth hole looked up from the tee and saw the flag on the distant green, so tiny that he said he felt in that moment 'overwhelmed by the whole tragedy of human existence' and was unable to lift his club. Unable even to walk, he was carried back to the clubhouse and thence to six months of psychiatric care. Fine now, but has never played golf since.

When I presided at the Eucharist for the first time after my ordination to the priesthood, I was wearing a special chasuble – the long poncho a priest wears at the altar to celebrate the Eucharist – made for the occasion, in wild scarlet silk with a hanging orphrey. As I processed down the nave I overheard one churchwarden, a solid Lincolnshire type, say to another, 'He looks like Shirley Bassey.'

In the Church of England, vesture has been the source of controversy since at least the Reformation, when the outward visible signs of inner invisible beliefs became critically important. With the Protestant ascendancy, out went knees-ups and bling; by the eighteenth century, clergymen looked almost indistinguishable from doctors and lawyers – professional, sober men in professional sober uniform, as boring and unimaginative as the business suit today. At Boston Stump, in spite of its size, there were no vestries, because for a long time there was no vesting, the clergy wearing in church what they wore out and about. Indeed, in Lincolnshire, a centre for Protestant and Puritan interests, a chasuble would have been no likelier to be worn in church than a pair of fishnet tights. It was only in the nineteenth century, with the rise of the High Church movement, that the wearing of vestments was revived. It caused a huge stink. Bishops were hauled up in court; there were riots in the streets of Pimlico. The problem was not simply that sober-sided people were outraged by flamboyance (a deep seam of this in the English psyche) it was that vestments were seen then as a capitulation to popery, a surrender to the Jezebel of Rome, prancing like Herodias' daughter in her gauds.

Those prejudices, if you like, endure today. At Evensong and most other services, whether in cathedrals or parish churches, you are likely to see us in what is called choir dress: a form of vesture in sober black and white, which owes more to Puritan than Catholic tradition. The only note of flamboyance is the coloured silk of our hoods, and this denotes academic rather than ecclesiastical distinction. (I once took a party of Romanian monks to Evensong at Wakefield Cathedral; when one of them asked me what the hoods were for, I told them it was customary for worshippers to put bottles of beer in them as offerings as they processed out.)

Vesture was still very much a live issue when I attended the National Pilgrimage to the Shrine of Our Lady of Walsingham in Norfolk. This High Church Jamboree, which takes place every May Bank Holiday, is to the world of vestments what Paris and Milan are to the world of haute couture. But not for all; at the village's medieval parish pump a party of Free Presbyterian protestors had assembled to preach, hand out tracts and get into arguments. Events reached a crescendo when the procession from the shrine passed by on the way to Mass in the ancient abbey gardens. Just as the Anglo-Catholic faction had turned out its heavyweights for the occasion – a praetorian guard of prelates in vestments so gorgeous they'd have made the most stylish Pope look like he'd popped out in his dressing gown – so did the Protestant faction, in the person of a marvellously eloquent Ulsterman. Black-suited, black bible in hand, pausing only to draw breath, his voice rose like thunder over the pilgrim hymn as he hurled passages from Scripture at the glittering pageant. 'Faith, reckoned to Abraham as Righteousness, is what will save you,' he roared, 'not your gewgaws and empty pomps!'

And at that moment, like the spirit moving over the waters, like St Swithun summoning a cold front, there came a great breath of wind. The trees shook, chasubles fluttered, banners flapped, purple skullcaps and Protestant tracts alike flew up into the air. Freeze frame.

One of the most commendable effects of the Reformation was a critical examination of the centuries-long accumulation of traditions in the Church. The ways in which we worship, read the Bible, function as a community, were both clarified and enriched – thanks be to God – but this brought impoverishment as well as enrichment. The High Church movement took hold in the slums of Victorian Britain because it offered a vision of something glorious in the grinding drabness of the East End of London, the docks of Sunderland and the mills of Manchester. 'Come, taste and see that the Lord is good,' it urged the working-classes. 'You may have nothing, but you may offer to God glorious worship, the God whom we cannot praise too extravagantly, and who chose to reveal himself to us clothed in human form, like ours.' Unfreeze frame.

Back in Walsingham, the sudden gust of wind died down and the skullcaps and tracts alike descended to earth in total confusion. Perhaps an ultra-pious pilgrim might have sneaked a skullcap into his bag and taken it home as a souvenir; perhaps another binned the tracts that fluttered to her feet; but most just picked them up and returned them to their owners. Presbyterians handed skullcaps back to grateful bishops, pilgrims tidied up tracts and handed them back to the protestors. When all was restored, we struck up with the pilgrim hymn again and the protestors continued their preaching. Normal service resumed.

*

I think of St Marcian of Constantinople, the patron of strippers. He was born to a noble and wealthy family in the fifth century but eschewed the world and its pomps to be ordained priest, and eventually became the treasurer of the great cathedral of Hagia Sophia in Constantinople. He had a tremendous flair for design and was always giving it, and other churches, makeovers. Personally, he was rather austere, giving all his wealth away, fasting rigorously, and basing his life on that of John the Baptist, of whom he was very fond. One day, vested as a priest in the gorgeous robes he had designed for the cathedral, he came across a beggar, naked and wretched in the street, so he stopped and gave him everything he was wearing except for his chasuble. It was so richly embroidered that when he arrived at the cathedral the Patriarch rebuked him for dressing so flamboyantly. Marcian, with a flourish, took off his chasuble and revealed his nakedness to all.

The anniversary of the Battle of Waterloo falls in the run-up to Petertide; not an anniversary much observed nowadays, but it used to be, and there is a reminder of it in the form of the Panorama Tower which stands on the Thrapston Road in Finedon. It was built by the Reverend William Alington, not only to mark the victory of Wellington's forces but also to provide a viewing platform for the Iron Duke himself, who was very friendly with General Arbuthnot of Woodford House down the road. While visiting, Wellington remarked that the country round Finedon was very like that of Waterloo. The Panorama Tower was built so that on future visits he might revisit, so to speak, the great field of battle. It also housed a Social Club, known locally as the Pam (after Panorama), but it became notorious for its home-brewed 'fighting beer', used to slake the thirsts of bare-knuckle boxers, gamblers, and rowdies, and eventually the establishment was closed down and the tower turned into a tannery. It was the location for one of the very first movie blockbusters, *The Battle of Waterloo*, directed by Charles Weston. It had a budget of £5,000 – colossal in 1913 – and the shoe factories were closed for two days so local men, two thousand of them, could recreate the battle under the direction of C squadron of the 12th Lancers, loaned from Weedon Barracks. They were paid sixpence per diem and the pubs were kept open all day for refreshments, but everyone got so drunk that filming had to be halted because Napoleon kept falling off his horse and someone stole Wellington's boots.

TRANSFIGURATION

The Feast of the Transfiguration is one of my favourite episodes in the Gospels. Jesus and some of his disciples ascend Mount Tabor in Galilee and he is there 'transfigured', lit with dazzling light, and is seen standing between Moses and Elijah, proclaimed as God's beloved son by a heavenly voice. It is one of those moments when the Gospel writers set out what we need to know, so plainly, so radiantly, that you wonder if it is a story from after the Resurrection that has been cut and pasted into the pre-Resurrection narrative.

In the Transfiguration by Theophanes – a fifteenth-century icon writer (writer, not painter) – we see for the first time Jesus in glory between Moses and Elijah on the mountaintop. The disciples, blinded, fall away from him; in order to see, like Paul on the road to Damascus, we need to be blinded, is the message, or one of them. But I love the detail to the left of the picture, the posse ascending Mount Tabor, unaware that they are about to see Jesus' identity revealed. Even more, I like the detail to the right: the posse descending Mount Tabor. Normal service is resumed – but nothing is normal after this. And then a chill note when you realise that the Feast falls on Hiroshima Day, and that it points to the other ensemble of three on a hilltop: Jesus crucified between thieves on Golgotha. The image of his humiliation and death, and the image of his divine glory, anticipate each other.

While on holiday, I visit a church to attend the Transfiguration service (with a baptism thrown in), taken by someone I vaguely know, a chaplain in the NHS. The congregation – larger, I feel, than usual – is full of handsome men in shirts chewing gum and looking a bit ill at ease, like gangsters at a funeral. I ask someone who they are and he tells me the mother of the baby getting baptised does the coat check at the local gay pub, so that community is well represented. 'And I wonder how many of the congregation have had the celebrant?' he adds.

A mountaintop in Wales, a hilltop really, where my friend's mother keeps sheep in a place so beautiful it seems not quite to be true. I am coming from Northamptonshire, my friend from Edinburgh, so I arrange to meet him at the airport. I park and go to the arrivals building where I am to meet Horatio Clare (now a celebrated writer, then a colleague at the BBC). He arrives, terribly hung-over, carrying a programme box – a sort of squarish, old-fashioned case made from cardboard with reinforced corners and stencilled with the BBC logo – a piece of kit, like those Bakelite headphones you still find in some studios, that dates back to the days when we not only made the programmes but the equipment too. Horatio, smelling like a pub carpet, embraces me stickily. We drive back along the M4 and then turn north for Abergavenny, Crickhowell and Cwmdu.

Horatio's mother, Sally, lives in an ancient farmhouse, two wings with a gable carrying the staircase in the middle, built 1607, altered once, in 1958, when rudimentary plumbing and wiring was put into its reluctantly yielding interior. It is more like a cave than a house: massive masonry flags on the floor, thick oak planks on the landing, shallow pointed arches over doors and windows. Best of all is Horatio's room, the renovated attic, which looks like a bohemian bomb strike: books everywhere, old records, a hi-fi, a bed on the floor, and on the windowsill a ship in a bottle and a soapstone carving of Horus. It is an archaeology of his life, from childhood books and jujus, through records to literature, to fags and drink and weed and condoms.

After lunch, we head down to the Usk, where Horatio makes me park illegally on an impeccably kept patch of grass at the gates of a posh country-house hotel. We walk through the wood and emerge into one of the most beautiful places I've ever been. The Usk, wide and shallow, ripples over and round the rocks through a valley of indescribable beauty, steep wooded sides rising to brilliantly green fields full of sheep and cattle, with the Black Mountains rising beyond them. We spend the afternoon in our pants in the river, me looking like Simon Callow in *A Room with a View*, Horatio looking like the faintly disgraced older English cousin of Tadzio from *Death in Venice*. We find a spot in the middle of the river, where it's at its deepest, and watch the eels swimming between clefts in the rock; then we sit on a sunny boulder, smoking and thinking of collective nouns for eels (an *anguillade*, a *syntax*, a *slide*).

Eventually we walk up to some higher rocks where Horatio had seen a pretty young woman paddling with some children. He wanders off to look at her and then we jump into the river at the fastest-flowing point and allow it to sweep us downstream. We swim around, me trying to look nonchalant at the mercy of a current that is stronger and quicker than I can manage.

We lie on a rock, smoke some more, and then pull on some soaking-wet and stinking clothes and walk through the woods up to the posh hotel, from whence I assume we'll be summarily ejected. But no, Horatio walks into the bar, orders two Campari and sodas, and we sit out on a sun-roasted terrace drinking and talking with our pants laid out to steam-dry on a bench, to the irritation of the other guests.

Back at the farm, Sally makes a picnic and we pack it into the BBC's programme box, along with a bottle of Bollinger. As dusk falls, we drive up to her high field on the mountainside and walk higher and higher through the bracken as the lamps come on in the valley beneath us, criss-crossed by headlights, and the gathering dusk leaches colour out of the landscape and then the sky. We eat hard-boiled eggs and sandwiches and drink champagne as grey-ghost sheep scamper past and fireworks burst in the sky above Bwlch, but far below us. Then Sally says, 'Look!' And we turn to see the orange moon rising over the top of the mountain, the sky around it emerald green and turquoise.

Sometimes, broadcasting on the wireless and broadcasting on the God frequency align, like when I am sent by Radio Three to seven lovely Italian cities in search of seven deadly sins for a series on that topic.

We take in Venice, Padua, Ravenna, Bologna, Florence, Siena and Rome, looking at fading frescoes and glittering mosaics, contrasting the bliss of those redeemed from their sins with the torments of those damned by theirs, set out in all their balanced glory and terror.

Two are particularly famous: the doom fresco in the Scrovegni Chapel in Padua, painted by Giotto around 1305, and the mosaic on the same theme in the dome of the Baptistery in Florence, made by Coppo di Marcovaldo around forty years earlier. Both show Christ in Glory, dispatching to his left the damned, who are consumed by a horned devil sitting on a serpent; to his right, he bestows blessings on the redeemed, assisted to heaven by an orderly squadron of angels. The chaos of hell and its gloomy pit is contrasted with the light and order of heaven; and in the Scrovegni doom, at the head of heaven's queue, is Scrovegni himself, perhaps with the example of Solomon dedicating the Temple to God in mind, offering the chapel to Christ with an expression of careful piety: the fortune that paid for it was made in the morally perilous world of banking.

In the Baptistery at Florence the same scheme – Giotto would have known it – and the parallels between the two versions are obvious. But there are differences too. The Scrovegni Chapel's doom is a fresco, painted on wet plaster, which when dry leaves a matt surface. The mosaic in the Baptistery, however, is formed of tiny tesserae of glazed ceramic and glass and gold leaf, which glister, like treasure. In the former, the light levels and corrosive breath and sweat of visitors oblige the custodians to limit the number of visitors, so the extraordinary drama reveals itself only gradually. The Baptistery, however, weathers far better the depredations of time and tourism and the mosaic is brilliantly lit for the benefit of the people thronging beneath it. And yet both are dazzling – not only our outer vision, by the skilful manipulation of light, but our inner vision too, by the spectacle of God's glory and power. In your light we see light, says the Psalmist. Coming away, I think of the apostles, dazzled, falling away from Christ at the top of Mount Tabor, blinded into sight.

Jonathan Edwards, the Olympic triple jumper, has made a documentary about St Paul. In the past, his earnestly expressed Christian faith has made him sometimes difficult for me to take seriously, especially when interviewed, panting beside a track, inserting Jesus into every answer as if he were name-dropping. But he is very good in this.

There are some daft things: a shifty seismologist says there may have been an earthquake somewhere near Damascus around the time Paul made his journey and that might have given him a migraine and that could possibly explain the hallucinatory epiphany. As Edwards shows, this explanation does not begin to capture the significance of the change it wrought in Paul, from persecutor of Christians to the greatest apologist of the Christian faith. We cannot resist looking for 'scientific' or objective explanations to account for religious phenomena; but these are *stories,* closer to poetry than reportage, and Paul's blindness was not a symptom of migraine but a way of representing his condition before he acknowledged Jesus as risen, the light of the world, the dazzling figure of the transfiguration. Paul must be blinded in order that he may see.

Not long after the Feast of the Transfiguration we remember the life of Nicholas of Cusa, cardinal, theologian, diplomat, astronomer and mystic, acclaimed by some as the first modern thinker. Born in

Kues near Trier (Cusa is its Latin form) in 1401, he was a brilliant student who became secretary to the Prince-Archbishop of Trier and was sent by him to Rome, where he distinguished himself both as a diplomat and as a scholar. He wrote of the impossibility of knowing Christ through the exercise of the organs of reason alone and urged a 'learned ignorance' as a proper attitude in those who would seek his truths and his service. He was not, however, in the least disengaged with the affairs of his time. Cusa's great work *De concordantia catholica* considers how the power of the State and the Church is exercised through hierarchy within a context of consent. He was one of the pioneers of textual criticism, showing that the *Donation of Constantine*, a highly influential document showing a transfer of powers from the Emperor to the Pope, was a forgery. A protégé of the reforming Pope Eugenius IV, he became known as the Hercules of the Eugenian Cause; although made a cardinal and Bishop of Brixen in the Tyrol by Eugenius' successor, Martin V, he fell from favour, especially after the debacle of the bleeding hosts of Wilsnack . . .

After falling out with the Bishop of Havelburg in 1383, one of the knights of Prignitiz, an individual known as 'Big Head', burnt down the church at Wilsnack. The parish priest discovered on the altar three hosts – wafers – untouched by the fire, and these hosts began to bleed. They were immediately hailed as miraculous and pilgrims (among them the Norfolk mystic Margery Kempe of King's Lynn, who visited in 1433) came in great numbers to venerate them. Nicholas of Cusa pointed out that if Christ was glorified in heaven, his blood could not appear on earth, therefore the bleeding hosts could not be genuine. This led to a tremendous row, bishops excommunicated each other, and in the end the Pope overruled Nicholas, who was imprisoned for a while by Sigismund of Austria before returning to Rome, never to see his See again. He died at Todi in 1464. The bleeding hosts of Wilsnack were eventually destroyed by reformers, but modern visitors to the Church of St Nicholas may venerate a vertebra from the whale that swallowed Jonah.

*

Christianity was invented by Jews. Our Scripture is Jewish – what we call the Old Testament are the sacred books of the Jewish faith – and of course the apostles, St Paul, and Jesus himself were Jews, *and they never stopped thinking they were.* In a way, the hostility which very quickly grew up between Christians and Jews was not because we were distant enemies, but because we were, and are, so closely related – the intensity of that hostility is in part due to that closeness. Sigmund Freud, a Jew, would have called it the narcissism of small differences; but you could call it a family fall-out (of the worst kind).

While that hostility, historic and contemporary, has obscured the deep roots we have in the Jewish faith, the Scriptures that we associate with the Transfiguration remind us how deep it goes. In the Book of Exodus we encounter Moses, shining with godly light, descending Mount Sinai with the Tablets of Law. He is almost as familiar to Christian congregations as Jesus himself, and if the image that comes most readily to mind is Charlton Heston, in all his square-jawed Caucasian virility, that only goes to show how deeply assimilated he is into Christian culture. Moses' story, which ends with his death in the land of Moab, prefigures the Christian story that is to come: a story of delivery from bondage, of wandering in the wilderness, and of a charismatic leader capable of amazing deeds. When Jesus is revealed to the apostles on the Mount of the Transfiguration, he appears between Moses and Elijah, the two pre-eminent figures of the Old Testament, showing that in Jesus Christ all their deeds and prophecies are fulfilled. Judaism is not incidental to Christianity, merely another competitor in the crowded market of the world's religions. Rather, it is essential to Christianity, for if we do not understand where we come from, how can we understand who we are?

Understanding where we come from has been for me a largely theoretical experience, but for David it is a lived reality. Invited to a friend's son's bar mitzvah in North London, we turn up in our dog collars, but David also wears his kippa and tallit – skullcap and prayer shawl – relics from his childhood. His family belonged to a church which followed Jewish law and Jewish festivals, keeping kosher and the Feast of Tabernacles; and then he lived in an ortho-dox Jewish community in Johannesburg for a surprising interlude in his twenties. No one bats an eyelid. At the lunch afterwards – how I love the Jewish impulse to mark everything significant with a special feed – he says the ha'motzi, the blessing over the bread, in fluent Hebrew (with an Ashkenazi accent, I am later told). I have never been to a bar mitzvah before and I love it. How clever to take a teenager on the threshold of maturity, when the faith of their fathers and mothers might fade, and put them not only centre stage but make them declare their life intentions in front of their peers. We should do this at confirmations of teenagers.

A clergyman – retired now and living in a tiny town in Burgundy – invites me to stay with him. I take an early walk and stop for breakfast at the Café du Commerce in front of the church, run by a very well-nourished lady who looks English but isn't. She is sitting with her friend at a table near the bar and, although she is scrupulously polite, I sense some irritation at having a customer. I soon see why. A theme tune strikes up from the television mounted on a bracket over their table and the proprietress comes running out as fast as her legs will carry her and hurriedly installs herself next to her friend in front of the telly. It's an American daytime soap dubbed into incomprehensible French, but you don't need to understand what is being said to get the gist. Soap operas, like adverts, are better for being in a language you don't understand, or watched with the sound off, or – best of all – in fast-forward. That way their meanings become clearer. In this show the men are all chiselled and the women are size oo. The scene builds up to an improbable encounter when the man, having removed his shirt for a reason so arbitrary you soon give up wondering why, stands in front of the woman, all glistening pecs and abs, and confesses to her that, first, he is sorry and second, he loves only her. At this point her eyes fill with tears and the soundtrack, in which a plangent oboe plays continually, swells and rises. The proprietress and her friend both sigh. Five minutes later another bare-chested man does the same to another liquid-eyed lovely. They sigh again.

A neighbour, a retired parson notorious for waspishness, comes round for coffee. I prattle on and he says: 'You do ask awkward questions. Everything's got to mean something.' We are talking about liturgy and my friend tells me of his departure from a post he once held at Westminster Abbey: Sacrist, responsible for assisting with the logistics of ceremonial rites. In his last week he was asked by the Dean to organise a Vespers for the Ecumenical Patriarch of Constantinople and the Archbishop of Canterbury, passing through London on official business. 'Nothing fancy,' said the Dean, 'it wouldn't be appropriate.' On the appointed day, the Dean, Archbishop and the Patriarch arrived at the west end of the Abbey to find within all the canons, the minor canons, the lay clerks, the vicars choral, all in full fig, and forty Queen's scholars in white tie, tails and college surplices. As they processed up the nave, the choir suddenly struck up with the Trisagion of the Improperia, and as the dignitaries approached the Shrine of St Edward, the doors were flung open to reveal the tomb of King Edward the Confessor lit by a thousand shrine lights ('I got them from IKEA'). The Ecumenical Patriarch of Constantinople burst into tears.

I say I find fussy liturgy distracting and prefer something plainer. 'Why?' he asks. I say, 'Isn't liturgy a means to reveal the saving truths of the Gospel and the mysteries of the sacraments? The rest is merely show business.' He replies, 'An onion, Richard, is only layers.'

Turns out he's actually called in to tell me about a dish in the antique shop up the road, the first ceramic made – and signed – by Jean Marais. My ears prick up because of the Cocteau connection.

After a decent amount of time following the retired parson's departure, I go and buy it.

On another occasion I take him out for supper and bet that one of the daughters of Cîteaux, the abbey from which the Cistercian Order spread, was Thoronet Abbey, in the Var. It isn't, which costs me thirty quid. He loves a bet, it's in the blood, he says. His mother once won a hundred quid when someone bet her she wouldn't pee down a chimney. She climbed a ladder up onto the roof, squatted over a chimney and peed – to the delight of her houseguests, gathered round the spattered fireplace beneath.

Mount Tabor in reality is nothing like the icon. The best candidate for the place the Gospel writers had in mind, Tabor lies in Galilee, not far from Tiberias, and it is on the itinerary for the pilgrimage to the Holy Land we are taking with a group of parishioners from Finedon and fellow travellers (a return visit for David and me, but as leaders this time). It is a proper mountain, not a rocky stage set, and being Galilee it is green and beautiful.

At the top of Mount Tabor is a church by Barluzzi, who cornered the market in building churches at holy sites for the Italian Franciscans in the 1920s. This is one of his more successful buildings, but the Franciscan spirit of welcome is wearing a little thin when we get there and find ourselves peremptorily bossed around by some friars. I find the friars irritating, perhaps, very faintly, because I detect in myself what I suspect is in them: a weariness that comes of being custodians of a sacred place for the benefit of those who lack the equivalent piety. This is common among clergy – not only with pilgrims to sacred sites but with congregations too. They talk when you would be silent, or seem unwilling to grasp an essential point. It is Pharisaism, I suppose, and we miss what they miss when our concern with propriety makes us blind – what we are is the reality of people. I sometimes think redcoats must feel much the same way, too busy chivvying people along to discover who they are and what they have to say.

We are invited to use an altar for our own Eucharist. It's a rudimentary outdoor altar, under a corrugated tin roof but open at the back to Galilee, spreading away into the distance. The friar who works as sacristan to Anglican pilgrims appears with a tray, like a tea tray, laden not with cakes but with wafers and wine and vessels and cloths – everything we need. We begin with a hymn, a fanfare from the Church of England to the Transfigured Lord: 'Immortal, invisible, God only wise; in light inaccessible hid from our eyes . . .' A crocodile of pilgrims – from the Philippines, I think – stop to listen to our attempt at four-part harmony, that distinctive Royal School of Church Music sound, imperfectly balanced, of mixed ability, rising above the lemon trees and pines.

I have connected on Facebook with an old school friend, not seen in forty years, and discovered we have had parallel lives; civilly partnered, living in London and Northamptonshire, blessed with plural dachshunds, and a love of Wagner. He texts me to say his partner cannot make it to the Wagner Festival in Bayreuth in the summer – would I like his ticket? Yes, I would. Bayreuth is to Wagnerians what Monaco is to fans of F1, and tickets can take a lifetime to obtain. So we are in Germany, Franconia, in the little town where Wagner built an ugly home and a magnificent theatre expressly for the performance of his operas, and where the Ring Cycle was first performed. It is a Ring Cycle we have come to see, and we've got to *Siegfried*, number three of the four operas in the sequence, and towards the end there's a passage which I have always loved but only now realise that it reminds me of the icon of the Transfiguration. It covers a scene change, between Siegfried's encounter with the watchful Wanderer and his encounter with the sleeping Brunnhilde, who wakes up into ecstasy. The passage begins with the violins playing the open G string at the bottom of their range, and then in unison they round an odd broken-backed figure, until they hold an impossibly high note very softly. And then a figure on the horns surprises you by shifting the harmonic centre to somewhere quite unexpected. As if to compensate for this, the violins rise a semitone, but resolution is out of reach and they descend again in unison, but differently. Up the hill one way, down the hill another, changed by the surprise they encounter at the top.

MATCHING

Three weddings back to back after Morning Prayer, Holy Communion, and a baptism rehearsal, and finally Evening Prayer, so I hardly leave the church from nine to five. I'm ready for the sofa by the end of the day, mostly because of the weddings, and mostly because I find I am working the crowd and cannot shake off a feeling of unease that I have become an Archie Rice to do so. I make them redo the responses if they're not loud enough or sound uncertain, I give prizes to the children for being helpful, and I tell jokes. I tell myself I am trying to get through to people so they'll go away having had a good experience and not a bad one, and will return more readily, if they return at all, but sometimes I think I am merely doing a turn. A friend told me about a wedding couple he had carefully prepared for marriage; the day before the wedding, with the rehearsal satisfactorily completed, he asked them if they had any questions. Just one: they had neglected to mention they were going for a pirate theme and would he mind dressing up as Long John Silver for the ceremony?

I'm off to Manchester for the wedding of a fellow seminarian, not the most red-blooded of our less-than-scarlet cohort, and rather an unlikely event I once would have thought, but the man continues to surprise us. I stop en route at Mirfield, where we both trained, to pick up one of the monks and then we sit for an hour in all but motionless traffic on the M62, making it to the church in the nick of time. I will be singing in the choir, so duck into the stalls just before it gets under way and look around a church unusually full of people in dog collars – men in dog collars, my friend being of conservative views – advertised by the Forward in Faith logo at the centre of the church's banner, out of place between the symbols of Peter, Apostle and Martyr, like a piece of clip art accidentally cut and pasted into a Romanesque tympanum. My friend, not in a dog collar, looks rather sweet and rather camp in morning dress, his bride is lovely, and it is a lovely occasion – with a ghost at the feast. Another of our cohort, now dying, sits hopelessly incapacitated in a wheelchair propelled by another, his partner. I cannot help but feel the anomaly of gathering to celebrate one version of faithful commitment while another, unacknowledged version, is also on show: the love that dare not speak its name.

It was Denmark that led the way with civil unions – as the proto-types for gay marriages were known – the law coming into effect in 1989. The first couple to take it up was Axel and Eigil Axgil, partners and activists who had participated in the campaign to change the law. They adopted the surname Axgil, a combination of their given names, as an expression of their commitment. Such partnerships were contracted at civil ceremonies only, but the Church of Den-mark allowed its clergy to perform blessings of same-sex couples on the grounds that it is people, not institutions, who are blessed. In 2010 the Danish parliament permitted same-sex couples to adopt, and in 2012 civil unions were replaced by same-sex marriage. These marriages are permitted to be held in churches, but clergy are not obliged to officiate at them if they do not wish to. Eigil Axgil died in 1995 aged seventy-three. Axel Axgil died in 2011 aged ninety-six. I often think of them when I'm marrying couples who fit the criteria the Church requires but on whose future even the most reckless gambler would not bet.

What makes a marriage? Is it conformity to the necessary sac-ramental character and canonical form? Hard not to feel the force of that. Is it rather, or also, an expression of the character of the relationship, no less enduring and faithful with the Axgils than with the many conventionally construed couples I have married?

You shall know them by their fruits, a phrase which in this context has a slightly unfortunate double meaning. I think my expectations are defined by my parents, whose marriage is the one I know best; in their case it was life-giving and life-long, as the marriage service puts it. At their fiftieth anniversary lunch, I noticed on their table they were joined by their bridesmaids, best man and ushers, all of whom were still with the spouses they had married at the end of the fifties. A table down, to my generation, and half were divorced.

A celebrity wedding in London, followed by a grand do at a smart hotel, with a celebrity chef and a celebrity best man. The bride's father made a speech expressing the view that life came down to this: the bringing together of man and wife in holy matrimony, for the begetting of children, in the turning cycle of life. I was sitting on the gay table and a friend whispered in my ear, 'It's not really for the likes of us, is it?'

At that time, between the arrival of civil partnerships and the possibility of an upgrade to marriage, the churches were parked in a layby, overtaken by ribbon-bedecked limousines heading for the registrar to solemnise the union of man with man and woman with woman. I was glad to see that happening; it seemed to me to offer people the best chance of sticking together, through thick and thin; but there was an irony that the generation of gay activists who raised the standard for radical difference in the sexuality wars of the eighties now planted it on the matrimonial lawn. Another irony that I should have chosen the one place still holding out against it.

At our friends Jon and Mike's civil partnership they asked me to give a blessing, which I could not do, the law requiring clergy, who are ex-officio registrars, to observe the rival jurisdiction of the civil registrar. He was an affable man, and eager to accommodate,

so he said after the ceremony he would close his book as a sign
to me that he considered his business done so that mine might
begin. I made a joke about the different gestures one might
employ for such an occasion, flapping my hands at my face like a
tearful diva before making the sign of the cross as a comparison.
Job done.

The present arrangements in the Church of England, which
allow me to bless my friends' dog but not the gay equivalent of a
golden wedding, are hard to justify. 'If your child asks for bread,'
Jesus says to the crowds at the Sermon on the Mount, 'who will
give a stone?' Depressing, but not surprising, that the Church
should be out of step with the wider world in this regard. Two
thousand years of thinking homosexuality a sin, rather than a mere
variation on the theme of being human, is not something easily
overcome, if you indeed think it should be. But I would rather be
uncomfortable for being more generous than we want to be, than
uncomfortable for being meaner than we need to be. Because in
a world where people go hungry, who hands out stones if asked
for bread?

I just sent anniversary congratulations to my friends Reggie
and Ray, whom I met thirty years ago just after they had got together. Three decades of objectively disordered unintegrated in-
trinsically evil sinfulness, to summarise the Church's traditional
teaching.

When arguments arise about redefining marriage, I often think of
Martin and Kate Luther. He was a priest, theologian and founding
father of the Reformation; she was a nun, Sister Katharina, one
of twelve he helped escape from the Nimbschen Convent in April
1523 by having them smuggled out, hidden in herring barrels. Both
had taken vows of celibacy and, while others in the Reformation
movement had broken such vows to marry, Luther had resolved
not to, partly because he expected to be burned at the stake and
partly because his personal hygiene left much to be desired and he

worried she might be put off even after emerging from a barrel that had been used to pickle fish. Nevertheless, in the spirit of reform they did marry in Wittenberg on 13 June in 1525, without ceremony and against the wishes of Luther's fellow reformer, Melanchthon, who thought it reckless. He was nonetheless one of the witnesses (as was the great painter Lucas Cranach the Elder, who painted the famous double portrait of the couple). They were given a former monastery, the unromantically named Black Cloister, by Elector John the Steadfast, and lived happily ever after, having six children but so little money they were obliged to take in lodgers. Nevertheless, Luther wrote to a friend, 'My Katie is in all things so obliging and pleasing to me that I would not exchange my poverty for the riches of Croesus.'

I solemnise the marriage of a couple who look like the beginning of a nursery rhyme, he with no fat, she with no lean. He works on the market in a rather fitful way and comes from a traveller background, as she does, but her side seem to outrank his in prestige. When they come for marriage preparation I have to sign his chit, which excuses him from the community service he's been sentenced to, after which his attention rather wanders. She is completely absorbed by the reception and the bridesmaids and her dress, which on the day is certainly splendid if a little démodé. It is built along the lines of Princess Diana's wedding dress, with big frilly shoulders and a plunging back, decades old now, but still dramatic. The bride's hair is huge, her make-up would not have disgraced Bayreuth, but I don't really get the full effect until we are lining up at the west end for her entry. The church is full, her father so drunk he has to go to be sick before he's capable of giving her away, but she is magnificent and poised and gets her attendants into position and we move off, stately as galleons, to the bridal march from Lohengrin. I detect a flutter of laughter as we pass the pews en route to the chancel step, but it's only after the marriage vows are taken and the couple turn to make their exit that I notice why. Across her shoulder blades, framed by the frilly diagonal of her dress, tattooed without skill in wonky dark blue, are the words FUCK OFF.

Candy, an old friend from school, phones to ask if I will officiate at her wedding. She and Nick, her boyfriend of many years, are about to emigrate to France and it seems timely, if not sacramentally necessary, to solemnise matters. I say yes, of course, and she seeks and gets the permission of the vicar of her parish church, next door to the photographic studio Candy's father started and which she has inherited. In the flat above, I'd spent many, many hours of adolescence with Candy and our friend Matthew, listening to Rod Stewart and Santana and later the 4 Be 2s and John Otway, while her German mother brought us tray after tray of sandwiches and coffee, unbothered by our incessant smoking. She would sometimes join us and reminisce about her days growing up in Dortmund during the war, where her father worked in the town – days which ended with the Allied bombing of the city, and a vivid memory of Dortmund in flames and her father's secretary running down the road carrying his files, which she dropped, sending pages fluttering out into the night and towards the furnace behind her, where they burst into flames like little fireworks.

The day before the ceremony, I drive there from Boston and call in at Mum and Dad's on the way. Mum has just had a new knee, and seems pretty much recovered from her operation, so that anxiety is over for the time being, but Dad's Parkinson's is progressing alarmingly. It's reached the point where his right arm and hand are now almost useless, the arm folding in on itself in a way that makes him look disabled – as indeed he is. My dear disabled dad.

At the church I meet the vicar, a nice man in a red-and-white-striped clerical shirt. He shows me where things are and introduces me to the churchwarden, who solemnly sets out the registers, the Church of England version of the Book of Life. Afterwards, a table for twelve has been booked at a pub in Higham Ferrers, but only three – me, Candy and Amanda, whom I remembered as a scowling punk with jet-black spiky hair, an image at odds with her title 'Matron of Honour' – show up. Candy takes this with good grace; everyone else is either not arriving until the morning or working to prepare the Bede House, where the reception will take place. So it's just the three of us – with me in a dog collar, which introduces a note of novelty to the proceedings.

On the day, I get to church early. People I haven't seen for years begin to arrive; a former master is among the former schoolboys and a long-buried reflex almost has me calling him 'sir'. Candy eventually arrives, late, and so nervous she's shaking. Nick is so nervous he can't get the word 'honour' out. But we get there in the end and the bells ring and it's lovely.

Afterwards, I have a fag with an old pal round the back of the church, shifty in cassock and cotta, although I take my stole off in, I suppose, an acknowledgement of conduct unbecoming. Then it's over to the Bede House, where I last half an hour before leaving for Boston, driving home almost cross-eyed with migraine, and go to bed for two hours.

Then it's out again for another wedding meeting. The groom, landlord at a local pub, tells me he lost a lot of weight recently. He looks to me to be about seventeen stone, so I casually ask how much he's lost. *Eighteen stone*, he replies. He'd been thirty-four stone.

A wedding enquiry at St Paul's, Knightsbridge. She is shy and foreign, he a big, gruff Scot. They do not live in the parish, seem unfamiliar with our ways, and I wonder if they are aware of what they are getting themselves into. I explain that they will need to attend regularly for six months, at least once a fortnight, in order to establish a legal right to marry – normally this is enough to deter the casual enquirer, but they insist that will be fine. I am also anxious they should understand that the full ceremonial they want will be expensive and I try, as tactfully as possible, to indicate that it could be done cheaper in a less smart part of London. No, they are sure.

Six months go by, and they dutifully attend, and as the day approaches we begin to put things in order. I need to sort out a special licence for them to marry, since she is not a UK national, and we need to get the final choice of music. It's only when we start to do this that I realise they are not what I thought they were. They want the wedding as late as possible and I explain that, legally, we have to be done by six; they tell me that will pose a problem, because their reception venue won't be available until seven. This seems odd to me, so I ask where it is. The V&A, they reply. I suggest that they ask again, because it shouldn't be too much trouble to open the restaurant. 'It's not in the restaurant,' he says. Where then? I ask. 'We've booked the whole thing.' And they have – the entire museum. They need it, too, as I realise when I see how long the guest list is.

I'm invited to the reception, which is as splendid as anything I've seen, and when the band come on I remark that they sound like Snow Patrol – then someone tells me that it is Snow Patrol.

The night before our own wedding – actually a civil partnership, celebrated not in church, with flowers and bells and choir, but at Diss Register Office – David and I went out to dinner with our witnesses, Jon and Mike, at whose civil partnership I had given the unorthodox blessing. I drove David's new car to the abbey to pick him up after Evensong, and would have parked it in the car park had not a fall of snow made me mistake a gap in the hedge for the opening. Eventually we managed to get it out of the ditch I'd driven it into, but perhaps for this reason – or more than usually conscious of the fragile goods onboard – the next day David drove us with unusual care from Wymondham to Diss. We'd asked Jon and Mike to be our witnesses because we had been theirs at a ceremony in a castle followed by dinner at a smart hotel. Just before pudding, the empty space next to David's had been filled by a glamorous black woman. 'Sorry I'm late,' she'd whispered. 'I got stuck in Brussels.' For some reason David thought she was a model, and asked if she had been on a shoot there. 'I'm a lawyer,' she said. 'I was at the European Court.' Is that your specialism? he asked. 'Sort of. I work for the government.' 'What do you do?' 'I'm the Attorney General.' Pause. 'Where of?' Pause. 'England and Wales.'

We had no guests at ours, apart from Jon and Mike, because being involved in big weddings puts you off them, or it does me. Besides, I rather like the municipal feel of a civil partnership. When the four of us got there, the registrar, anxious to be helpful, wanted to discuss what we wanted, the music and the poems and the rings, but we did not want any music or poems or rings, just to make the declarations, and sign the forms, and take our certificates away. He seemed disappointed and marked the solemnity of the occasion himself by wearing a Battle of Britain tie. The ceremony, about as romantic as applying for a TV licence, took about ten minutes; then we went to the pub and had a row when David decided unilaterally to phone his mum and tell her the news. I hadn't wanted to get civilly partnered at all, or not then, certainly not until we were living together. It seemed absurd to me to make this step when he was living in Norfolk and me in London. The proper time to do it would be when we had rearranged our lives to spend them together, and could return from the Register Office to our marital home, but David, ever impatient, thought differently. He'd phoned me one day, demanding to know my intentions, because, he said, if I did not wish to commit myself to him there were others in a queue who did. And so it was we stepped, conjoined, through the light grey slush outside Barclays, got into the car and drove to London, where Jon and Mike took us, rather fittingly, for supper at the Ivy. My grandfather used to take my grandmother there when they were first wed.

There were lovely weddings at Knightsbridge too. I remember one of an English woman to an Iranian man, both in their twenties, young to get married now, but when I asked them if they were sure that they were ready there was no trace of doubt in their unison

'Yes'. When the day arrived, I walked into the church to find it asymmetrically arranged, a crowd on the bride's side and a handful on the groom's. It was so unbalanced, I suggested their friends fill up the emptier side. As part of my preparation for the ceremony, I put a Kleenex in my folder lest the bride get tearful, but it was not needed for her. In the middle of the exchange of vows he started to weep, and sobbed his way through, which was so affecting I had to compose myself too. Afterwards, I said to the bride how unusual it was for the groom to cry and she told me he had been an activist in Iran and had been arrested and imprisoned and tortured and only just escaped with his life. Most of his relatives were either dead or in prison or unable to travel, which explained the asymmetry, and in the moment he plighted his troth to her, he was overwhelmed, knowing that it could so easily not have been, and that it was love and champagne and canapés at the Berkeley rather than fear and rubber truncheons and a desert jail.

I saw in the paper a picture of the marriage of the Queen and the Duke of Edinburgh. Princess Elizabeth, as she then was, met Prince Philip of Greece and Denmark, as he then was, when she was thirteen and he eighteen at Dartmouth Naval College. They are second cousins, once removed, and among his German relations there were several prominent Nazis, which was awkward. When in due course news of a romance spread, some of the newspapers were less than enthused about a suitor they saw as a foreigner. But *amor vincit omnia*; they announced their engagement on 9 July 1947. The Prince renounced his Greek and Danish titles and converted from the Greek Orthodox faith to the Church of England. The wedding took place on 20 November that same year, a lavish affair for austerity Britain, held in Westminster Abbey and conducted by the Archbishops of Canterbury and York. The Queen's dress, by Norman Hartnell, required extra clothing coupons and was very much admired.

Weddings always bring to the surface family tensions and this was no different; Prince Philip's sisters, who had married Nazis, were not invited, nor were the Duke and Duchess of Windsor. The Queen Mother, however, came round to the match and I am told that when her new son-in-law was made HRH Prince Philip, Duke of Edinburgh, she promised to stop calling him 'the Hun'.

MICHAELMAS

September, month of Michaelmas, the Feast of St Michael and All Angels, commemorating the Archangel Michael's victory over Lucifer, when he and his infernal band were cast out from heaven – a rather loose interpretation, as it happens, of events in the seventeenth chapter of the Book of Revelation. Michaelmas has acquired a more prosaic sense in the secular world, in England marking a Quarter Day when accounts may be presented; traditionally the time when the peasantry elected reeves, whatever they were; and the beginning of academic and legal terms. All of these derive from its position in the calendar, at the point where autumn sets in, the nights lengthen, and we turn to face the winter. Popular culture draws together these themes in the belief that Michaelmas should mark the end of blackberrying, for when Lucifer fell from heaven it is said he landed in a blackberry bush and went to the lavatory in it.

The Book of Revelation promises an apocalypse, preceded by signs and portents, so the book's mysterious symbolism has often been invoked at times of crisis as signs of the approaching end. Among those who have been said to bear the Number of the Beast (666) are Napoleon, Hitler and President Obama, which tells us just how open to interpretation these symbols are. Some fundamentalist Christians in the United States, informed by Revelation and a number of other New Testament writings, have such an urgent sense of the coming crisis that they carry cards in their wallets to notify those who might be distressed in the event of their disappearance that they have been taken up in the Rapture. We might think something else is going on there, but the Church's tradition, and the witness of Scripture, point to a decisive, dramatic, definitive end that awaits us all, and Christian history is full of examples of those so overwhelmed by the imminence of the second coming that they begin to live, to attempt to live, in the new reality it inaugurates.

C. I. Scofield was a former Confederate soldier and lawyer from Tennessee who, after the Civil War, married an heiress of French Catholic heritage in St Louis before moving to Kansas and taking up politics. He became State District Attorney aged twenty-nine, the youngest in the country, but fell from grace after being accused of bribery, forgery, theft and alcoholism. His wife divorced him in 1883 and, on his uppers, Scofield experienced a conversion to evangelical Christianity, to which he devoted his formidable and now restored energies. While his divorce was still going through, he became a Congregationalist minister, remarried, and took on the role of pastor in what is now the First Congregational Church of Dallas. There he styled himself the Reverend C. I. Scofield, DD, though there is no record of an academic institution having awarded him a doctorate in Divinity or anything else. His pamphlet 'Rightly Dividing the Word of Truth' set out his doctrine of dispensational pre-millennialism, which teaches that God relates to humanity according to Biblical covenants expressed in a series of 'dispensations', different historical periods, so the Book of Revelation is understood not as an account of past events but as predictions for the future, looking forward to Christ's imminent return to earth to inaugurate a thousand years of peace and the taking up of the redeemed in the Rapture. Scofield published his magnum opus, a Reference Bible, in 1909; it very quickly became a bestseller, setting out the text of the King James Bible with annotations revealing its message to be consistent with dispensational pre-millennialism. Its influence is hard to overestimate; the speculative, eschatological character of American fundamentalism, and its influence on evangelists and preachers such as Hal Lindsey – who believes the European Union is the work of the antichrist – and more widely on domestic and foreign policy, has been enormous. Scofield himself became rich from its sales, invested in real estate and became even richer, before dying at his home on Long Island in 1921.

Long before Scofield came on the scene, another American, John Humphrey Noyes, attempted to live in the Kingdom before its arrival. He was a preacher and theologian who came to believe that Christ had returned to the world in AD 70 and that therefore those who followed him faithfully were living in a new perfected age. He proclaimed himself free from sin on 20 February 1834, but this did not prove persuasive with his peers, and he eventually founded the Oneida Community in New York State in 1848. The members lived communally, sharing in all tasks, and manufactured hats, travel bags and silverware to make their living. They practised complex marriage, in which men and women took various sexual partners, partly for pleasure, and partly to produce children, bred according to a system called stirpiculture, an early exercise in eugenics. Older men initiated younger women in sexual activity, and older women initiated younger men. This sometimes produced tensions within the community, whose members showed a very durable interest to live in exclusive marriage, so they developed a system of ritualised denunciation called mutual criticism, which it was hoped would purge members of selfishness. There were advantages in this for women, who shared childcare with men, but 'selfishness' eventually became too powerful and when Noyes attempted to ensure the succession of his son Theodore as leader, those tensions overflowed. Noyes heard that a group of local clergy were planning to bring a charge of statutory rape against him, so he fled to Niagara Falls in 1879 and never returned. The community soon fell apart and all but folded, save for the silverware manufacturing company, which exists to this day as Oneida Ltd, the largest supplier of dinnerware to the food service industry in North America. Among the community's alumnae were Ella Underwood, its last surviving member, who died in 1950 at the age of one hundred, and Charles Guiteau, the insane poet who achieved notoriety when he assassinated President James A. Garfield.

I thought of Scofield, Noyes and their followers, agonising in Dallas and Oneida, when I visited the seven churches of the Book of Revelation. These churches, in modern-day Turkey, were established by the apostles (and those who came after them) very soon after the events of Jesus' life. Revelation contains letters addressed to them, full of anxiety and reproach, attacking them for lacking faith and courage and strength, and warning them of what will happen if they didn't buck their ideas up.

They were founded in cities that were among the most important of their day. Ephesus, Smyrna and Pergamon vied for the title First City of Asia, with populations of around 200,000 and most of the trade of the Eastern Mediterranean passing through. The first Christians there lived alongside Jews and Greeks, and the Roman authorities who controlled the region tolerated this cosmopolitan mix as long as they caused no trouble.

The Book of Revelation was written when trouble broke out. The Romans insisted that all subjects must pay homage to the Emperor, but when he was raised to the status of a god, Christians found themselves in an impossible situation. How could they worship the Roman Emperor as a god, when their faith insisted there was only one God, and he didn't live in Rome? Dissent spread and the Romans acted, forcing Christians either to offer sacrifices to the Emperor or face the consequences. For some, this meant death; for others, like the author of Revelation, it meant banishment – exile to the island of Patmos, where he wrote to the churches, urging them to stand fast in the face of the Roman threat. It was these dramatic circumstances which drew forth from the writer that symbolic language of angels and devils and fiery judgements.

Today, those once-proud cities are just heaps of stones. This did not come about, as the writer feared, because they were put down by the Roman powers. On the contrary, it was Christianity that conquered Rome, not the other way round. Nor was it because the final judgement had come. Ephesus and Smyrna and Pergamon were reduced to ruins by earthquakes, and invasions, the collapse of trade and the relentless cycles of history, just like the many other civilisations which have waxed and waned, leaving only piles of stones for archaeologists to ponder over. Meanwhile, we're still here, awaiting the Apocalypse, the day when Christ will come again in glory to judge the living and the dead, as the Creed has it.

Misguided people who meet on a hilltop in anticipation of the end of the world that never comes are figures of fun, but I sometimes think they're right, not wrong – it's just that they're right in the wrong way.

Judgement need not come screaming down from the clouds like a squadron of jet fighters. It could be the moment when we finally understand who we are and what we are for.

Around the beginning of September each year, when the wedding season has died down and the long weeks of Trinity begin to stale, David and I take our holiday. We go with our menagerie of dogs – and now a cat, left on the doorstep in a bag and rechristened Moses – to Scotland, to the same place on the Kintyre peninsula, about as remote on mainland Britain as you can get. This remoteness appealed to Paul McCartney, who bought a farm here at the end of the sixties – and you can see why. To drive there, even the most dedicated paparazzo has to go first to Glasgow, then north past Loch Lomond, up to Inverary, then down again, past Lochgilphead then Tarbert to Campbeltown, from where whisky once sailed out to the world, but no longer. The merchants' houses there stand on a high road leading north; handsome sandstone villas looking down across the town, facing, on the other side of the loch, two streets of tenements and a housing scheme. It is not a big place, but it is the biggest around, with a rather decayed suite of civic buildings, churches of virtually all denominations, and a Boots so full of made-up prescriptions it looks like the medical tent at a refugee camp. Our destination is a village about ten miles away on the east coast, better arrived at via ferry from Ardrossan in Ayrshire to Brodick on the Isle of Arran, then from Lochranza on Arran via another little ferry which takes you to Claonaig on the peninsula. Either way, by road or with seafaring, it feels like an epic journey, but it is worth it because it is so beautiful.

We stay at the edge of a bay, the one where they filmed the video, although it was before the era of video, for 'Mull of Kintyre', McCartney's misnamed hymn to his adopted home. The Mull is actually the southern tip, where the Chinook helicopter crashed, killing half the UK's senior military intelligence officers in the nineties. There's a cairn there now to mark the spot, and the odd golden eagle flying far overhead. The bay where we stay is part of a private estate with a castle and four or five other houses that you can rent. The one we rent is a cabin really, not of clay and wattles made, but of corrugated iron and tongue and groove, built in the twenties for a retired schoolmistress to see out her days. No bee-loud glade either, but a rocky bay noisy with oystercatchers, patrolling the rock pools at low tide like snooty maître d's.

And peace comes dropping slow: the cabin is not on the road, cannot be seen by the other houses, and stands on a patch of grass at the edge of a steep shingle beach leading to Kilbrannan Sound, facing Arran and, in the distance, Ailsa Craig, the volcanic plug of high-grade granite from which the finest curling stones are made. Inside, the house is panelled with pitch pine, has a fire in the kitchen and another in the living room and a view that could break your heart. I have sat in the front room and watched sea otters swim out beyond the rocks, and a deer walk past, and a heron lazily spear its breakfast, and once a fluke as it reared and disappeared in the waves. We have loved it from the moment we first arrived, and with each visit relearn to do nothing but look out of the window, walk along the bay, sit on the rocks looking out to sea, allowing the magic of the place to work.

It has become a place we go to in order to restore the energies of our relationship, expended in the dynamics of vicarage life,

unbalanced by my moth-to-a-flame attraction to the limelight and
David's owlish preference for the shadows. As a measure of our difference and our effort to resolve it, we have learned to travel there
separately because I insist on doing the journey in one go, stopping
to exercise the dogs on the Ayrshire coast, while David takes two
days and likes to stop for tea and Burger King and, mostly, fags. So
if we attempt a journey of more than an hour in the car together
we fight so bitterly that it takes a day for détente to prevail, and I
do not want to lose even a day from the straitened budget of what
some would call quality time.

Quality time: time together with no callers, nothing in the diary,
no phone, no television, no screens, even social media abandoned
for the few days we spend there each year. David would never leave
the bay if it were up to him, but I have to; seclusion for me always
has to be varied with society, and in the mornings I go into town
and buy a *Guardian* and sit in a café on the esplanade watching the
boats in the harbour. Afterwards I call in on a friend living in one
of those merchants' houses on the hill, who runs a charity restoring
a completely unexpected cinema done out like the Alamo. There's
another friend, on the island of Gigha, which lies off the west coast
of the peninsula, but that is the full extent of our social life, save the
odd invitation to drinks from other people staying on the estate.

It is also for me a place where I can restore some shape and discipline and dimensions to a prayer life which, ironically for someone
paid to pray, is so easily lost to the less consequential aspects of
ministry. Being a parish priest is in some ways like being the host
of a party. Serving your guests comes at the cost of your own enjoyment – or, rather, provides a different kind of enjoyment – and the
terrible tendency to lapse into the Master of Ceremonies role which
befalls those of us called to be shepherds and pastors of Christ's
flock is one in which prayer withers.

I learned the rudiments of my prayer life in a monastery, in which
prayer is caught up in the tide of a patterned life, lived corporately.
The rhythm of Matins and Vespers, Morning and Evening Prayer,

repeats in parish life too, or should, but what is harder to achieve is the regular period of silent prayer without which corporate prayer drifts. In the monastery, I spent half an hour every morning and evening, perched silently on a prayer stool, in a side chapel in the community church, which never seemed fuller than when empty. It is like being underwater, in an invisible medium which only reveals its distinctiveness when you encounter resistance, or weightlessness, or hear the ping of prayer returning in endlessly surprising ways from what you thought was silence.

Something rich and strange, the returns of prayer, encountered most often now beside the sea. I sometimes think reflection began with someone on a foreshore, that littoral place, getting caught up in the rhythm of waves coming in and going out. Matthew Arnold, gloomy on Dover Beach, heard only the melancholy long with-drawing roar of the tide and diagnosed the departure of the age of faith; but tides go out and come in and go out and come in.

On the rocks in front of our Kintyre cabin, Anthony Gormley has installed one of his standing figures, life-size, lapped by in-coming and outgoing tides, looking out to Ailsa Craig and the sea beyond. It is for me an image of the priest, a figure occupying the in-between space, feet on the ground but looking out to the far horizon, to the big glitter.

To Mirfield for a Michaelmas ordination – that of an American friend studying at the College of the Resurrection, deaconed here before his priesting back home in Philadelphia. I fall at once into the mysterious swirling undercurrents which characterise life for me there, X's dislike of Y, already an issue, brewing like a storm in a sherry glass. We drink filthy sherry before Evensong and then head to church for re-entry into Mirfield liturgy. As I am leaving, a figure of gothic horror limps towards me out of the dark. An old man, walking with a stick, his face horribly smashed up and bruised, a bandage stuck to his forehead. It turns out to be my friend's dad; he'd fallen down the steps at St Giles' in Edinburgh the week before and opened an artery in his head. The family party has a table to itself at dinner. Later, I go down the road for a drink before Compline and talk to another American seminarian from Connecticut, who looks like Central Casting had answered the call for an American Episcopalian seminarian from Connecticut.

Dramas: the Bishop misses a connection and ends up stranded in Chicago; he's hoping to arrive at Manchester in the early morning. Will he make it? If not, Bishop Anselm, one of the brethren at the monastery, will do the necessary. Then Compline, then a drink with a friend who tells me his granny ran into a parishioner from Boston at a do in Sleaford and asked how I was getting on. He'd told her, 'We hardly ever see him, he's always away.' News to me, unwelcome news.

I get up early, go to Lower Church, and have half an hour in front of the Blessed Sacrament before Matins. It is both familiar and strange to sit in the guest pews for the liturgy you once led; I feel the same old configurations of strength and weakness, of affection and dislike, of expertise and inexperience, but you don't know the backstory; who's in with whom, or out with whom, who's the pack leader, who's the runt?

Breakfast – fried egg with a jolly principal, who makes a joke of holding his fingers over his mug as if for an ablution when I offer to pour the milk – and then to Wakefield station to pick up guests, then into my cassock and scapular for singing practice in Upper Church – Gelineau psalm, nice hymns, Palestrina 'Sicut Cervus' – and then it begins.

Gorgeous service, although the Bishop – who made it from Chicago in time – looks tiny and fussy in a red chasuble and huge gold mitre. It is full fig, a prostration for the litany, the works, but very moving, although the Episcopal Church's Eucharistic Prayer is verbose (and close, I later discover, to the non-juring Scottish bishop's prayer book version that kicked off Anglicanism in the States). My friend is vested in a dalmatic; bit of a struggle because he is portly and the Bishop is small and slight and the dalmatic nearly got the better of them. Then down the hill for Prosecco and lunch, then home through long queues of traffic to Boston and a takeaway from Masala Zone, where a woman, seeing my dog collar, asks if I am a vicar. I say I am and she asks if I could help her with something. I say I'll try, and join her at the bar. She thinks for a moment and I ask myself, What's this going to be about? Then she says, 'What's the difference between a vicarage and a rectory?'

Michaelmas 1978, the first I really remember, not because of fallen angels but a dead Pope, John Paul I, who reigned for thirty-three days. In spite of a short incumbency, he was known as the Smiling Pope, and, rather like Pope Francis, very quickly endeared himself to many. Patriarch of Venice at the time of the death of Paul VI, he was the last Italian Pope, ending a run that had begun in 1523. As a bishop he had attended the deliberations of the Second Vatican Council, and in the spirit of *aggiornamento* established clinics for the sick and those in need, instructed churches to sell their gold and silver gewgaws and give the money to the poor, and strove to relate the Gospel to contemporary life in a series of letters addressed, whimsically, to Dickens, Maria Theresa of Austria, Pinocchio, the Pickwick Club, King David and Jesus. He was conservative, as Popes inevitably are, in other matters, perhaps one of the reasons why he did not want the job. Visiting Portugal while a cardinal, he met one of the visionaries of Fátima, then in old age, who addressed him as 'Holy Father', which caused him severe anxiety. And when the Conclave met to elect a successor to Paul VI, he explicitly ruled himself out. It was not to be. He took the name John Paul, the first Pope to use two names, in honour of his immediate successors, and also chose to be known as 'the first' (unlike Francis, who also used a name not used before). He declined coronation, refused to wear the papal tiara, and was the last to use the Sedia Gestatoria, the throne carried around at shoulder height which preceded the Popemobile. When the news was announced, Mother Teresa described him as 'a sunbeam of God's love shining in the darkness of the world' and the leader of the delegation for the Orthodox Churches, Metropolitan Nikodim of Leningrad, dropped down dead. Thirty-three days after his election, having retired early to read *The Imitation of Christ*, John Paul I also died and was discovered the following morning, sitting up in bed, by one of his nuns. Conspiracy theories abounded, but to any close observer of Church matters the likelihood of clergy organising anything that effectively is so infinitesimally small they need not trouble us for long.

DISPATCHING

All Saints', All Souls'

Behind the high altar at Boston Stump stands an enormous carved reredos, boasting, like Heinz, fifty-seven varieties: fifty-seven varieties from the great multitude of saints, holy men and women and children acclaimed by the Church as citizens of heaven in advance of their actual arrival. There are apostles, evangelists, martyrs, teachers of the faith, local saints, doubtful saints, all ranked around the central figure of Christ in glory. When we had school parties in, we'd set them a challenge to find a particular saint, and it would keep them occupied for hours. Parishioners' deep attachment to that reredos seems an irony in a church that so visibly showed the vandalism of the Reformation with its empty niches, evicted of their saints as ruthlessly as the aristocrats of Revolutionary France during the Terror. Eastern England, once a place of pilgrimage and guilds and relics, was purged, although some old-fashioned customs persisted in altered forms (at the Stump, a Puritan stronghold, they left the image of St Botolph, the patron, untouched). Communities need culture and in the seventeenth century ancient customs were reconfigured to meet prevailing opinion, just as, a thousand years earlier, Christianity, newly arrived, grafted itself onto an existing pattern of rituals and religious belief. Churches were built on the sites of pagan temples, Easter took its name from an Anglo-Saxon goddess of the dawn, wells sacred to the druids were Christianised by attaching a story about a local saint.

*

The publication of the second volume of my *Lives of the Saints* falls, in a timely fashion, on All Saints' Day. At BBC Northampton, in an airless cube with nothing but a microphone and a set of headphones, I talk to local radio stations from the Tamar to the Tees. Asked by interviewers for examples, as I leaf through the book I am reminded of the sheer variety and diversity of the men and women and children the Church has decided to acclaim as citizens of heaven. Among my favourites are St Edith of Wilton, who knocked out the devil with a vicious right hook, and St Benedict Labre, who ended up a beggar in Rome in the 1770s. He would spend his days in ecstasies, floating in the air, which pleased the vergers of the churches he visited because they could sweep under him rather than round him. We'd all like one of those.

Some of these stories are harder to swallow than others, but All Saints', with its rank on rank of holy ones, asserts that there is something irreducibly strange about people who live the life of heaven on earth, so often they seem peculiar or unsettling or hard to fathom.

Here's another, an English saint, William of Rochester. Already it's controversial, for some would say a Scottish saint, and know him as William of Perth. He was certainly born there in the twelfth century and, according to tradition, was rather a wild youth. This burned itself out, and in maturity he became a baker, devoted to his customers and to the service of God. One in every ten loaves he baked was given to the poor, a tithe he exacted upon himself, and he observed the discipline of daily Mass, going to church very early in the morning.

One day he found in the church porch an abandoned baby boy. Rather than leave him to the mercy of the authorities, he adopted the child, named him David the Foundling, brought him up as his own and taught him his trade. William vowed that he would one day take the boy on a pilgrimage to the holy places of England. They travelled south, to Rochester, where they stayed three days, and thence to Canterbury. But on the way, young David, filled with evil, turned on his father and killed him, stole his purse and left him there by the edge of the path. Next along was a madwoman, who plaited a garland of honeysuckle and placed it first on the head of the corpse and then her own, whereupon the madness left her. As so often happens in the stories of the saints, a miracle follows a tragedy. Cured, she told the monks of Rochester what had happened and they carried the body to the cathedral, buried it and built a shrine to William, which became famous. Others followed the madwoman in seeking his prayer in their distress and many were cured. Before long, William was acclaimed as a saint. The bishop took up the cause and in 1256 Pope Alexander IV made it official.

A happy ending, then, to a sorry tale? You might think being murdered by your adoptive son is nothing to feel cheerful about, but it is a happy ending, for William ends up in heaven, and is now the patron saint of adoption.

It's the Mothers' Union Christmas dinner, held in the Mission Room, and over the Beryl Woods china we fall to talking about schooldays. Mrs Peet remembers in the fifties being taught English at Kettering High School for Girls by a Miss Sharf, who was rather statuesque and mysterious. I put two and two together and realise Miss Sharf went on to become Mother Thekla, Abbess of the Community of the Assumption, and the late Sir John Tavener's muse. She wrote the words for his 'Song for Athene', which was sung at the funeral of the Princess of Wales. I saw her once, sitting in the pitch-dark, still statuesque and mysterious, at Compline in the Whitby Sisters' church a year or two before she died.

Visiting Norfolk with a friend, one of the monks from Mirfield, we head off to Hoxne, the site of the martyrdom of St Edmund, King of East Anglia in the ninth century. Edmund arrived at Hunstanton from Germany when he was fourteen and unexpectedly found himself proclaimed sovereign, and crowned on Christmas Day. He then went back to Hunstanton and sat in a tower learning the Psalms until he had them by heart. He was said to be a just and wise ruler, unmoved by flatterers. Unfortunately, East Anglia was being ravaged by Vikings at the time and the great heathen army invaded. Edmund put up a stout fight, but eventually the Vikings chased him to Hoxne in Suffolk, where he hid under a bridge. There was a wedding taking place in Hoxne that day and as the bride and groom crossed the bridge they saw Edmund's spurs glittering and gave away his hiding place to Ivar the Boneless. Ivar insisted he renounce the faith, Edmund refused, so he was beaten, shot with arrows until he looked 'like a hedgehog', and finally beheaded. They threw his head into the forest and when his followers went to look for it they discovered a wolf shouting 'Hic! Hic! Hic!' – Here! Here! Here! – holding the king's head in its paws. The body was buried, but when exhumed so it could be moved to a special tomb at Bury, the arrow wounds had healed and his severed head had miraculously become reattached to his body. He is the patron saint of pandemics.

I stand on a little bridge, Victorian, near the place where the one beneath which Edmund sheltered stood – or so it is said. The stream is fast running, good for Pooh sticks, I reckon, but as I stand by the water's edge, the running of the water, the twitchy movements of the overhanging branches, the cold, the clear light, begin almost to hypnotise me, and I am for a moment transported, not out of the place – it is being here that made it happen – but out of time, conscious of the cross-rhythm of the here and now and eternity, like the twitching branches and the running stream.

'It's a thin place,' says my monk friend. A thin place? 'A place where the membrane between this world and the next is thin.'

Saints are tricky for churches that have been through the Reformation, which for theological and political reasons displaced and discredited them and the cults they gave rise to. Though their continuing witness is tolerated grudgingly, when they have become identified with a place or a season or a profession, saints can prove impossible to eradicate. But in some cases heroic virtue is over-looked or not recognised for what it is. One of my favourites is John Mill, who produced an early edition of the Greek New Testament. Mill was born in 1645 or thereabouts at Shap in Westmorland, went to Queen's College Oxford, where he was made a Fellow, and gave the 'Oratio Panegyrica' at the opening of the Sheldonian Theatre. He subsequently became chaplain to the Bishop of Oxford, and, in 1681, chaplain to Charles II and Principal of St Edmund Hall, where he spent the rest of his life. His great scholarly achievement was the meticulous analysis of more than thirty thousand discrepancies – or textual variants, as they are known in the trade – in the hundred or so New Testament manuscripts available to scholars at the time. This may sound a dull enterprise, but it was in fact a revolutionary one at a time when the stability of Scripture was presumed. How do you account for discrepancies in a text upon which salvation depends? These differences, the work of man rather than God, and in a sense mere jots and tittles, can have dramatic consequences, partly in expressing differences of meaning, but most significantly in showing that Holy Writ may be less than pristine, subject to the same dynamics of transmission and editing as any other text. For some, this merely releases fresh energy in the study of Scripture, for others it threatens the very foundation of the faith. Mill was attacked by scholars and divines, and died only a fortnight after his work was published.

An icon of the Virgin of Kazan was discovered in the sixteenth century by a little girl called Matrona, who was led by the Virgin Mary to the place where it was buried. Of the highest importance in Russian Orthodox tradition, it shows the Virgin Mary holding the Christ child. The icon was entrusted to the care of the monks of the Theotokos Monastery, built on the spot where Matrona discovered it. Framed magnificently in gold and jewels, it was venerated as the protectress not only of Kazan but of Russia, where it achieved the status of Palladium, paraded ahead of armies and defenders of Russia when threatened by hostile powers. The efficacy of her intercession was cited by army commanders in the defeat of Russia's enemies during the Polish invasion of 1612, the Swedish invasion of 1709, and Napoleon's invasion of 1812.

Alas, during the night of 29 June 1904 the icon was stolen by thieves, who were after the frame rather than the icon; although they were apprehended and the frame recovered, they confessed that the icon itself had been chopped up and burnt. One of them later said that it had actually been spirited away to a monastery in Siberia, but the police, unconvinced, refused to investigate this on the grounds that if it were a fake it would be disrespectful to treat it as if it were the real thing. The Church regarded its loss as a judgement on Russia, and a sign of tragedies to come – the Revolution of 1905 and defeat in the Russo-Japanese War. After the 1917 Revolution, however, belief spread that the icon had in fact been preserved, not in Siberia but in St Petersburg, and there were stories of its appearance on the fortifications during the Siege of Leningrad, which kept the Wehrmacht at bay in the 1940s. Her usefulness in this magnificent enterprise did not save her from being sold by the heathen and opportunistic Bolsheviks; she was eventually acquired by the Blue Army of Our Lady of Fátima in Portugal and enshrined there in the 1970s. Scientific examination revealed that the icon was in fact a copy, made around 1730 (it was not unusual for icons to be copied and distributed around Russia). The Portuguese, unpersuaded by this unromantic evidence, gave the icon to Pope John Paul II, who kept it in his private study and declared, 'It has found a home with me and has accompanied my daily service to the Church with its motherly gaze.' Nevertheless, he resolved to make a visit to Moscow or Kazan to take it home, but the Patriarchate declined. In the end it was 2004 before the icon was returned unconditionally to the Russian Church and placed in the Annunciation Cathedral of the Kazan Kremlin.

*

Remembrance Sunday in Finedon and we meet at the War Memorial, the only one I know of which has an exhortation to 'cheerfulness' above the names of our Glorious Dead. Everyone turns out, from Rainbows to Veterans, for this centenary year, although I have noticed the numbers rising for a few years now. Perhaps it is the Wootton Bassett effect, the thrown flowers and respectful applause greeting the repatriated bodies of our service personnel who've died in 'Afghan', as they call it? Perhaps also because there are no veterans of the First World War left (although I have a parishioner who remembers the Zeppelins over Burton Latimer) and few members of the generation that fought in the Second World War, many of whom I have buried since I've been here. Maybe we sense their absence and seek to fill the thinning ranks? I have come to love the veterans, their comradely help for each other, their reliability, their reluctance to make a drama out of things.

They are very much in my mind this centenary year. The BBC has invited me to visit the First World War battlefields of northern France and find the grave of my fellow priest and former chaplain of my school Bernard Vann, who – unusually for a High Church parson – won a VC, awarded posthumously. I find it jarring. How could a shepherd of the sheep, even a public school chaplain, charge into battle with his bayonet fixed? He did exactly that, often, having enlisted in the Artists Rifles – not as a padre but as a private soldier – and then been swiftly promoted up to lieutenant colonel, collecting an MC and bar and a Croix de Guerre as well as his VC. He seems to have been one of those people who only came fully alive on the battlefield. Vann had no doubt that he was fighting a righteous war, in defence of Christian civilisation.

When I look out over the graveyards, not only of British troops and their allies but of Germans too, lying, equally dead, in the heavy soil of Picardy, it strikes me that the enemy, too, had thought God was on their side. Kaiser Bill said, 'I look upon the people and the nation, as handed on to me, as a responsibility conferred upon me by God. And I believe, as it is written in the Bible, that it is my duty to increase this heritage, for which one day I shall be called upon to give an account. Whoever tries to interfere with my task, I shall crush.'

This is not my idea of a Christian civilisation we would want to preserve, but neither is old maids cycling through high-hedged lanes to Evensong, which sounds more like the title sequence for a whimsical sitcom than a civilisation a kaiser would want to destroy.

The film crew and I stay at a hotel in Arras. We arrange to meet in the bar and then go for dinner. I come down early, in my dog collar, and perch on a stool, trying not to look self-conscious. My drink arrives, and as I lift it to my lips with unhurried *savoir faire* I lean backwards and very slowly the stool teeters, then tips over. No one says anything.

At Thiepval, the Lutyens memorial to the 'glorious dead', I get talking to two Englishmen who turn out to be instructors from Sandhurst doing a recce before bringing their students out for a tour of the battlefields. I say that I find it hard to imagine something like this ever happening again.

'What do you mean?' he asks. I can't imagine infantry and tanks facing each other across churned battlefields any more, I say. It's all intelligence and drones now, isn't it? He tells me, 'I give it twenty or thirty years.' Till what? 'Till infantry and tanks meet again and churn up some battlefields.' Why? 'Russia and China are looking to extend their borders?' he says.

Somebody shows up wearing a white poppy and I bridle a little. Not because I object to people expressing a commitment to peace, but because it implies that those who wear red poppies are not equally interested. According to the Peace Pledge Union and the Quakers, the kind of remembrance red poppies promote is un-Christian, embodying the idea that violence can serve the cause of good, while the white shows that absorbing rather than inflicting violence is what lies at the heart of the gospel. To me, the red poppy, so fragile, the colour of shed blood, recalling not banners and trumpets but the dead of Flanders, does anything but glorify violence. I had this conversation with a veteran in the shopping centre in Welling-borough the other day, selling poppies there. He seemed to think that anyone who had experienced war would not think it some-thing to glorify at all.

And then I remember, years ago, going to Boston Grammar School's Remembrance service. After the names of fallen Old Bos-tonians were read out, an Old Boy spoke about two local men, the Staniland brothers, whose names are commemorated on a brass plaque in the Stump. Staniland is an honoured name in Boston, and one of these two brothers was the Town Clerk. When war broke out in 1914, he and his brother were commissioned as officers in the 4th Lincolnshires and in due course were sent to the Western Front. The younger brother, Geoffrey, a second lieutenant, was killed on 12 April 1915, aged thirty-four. Three months later his brother, Captain Meaburn Staniland, followed, dead at thirty-five. You'll find similar stories recorded baldly in a line or two on war memorials the length and breadth of Britain.

Did their families put out more flags, stiffen the upper lip, raise up sons to follow their fallen kin into battle? Yes – another Stani-land, I noticed at the Grammar School Remembrance service, was killed in the Second World War. The family chose to remember their dead sons not with trumpets and blood and glory, but with the text: *Greater love hath no man than this, that he lays down his life for his friends.* In answering the violence of the world with the sac-rifice of their lives, the Staniland brothers, and millions like them, did not glorify war, but transcended it.

Driving through Picardy we keep coming across villages with names more famous than their size justifies, names made famous by the titanic battles fought there a hundred years ago, but today returned to a sort of innocence. I am at Bellenglise where Bernard Vann won his VC amid the din of bursting shells, their fragments still turned up by the plough. Today we hear a skylark spiralling up where those shell fragments in October 1918 rained down.

One of my favourite soldier-saints is Ernesto de la Higuera. A saint by acclamation rather than canonisation, he was born in Argentina in 1928, of Basque and Irish descent. As a youth, he excelled at sport in spite of his asthma, becoming the most feared fly-half in Buenos Aires. He also showed an extraordinary 'affinity for the poor'. As a medical student, he saw terrible hunger, poverty and disease in his travels through South America and was so radicalised by these experiences he threw in his lot with the liberation movements in Guatemala and Cuba, but was eventually martyred in 1967 when wicked soldiers captured him and shot him on trumped-up charges. Immediately, stories of his holiness began to circulate. The nurse who laid him out compared him with Jesus after the Crucifixion and locks of his hair were cut and taken as relics. Those close to him, devastated by his murder, began to sense his continuing presence among them, and it was believed by local people that his spirit walked abroad. The *campesinos* thereabouts venerate his image, placing it alongside Jesus and Mary in shrines, and if their goats should stray they pray to him for their safe return, very efficaciously it seems. One man, a Señor Calzadilla, who was paralysed, recovered his ability to walk after praying to St Ernesto. Indeed, so revered and venerated did he become that he was one of the most recognisable figures of the twentieth century, though better known under his other name: Che Guevara.

I am fond also of St Sergius and Bacchus. They were soldiers, and some have suggested lovers, in fourth-century Syria. Roman citizens, they served as officers in Caesar Galerius Maximianus's army, and were inseparable. One day he asked them to come on a day out to the pagan temple; when they refused to enter, he realised they were secret Christians and lost his temper. He dressed them up as women, paraded them around while everyone mocked them in falsetto. Bacchus was then beaten to death. The next day his spirit appeared to Sergius, beseeching him to hold fast and promising that they would soon be together forever, in the words of the Rick Astley song. He was then brutally tortured and eventually murdered, but did not renounce the faith. They became immensely popular after their martyrdom and the hagiographies make such mention of their closeness, even describing them as ερασται, which can mean 'lovers', that the controversial American scholar John Boswell has suggested they were joined to one another by the rite of αδελπηοποιεσις, 'brother-making', which he argues was a sort of early same-sex blessing.

In Boston I officiated one year at the Act of Remembrance at the Obelisk, for which I put on cassock, surplice, scarf and hood, and was ceremonially verged – led by a verger carrying a staff – along the main shopping street, Strait Bargate. Odd to be dressed up like that in ceremonials while shirtless lads looked on, though not unkindly (they always acknowledge me when I say hello out and about in town, unlike the middle-aged, who usually do not). After the service I went to lunch at the Church Hall to celebrate the sixtieth anniversary of the end of the war in Japan with veterans of that conflict. They were a nice lot, about thirty veterans and their wives and some widows, and I sat next to the chairman of a neighbouring branch, a lovely man, aged eighty-nine, an old soldier wounded five times in Burma. He married late, at thirty-eight, and told me that his wife Audrey, with him at the lunch, had 'never once complained in more than fifty years of marriage'. She sang along to songs from the forties in her wheelchair with a passion that made people on the next table look over, one a little crossly. A man told me that he'd been invited to Japan by the Veterans Society, him and nine others, all expenses paid; but all of them, unknown to each other, declined. 'I can't forgive them,' he said. I observed that I was professionally involved in forgiveness and reconciliation and wondered if he ever felt that might change;

he said he was sorry, but he simply couldn't do it.

On my left was a former Spitfire pilot who'd served in Burma, flying from London to Rangoon via implausible places like Alexandria and Karachi. He had also served in Sicily, where he was surprised one morning to be shot down by a Messerschmitt. He bailed out, exactly as trained (pull your helmet off, roll the plane to the left, jettison the canopy and fall out), and landed safely; or so he thought. He wandered around a bit before being picked up by some Americans, who noticed that he was limping. When he took his boot off, he saw he'd been shot through the foot but hadn't realised.

Notice in the paper: *Jack Warwick, funeral director, has died in hospital in Australia, where he was holidaying.* At the bottom it says *All enquiries to Jack Warwick, Funeral Director.*

I suppose every religion must have something to offer for the commemoration of the dead, especially ones that situate themselves on the earth in which the dead repose. In spite of endless revision, even the Church of England, which sometimes seems about as mysterious as S Club 7, maintains some sort of lookout beyond the far horizon of our lives. Four hundred years ago, when the reformers were taking charge of places like Boston, men on a mission, disgusted with the corruption of the Church, came to the Stump, then one of the greatest churches of Medieval England, with hammers and axes, smashing windows and pulling down statues, imposing their own radical rewrite of Christian faith on buildings and believers. Out went the Mass and in came the sermon, out went the stained glass and in came whitewash, out went Christmas and in came catechesis. In parts of England, particularly in the east, they swept all before them; but it's difficult to sweep away our habit of thinking of our dead, especially marked, then and now, on All Souls' Day.

The Christian custom is at least a thousand years old. Even today there are places in continental Europe where food and drink is left out at night for the dead. In the Austrian Tyrol special cakes are baked and set in front of the fire when the family goes to bed, and in Brittany people meet in cemeteries to pour milk on the head-stones of their family tombs. I expect these practices go back in one form or another much further than Christianity. The Christian faith appropriated them and made them its own, but never wholly its own; and maybe that is why the rigorist Puritans sought to eliminate them. Unlike most other pre-Reformation red-letter days, All Souls' remains in the calendar – not in its original place, after Easter, but on the day following All Saints', as a nod to the new orthodoxy, which appropriates it to the maxim that souls follow saints, the faithful departed who endure in God's favour in the life beyond this life. So when Christians remember the dead, we do so paradoxically, with grief and with hope. I love the Russian *Kontakion* for the Dead, which gets this exactly: 'All we go down to the dust; and weeping o'er the grave we make our song: Alleluia, alleluia, alleluia!'

Marge was housekeeper for my grandmother, 'Mrs Coles', and my mother 'Mrs Nigel', and I knew her all my life and half of hers. I played the organ at her funeral, in the village where she had been born, baptised, schooled, went into service, married the estate carpenter, brought up her children, endured widowhood, and would have died, had not dementia obliged her to move into a home. It was a lovely afternoon, the sun came out, and everything was cool and fresh after heavy rain. The vicar officiated in a packed church, which had been cheerfully done out in orange gerberas – Marge would have loved it. Her son Roger gave the address. He said he remembered how they'd 'walk across the fields to the Jolly Friar in Twywell on a summer evening. Crisps and Vimto for the kids and mum's favourite, a lemon and lime, for her. Then we'd all get the bus home. It doesn't sound like much today, does it?' he said. 'But we couldn't have been happier.'

*

A fortnight before Christmas and in between carol services I am on the phone to a funeral director, going through the order of service for a friend's mother, who I will be consigning to eternity at a crematorium in South London. As we're going through hymns and music, she asks me what I want the organist to play when the coffin comes in. 'I Know That My Redeemer Liveth', I tell her. On the day, I open my order of service and see printed therein: *As the cortège enters, the organist will play 'I Know That My Reindeer Cometh'*.

One morning in Stamford, back when I was a new pastoral assistant, I got to church to find the churchwarden, a candle burning in front of the screen, as if for a funeral, but no vicar. 'Looks like a funeral,' the churchwarden said, 'but I'm sure he said the funeral was on Friday.' The vicar arrived in a foul mood; there was indeed a funeral scheduled for ten, so I got into a cassock. He gave me a few terse instructions and then, just before the cortège arrived, told me to go and play the organ, because the organist hadn't turned up. So I did, never having played it before, not even knowing how to turn it on. We got through the service, and I was improvising on the *kyrie eleison* at the end when the churchwarden came and said I was to 'come immediately'. I got stuck in a bottleneck at the north door, but the vicar appeared and signalled, rather less than graciously, for me to push through. I did and got in my car and he told me to wait for the limousine carrying the family party to overtake us and move into position behind the hearse. But I could not work out a signal that would indicate this to the limousine driver, or he was disinclined to understand me, so I had to pull out first and off we went, making an odd procession through the town: the hearse bearing the coffin, a top-hatted man in front, a shiny black Daimler behind, carrying the family, and me and the vicar in the middle, in cottas, him in a biretta, sitting in a bright blue Beetle with a bunch of snowdrops in the dashboard vase.

We got to the cemetery and processed with the coffin and the family to the graveside, where the vicar scattered some sand onto the coffin, they all threw in flowers, and they all cried. It was very moving, standing round a graveside on a cold and frosty morning, as these people mourned their mother, their grandmother, their friend, and my eyes filled too. Sharing in the grief of the bereaved wears off quite quickly, I found. Your job as officiant is not to weep but to lead the service. And grief belongs to mourners. I once experienced that the other way round, taking the funeral of someone I loved, and decided I would not do it again.

After the funeral we went to see a parishioner in hospital, admitted weeks ago without anyone at church having been informed until now. I drove us there – 'Can we have radio silence, please?' – and when we arrived, parking in the Pay and Display with everyone else (clergy privilege long abolished), I asked for her at reception. The hospital clerk had no record of her admission. We were about to leave when the vicar spotted her husband in the car park. 'She's in ward one,' he said. 'Under a pseudonym?' I asked, gormlessly. He looked at me and snapped, 'Of course not!' I realised, in a moment of hot shame, that he was in pain. The vicar saw it too and after I had followed them back into the hospital, I was sent to wait in the car park until he was done. She was in the mental health ward and that's why her name hadn't shown up in the records.

I go to see a man who lives in retirement in a bungalow behind a garden that's beginning to get out of control; it is overgrown, but a double row of grape hyacinths is springing up, intensely blue, marking out what had once been a well-tended path. I ring the bell once, then twice, and eventually he comes to the door in a shabby old pair of trousers which he is trying to do up as I watch him fumble for his keys through the frosted glass in the front door – I'd caught him on the loo, I realise. He lets me in and with gentle charm ushers me into the sitting room, which is less than cared-for, with a grand piano taking up half the space, pushing the sofa and the armchairs into a cramped semicircle round the television. He sits down heavily on the sofa, does his flies up without evident embarrassment, and I ask him how he is.

Not good: he's been ill, with anaemia, and the iron tablets the doctor's put him on have upset his stomach and given him terrible constipation. I wince, remembering his hurried appearance at the door. But that isn't what's really ailing him. He says in his gracious voice, 'You see, the real trouble is that I miss my dear wife.' He begins to weep. 'I'm sorry, I get emotional when I think of her.' I say, as gently and as evenly as I can, please don't apologise. She'd been diagnosed with breast cancer when she was forty-eight, but had survived until their fiftieth wedding anniversary, when she'd finally succumbed. 'It had been a lovely summer afternoon,' he tells me, 'we were at home, the door was open, leading out into the garden. I was with her, talking to her, and I saw her take her last breath.' He pauses, his eyes running with tears, and gathers himself to say, to heave out, 'When I saw she'd died, I went outside and stood in the garden. Why did I do that? I don't understand why I didn't stay with her. Why didn't I stay with her?' He looks at me, in agony. I look back steadily, but say nothing – what can I say? – and he says, 'But she was gone, she wasn't here any more.'

The florist is unexpectedly open because a young man died at Christmas when his car left the road at midnight and ended up in a ditch. He lay there undiscovered until a farmer found him at half past seven in the morning. The florist has been under siege from people wanting to send flowers, and she feels she couldn't refuse. So she drove to the wholesalers at five o'clock on Christmas Eve to pick up armfuls of lilies and white roses – anything she could get her hands on – for the funeral. David and I walk round the churchyard and run into a man with his weeping daughter outside the closed electrical shop, where he is trying to replace a burned-out fuse for her Christmas present, an Xbox. The first casualty of Christmas, I think; and then I remember the dead boy.

*

Someone tells me about a friend, a funeral director, who was preparing a body for a viewing in the chapel of rest. The family were outside and, before bringing them in, he went to light the two candles beside the coffin. Unfortunately, when he struck the first match, the top flared up and flew off, he knew not where. He struck another, lit the candles, and went to collect the grieving widow and children. When he returned, he found the body and the coffin on fire. The match head had landed in the coffin's synthetic lining, which had gone up like a firelighter.

At Theological College during Death Week, a week devoted to the ministry we would exercise for those at the end of their lives, we went on a trip to a funeral director's and thence to the crematorium. The company we visited was run by a likeable man called Tim, who generously gave half a day each year to show ordinands round. The company was based in an old Methodist Sunday School, a huge place hurriedly converted, so the walls suddenly met the ceilings in surprising ways, and in the stockroom upstairs dozens of coffins were stacked upright, head at the bottom, in a room where the Sunday School used to put on pantos, so the caskets were bizarrely surrounded by childish paintings of Jack and the Beanstalk and Puss in Boots.

Tim told us how the place functioned, what clients wanted and didn't want, and, most usefully, what made for a good relationship between clergy and funeral directors. What exasperated them most, he said, was clergy not letting them know in advance when they were away, and incumbents and curates taking the same day off. Another thing that exasperated them, he told us, was clergy phoning with fait accompli funerals, no consultation over dates and times. He said organising a funeral was like organising a wedding, only you had a year to do a wedding. For a funeral, you were lucky to get a week. I wondered what it must be like to look after Jews or Muslims, who need to be in the ground in twenty-four hours.

Then an extraordinary visitor arrived – the Coroner's Officer, a huge man with the biggest belly I'd ever seen. Shaven head, moustache, an oddly delicate, slightly fastidious way of moving, and bright red braces, which he twanged. He was an ex-copper and lugubrious as ex-coppers were; having explained what the Coroner's rights were and why they were interested in bodies, he told us that coroners ranked after the Lord Chancellor, who appointed them, so on state occasions those small-town solicitors and country doctors followed the Lord Chancellor in procession, ahead of far more illustrious dignitaries.

Both Tim the undertaker and the Coroner's Officer were at pains to tell us that their duties were carried out sensitively, with regard for the feelings of the bereaved – they described themselves, or their role, as pastoral – and I was impressed by the practical care Tim took of his customers, as a professional and as a decent human being. His sympathies were wider than his commercial interest, so he didn't flog people expensive coffins, nor did he embalm bodies that were only slightly delayed between demise and disposal. He took us into the cold room, where three bodies wrapped in shrouds were stacked on shelves and three more were lying in coffins awaiting viewing. There was a little old lady done up to her chin in a pale yellow zip-up shroud and a thin man dressed in a suit and a baseball cap, and a big man in an England shirt, his face covered by a flap of some shiny synthetic material. Someone forgot to prop up his head after he died and the blood had settled in his head, so he was a bit discoloured. Back came the flap to reveal his puce face, as if he'd died in a moment of apoplectic anger. The dead, though, were unnerving but not frightening. They looked like waxworks, not human somehow. There's something in our psyches which says, Don't go there.

Much more affecting was the junk lying around the place: pieces of statuary and woodwork carved with names now unknown, in spite of the 'always in our thoughts' and 'never forgottens'. Most affecting of all was a set of shelves stacked from top to bottom with plastic receptacles containing as yet uncollected ashes. Some had been there for twenty years, the earthly remains of a mother or grandfather or a son abandoned not in life but in death.

We went on to the crematorium, a handsome slightly Lutyens brick building covered in ivy and set on a wooded hillside. Tim conducted us in via the back entrance, past a group of mourners, uncomfortable as defendants in unaccustomed jackets and ties. We saw the arrival of the coffin, not in the wood-laminated carpet-tiled front-of-house but on CCTV in the grubby, janitorish backstage area. The operator followed the funeral on monitors, and when the officiant pressed a button, a bulb lit up on a panel prompting him to play the music, operate the curtains, close the doors.

We were then taken to where the coffins arrived after their departure from the chapel. It was functional, a workplace with none of the softening design elements of the front-of-house. The distinction is carefully preserved, for example, by double doors between the furnaces and the chapel, so relatives don't have to hear the sound of the ovens as the coffin trundles away. This area was run by an affable skinhead in T-shirt and jeans, with elaborate tattoos covering his forearms. He was very helpful and told us how it worked, explaining the digital readouts on the ovens showing the temperature, the bye-laws concerning emissions (no plastics, no nylon), and how they make sure that the ashes you receive are the ashes of your relative and not another. There were some gruesome things, like the cremulator, which looked and sounded like a big coffee-grinder, grinding up the bits of bone among the ash. And when he opened an oven to let us see the almost consumed body within, everyone pushed forward to see a red-hot skull looking back at us.

Weird funeral coincidences: Yasser Arafat in Ramallah and John Peel in Bury St Edmunds.

Funeral in church for John, who in his salad days downed tools at the building site at noon on a Saturday, got the bus to Northampton, ran to Franklin's Gardens, changed into his rugby kit, played in the back row for the Saints, got the bus back to Finedon, went to the Prince of Wales for a pint or two before heading for home, his return announced by the click-clack of his Blakey's on the yard flags. Our goings out and our comings in.

Robin, my training incumbent in Boston, told me that when he was in a parish in North London there was a funeral director with whom he got very friendly. One day he phoned up in a flap and said he had a last-minute problem and could Robin take a funeral for him. Robin said yes, he could, and asked for details. The name of the deceased was Goldstein and Robin gently enquired if the gentleman was of the Jewish faith. Yes, the undertaker said. Robin reminded the undertaker that he was a Christian priest and therefore not really suitable. The undertaker thought for a moment and said, 'Couldn't you just put on a hat?'

We once called in at a nursing home, where the manager waited until Robin finished introducing me, then laughed and looked at me a bit quizzical as he said, 'Not the famous Richard Coles, who used to be in that band?' I said yes, but by then he'd turned away in embarrassment. We went to anoint a man very close to death, breathing raspily but awake and able to respond. Robin spoke to him a bit like an adult to a child and held his hand – the former was awkward, but the latter was not – then anointed him and we said prayers. On his bedside table was a photograph of himself, still recognisable as a young man in Second World War army officer's uniform, arm-in-arm with a young woman. They were both smiling and delighted to be with each other – his wife, I presumed, no longer on the scene – and the contrast between that and his circumstances now was poignant.

He died in the night, and when it came time for his funeral we discovered from a friend of his that the woman in the photograph was indeed his wife, who had died not long after the photograph was taken, leaving him a widower for over fifty years. He also turned out to have been a war hero, decorated more than once for bravery. After the war he'd gone into business and eventually became a director of a big and successful company. So, a man of substance and character, and a bedridden, all but unvisited, ancient who died alone in a nursing home in the fens. All our journeys end at the same terminus and we can decorate them this way and that, but it makes no difference. The thought produces in me Schopenhauerian good cheer.

A cremation at Mortlake, so the funeral directors offered to pick me up at St Paul's and drive me there. They arrived in the van, or the private ambulance, as it is coyly called, which picks up bodies from hospitals. It was driven by one of the most taciturn members of that profession, a tall Jamaican of few words, who I rather liked. He nodded hello and we sat in agreeable silence until he said, 'Jeremy Beadle?' I replied, 'Yes?' There followed a pause. 'Him in de back.' And so I learned of the untimely death of television's favourite prankster.

I was in the gym on the running machine when I saw on the telly, sound down and accompanied inappropriately by thumping disco, that Mo Mowlam had died. Mo was that rarest of things, a genuinely loved politician, Northern Ireland Secretary at the time of the Good Friday Agreement. I had become friendly with her and her husband Jon in the nineties and spent a couple of weekends with them at Hillsborough Castle, her official residence in Northern Ireland, a smart country house which seemed normal until you tried to open the French windows and realised they were bullet-proof glass and needed more push than you could give them. She had been ill for a while, and I knew she was dying, but I still felt a jolt of shock when I saw her face on the television. I called her husband Jon with condolences and he asked me to conduct Mo's funeral – but with no religious element, if that was something I could do. I didn't need to think before saying yes; the components of it were entirely up to her and Jon. Afterwards, I wondered if it was strictly proper for me to conduct a non-Christian funeral? As a private individual, rather than as a clergyman of the Church of England? Am I a private individual as a clergyman of the Church of England? I agonised about this for a bit and said Evening Prayer and almost immediately found myself mentally rehearsing my performance. The Old Adam.

The day before the funeral, as I took the train cross-country to Sittingbourne, I read everything from the *New Statesman* to the *Spectator*, to *Prospect*, for balance and detachment. Jon was there with his children and we talked till late, drinking Balvenie and red wine, which I knew I'd pay for the next day. Jon seemed compos mentis, although he repeated himself several times, funnily enough just like Mo did, and told me three times, until his daughter gently interrupted, about his conversations with Tony Blair about the re-action to Mo's death. Jon showed me letters of condolence he'd re-ceived, a generous one from Gordon Brown (terrible crabby writing in thick felt-tip), lovely ones from Prince Charles and Madeleine Albright, and a sober typed note from Elizabeth R. We recalled, too, the times Mo had been harder to love, her off-stage bad temper, and exasperating habits, and unrestrained willingness to milk her popularity, which made us laugh. We decided what we were going to do at the service – including singing two timeless funeral classics, 'Working Class Hero' and 'Mad Dogs and Englishmen' – and then watched *Lost* on E4.

I woke up with a terrible hangover and was sick, not a great start to the day, but recovered and got into clericals and went to see the crem with Jon. It looked like Southfork in Dallas, a modern fake-gabled single-storey building in a windswept field surrounded by young trees. The staff were helpful and showed me the buttons and stuff I needed to know, including Button 2, which made a bright light shine on the coffin, growing in intensity and then going out as the curtain curled round the catafalque. A bit showbiz, I said, and they said, 'Yeah, we call it the "Beam Me Up Scotty".'

Back at the farm, Mo's relatives had arrived in a camper van, her nephews and nieces changing from sandals to shoes, from T-shirts to suits, and then the hearse appeared, ponderously unsuitable on the track that led to the main road. The funeral director was one for walking in front of the hearse with his top hat in his hand, to the end of the land, where he got in beside the driver and we drove through Sittingbourne's streets of filter lanes and budget off-licences and crossed dual carriageways, talking about embalming until we got to the crem.

I officiated in clericals, accompanied 'Working Class Hero' on the organ, and in my address thanked Mo for having made me, in my dog collar, at a service, sing the word 'fucking' not once but twice. That made the funeral director laugh. We had a minute's silence and a carefully worded commendation, and that went some way to providing for the thing religion used to provide for, and that was that. Goodbye, Mo, not with a fanfare, an unseemly showing from the media, a choking reading of 1 Corinthians by the Prime Minister, but with something domestic, recognisable, un-wrenched-out-of-shape.

An odd thing: when I told my colleagues that I was going to take Mo's funeral, their first reaction was to congratulate me, as if I'd pulled off a coup, rather than to offer condolences.

This happened too at St Paul's, Knightsbridge, when we took the funeral of Alexander McQueen the fashion designer, perhaps the most weirdly glamorous funeral in a church where glamorous funerals were not unusual. I knew Alexander McQueen a little before he was famous, when he was Lee and used to hang around the same nightclubs as me. He was a nice man, a working-class boy from Bermondsey with a wonderful talent. The fashion world turned out in force for the funeral, which was arranged not by the family but by Gucci. This was probably wise, because media interest was high and the houses opposite, most of which were permanently being done up, emptied of builders and filled up with photographers, the more enterprising of whom arranged exclusive access to the upper floors overlooking the church. They were not enterprising enough, however, to catch the coffin arriving, because in keeping with ancient custom it came in on the eve of the funeral to lie on a catafalque overnight draped in a pall, a big purple cloth, with four giant yellowish beeswax candles burning around it. Less in keeping with ancient custom, a security guard, ex-SAS – whom we provided with coffee and cakes from Ottolenghi's round the corner – was locked in with it overnight, while a team of – tactical gardeners? – arrived to build a temporary screen of foliage round the churchyard to make the paparazzi's life a bit more difficult.

In the morning I got into church early and prayed before Matins for the Lee I had briefly and glancingly known, lying in his coffin. Then the flowers began to arrive, the most extravagant I have ever seen, from David and Iman, and Elton and David, so luscious and abundant it was difficult to see how anyone could top them, but someone did when a giant tray of white narcissi arrived, like a field of virginal perfection only slightly spoiled by the faint smell of piss you often notice with narcissi. The thick accompanying card was signed 'Anna Wintour'.

The curate down the road went into her local primary school to take assembly and as she was preparing to leave the Head appeared and asked her to come to the office. One of the children, a nine-year-old boy, had lost his mother the previous year, just before Christmas, killed in a car crash. His grandmother had just called to tell them that morning, while the boy had been coming in to assembly, his father had been killed in an accident at work, almost a year to the day after his mother died. The Head asked her to break the news to him, while the pastoral team supported her. The little boy was called to the office, walked in, looked around, and said: 'My dad's dead, isn't he?'

*

One of the sofa-surfing young men of the parish was hanging around in church, so I sat with him in the Cotton Chapel, deflecting his requests for money and talking him through his problems. His eyes grew wet and then he began to cry, burying himself in his army-issue parka in shame. Hard to tell how much grief and how much calculation was in it. I had to move him on, because we were waiting to receive Jean, who died last week, into the Cotton Chapel on the eve of her funeral. Robin and I covered her coffin with the pall and put on a bible and a crucifix while her unchurched girls sobbed in the back row.

A good turnout of town and church the next day. It was not a requiem, at the request of the daughters, but it was a proper funeral, with sprinkling and censing of the coffin. As I produced the thurible and handed it to Robin, the little fusillade of protesting coughs broke out, as it always does, and it was my turn to be incensed. Three things I am going to hold in reserve on this: first, around a billion Christians, from San Francisco to Shanghai, seem to manage quite well with incense, certainly without succumbing to respiratory failure. Second, it did very well for Jesus and the apostles, and is recommended to us by Holy Scripture. Third, if anyone brings up the coughing, I'm going to say, nonchalantly, yes, the children at the primary school do that too. As we processed out, the servers stopped at the north door to let us pass out to the cars and I saw they were all in tears and my irritation subsided and I felt chastened.

After Evening Prayer, I was walking down West Street, it was dark and clear and cold with a frost coming, and I came across a young man, in his twenties, about six feet six tall, skateboarding bare-chested along the pavement. I stepped to one side to let him pass and trod in a human turd.

Someone called to say Harry Williams had died. He was the most celebrated brother of the community, and once one of the most celebrated clergymen of his day, and the author of *True Wilderness*, which made a great impression on many, including me. The day before his funeral I drove up to Mirfield, arriving in time for Evensong and to receive Harry's body into church. I was co-opted as a cantor; it felt good to be back in a scapular and on a cantor's stool singing the office. Harry, lying in an open coffin in the porch, was boxed up and brought in and put under the giant pall the community uses when one of its own dies, held up over a frame, and known inevitably, in community slang, as the Wendy House.

The next morning, I joined the choir for Harry's requiem, which was glorious, all the more so considering he didn't really believe in anything. There was the oddest mixture of mourners: some handsome toff boys, who bawled through the Kontakion; a scattering of smart ladies; and someone representing the Prince of Wales. Before the service one of the new students was sitting in his stall trying to pray while two women sitting behind him were chatting. Unable to bear it any longer, he turned round and snapped at them that it is the custom of the house to observe total silence in church. They looked chastened and obeyed, which was lucky, considering, as he found out later, they were Lady Runcie, widow of the Archbishop of Canterbury, and the Dowager Duchess of Devonshire. We sang 'Coe Fen', which as usual I couldn't get through, and a glorious Kontakion as the body left the church.

Funny thing: the two former students who turned up for the funeral were me and my friend Ed, neither of whom knew Harry, though we both admired him and particularly *True Wilderness*. I say we never met him, but we saw him every time we passed his room on the ground floor. One of my fellow students told me he used to wave at Harry every time he went past, and he would smile and wave back. Then a note came down from the House asking all students not to wave at Fr Harry.

At a funeral visit I try to phrase a question tactfully: 'Would it be fair to say your grandmother . . . knew the value of a pound?' Her grandson replies, 'She'd have skinned a fart.'

*

Prayer on the board in the Stump:

> Please pray for Joan in her confusion and possessiveness and make her realise that no one is perfect and that if she carries on this way she will be left a very miserable old woman.

*

Funeral today, and just as I am about to commend the departed there is a little commotion at the back of the crematorium chapel. The doors swing open and a man in shackles with a prison officer on either side and one in front, and two uniformed plods behind, comes in, the youngest son of the departed. It calls to mind the final scene of the American Civil War film *Shenandoah*, with the young son staggering up the aisle at the wedding, only the moral polarity has been reversed.

We buried Bob today, a stalwart of the church, the cricket club, the school, the town and everything. He was a plumber by trade, his apprenticeship interrupted by the war. He used to tell how, one afternoon, working his allotment, he saw a Dornier chased by a Hurricane fly so low he could see the terrified faces of the German crew, followed by a rattle of machine-gun fire, an explosion, and a scorched glove fell at his feet. When he picked it up, a hand fell out. Bob was also summoned, in his professional capacity, to Harrowden Hall, seat of the Vaux family (of Gilbey's Gin), which overlooks Finedon. There he was required to line with lead the late Lord Vaux's coffin before he joined his ancestors in the family vault, and was surprised, when the job was finished, to discover that his Lordship had been lying alongside the whole time under a sheet on a table. He was lifted like a scarecrow into his newly leaded home with such insouciance that Bob's apprentice fainted.

Bob's grave is next to the cricket club where he was opening bat for many a year and played for the county on more than one occasion, 'impressing the visitors with his neat play', according to the *Kettering Evening Telegraph*.

Someone I go to see on a funeral visit shows me a pile of old *Church Times* from the fifties that had belonged to his devout mother. In the classified section there is an advertisement which reads: *Curate seeks motor car to broaden experience of life (pre-1938 models only)*.

And then a good headline: *Russian Patriarch Reappears – I Am Not Dead*.

And in the following week's *Church Times* a notice from Bishop Stephen Venner in which he makes it known that he is not dead either.

Conducting the funeral of a lady who ended up living in a caravan surrounded by bags of bought but unopened shopping. There she contracted cancer and died aged fifty-six. She asked for me on her deathbed and she was composed and not in distress. I went to see her sister to discuss the funeral arrangements and she had emptied out the contents of the caravan and found details of thousands of pounds' worth of bank loans, money that she'd then donated to animal charities. She couldn't bear the thought of someone paying a tribute at her funeral, but had found a poem, lovingly laminated, in a bin liner, which she wanted read instead.

> *I may never see tomorrow,*
> *There's no written guarantee;*
> *And the things that happened yesterday,*
> *Belong to history.*
>
> *I can't predict the future*
> *I cannot change the past.*
> *I have just this present moment.*
> *I must treat it as my last.*

I must use the moment wisely,
For it soon shall pass away.
And be lost to me forever,
As part of yesterday.

I must exercise compassion,
Help the fallen to their feet;
Be a friend to the friendless;
Make an empty life complete.

The unkind thing I do today,
May never be undone;
And friendships that I fail to win,
May never more be won.

I may not have another chance,
On bended knees to pray;
And thank God with a humble heart,
For giving me this day.

Donations to the Cat Protection League.

*

Tony, not a parishioner but a fellow member of the Cycle Touring
Club, was killed in a collision while on his bike. He was a parishioner before my time, running a specialist steel-manufacturing
company where the Finedon Road furnaces once roared. He gave
the church the fireproof doors behind which we keep our parish
records, the last church in the diocese to do so, to the chagrin of the
County Records Office. They date back to the 1540s, preserving in
the copperplate script of the eighteenth and nineteenth centuries,
and the tiny brown inked handwriting of my Jacobean predecessors, and the smart italic of a predecessor still with us, Finedonians
hatched, matched, dispatched, in every degree. That's the admin

end of what we do, preserving a community's memory. The holy end, I think, is more about releasing it. 'Don't cling to me,' says Jesus to Mary in the garden early on Easter morning, for although love binds us he has somewhere to go, and so do we.

We lead Tony from church up the hill to his grave, as spring bursts forth; but we're destined for grace, beyond nature, and not for renewal, but resurrection.

ADVENT

On a weekend break away from the parish in the Christmas rush, David and I go to church on a cold morning, where Matins is taken by a lugubrious clergyman who ascends the pulpit and says, 'As Christmas approaches on this fourth Sunday of Advent, I want to preach about the end of the world . . .'

In London I run into an old friend, a priest. He is vicar of a parish no less smart than St Paul's, Knightsbridge, the very pattern of a town priest, and I cannot think of a cleric more suited to life and ministry in the middle of London than he. One of the great pleasures of living in London, he says, is the opportunities it offers to do things that are only possible in a city of its size. If you want to yodel, or play ice hockey, or dance the tango, or do all three together, there are enough people wanting to do the same to turn the idlest of wishes into reality. Once he called to tell me about a group he had found on Facebook: *Dachshunds in London*. 'It meets at two on Sunday afternoons at the bandstand in St James's Park,' he said. 'Do you fancy it?' Yes, I did. David and I, with unintended good timing for our civil partnership, had been given a miniature long-haired dachshund by an eccentric millionaire whom I met once. Daisy, unusually dappled in white and tan, with eyes like blue marbles, qualified us for membership, and my friend's wire-haired version, called Fritz, qualified him.

We tried it out one Sunday in late autumn, and although it had chucked it down that morning, the sun came out after lunch and the whole park glowed with the reds and yellows of fallen leaves. When I arrived, with Daisy tugging on her lead, the only person there to meet us was a Russian dog photographer who looked a little crestfallen at having come such a long way for such a small turnout.

Then, in the distance, the low profile of a dachshund snaking through the wet leaves appeared, then another and another, dragging their owners behind them, and then I heard someone call my name. It was my friend and Fritz. The dogs ran off, and – typical clergy – at a meeting of sympathetic and varied strangers with one big thing in common, we talked only to one another, swapping news and church gossip while Fritz and Daisy scampered with their peers. We compared plans for Christmas – How many carol services have *you* got? – but then my friend said, 'Thank God we've got Advent first.'

'Advent first, thank God,' I agreed. 'My favourite season of the Church's year.' He said, 'Mine too.'

If you are a member of the Church of England, a feast of Advent music, hymns, readings and customs is your heritage, from 'Come, Thou Long-Expected Jesus', to Isaiah's promise of a miraculous birth, to the Blue Peter Advent Crown, so complicated to construct it caused the worst row my parents have ever had in the Christmas of 1971, still not mentioned in our house. My favourite ritual when I was a boy was opening the Advent calendar. Back then, it was all scenes from the Christmas story, or of Christmas traditions. Now, it seems to be mostly chocolate Daleks; but for those past the age of confectionery, the services of Advent are themselves a sort of calendar, a look at the great themes of the season: waiting for Jesus, the judgement he brings, light breaking at the edge of the night; and a preview of the joy that is to come.

Some of these themes are more familiar than others; joy coming to the world is one we can all respond to, but I suspect the coming judgement is less readily embraced. The Bible readings throughout Advent are full of a sense of impending crisis and a call to watchfulness, quite startling in its urgency and at odds with the mood abroad. We look forward to the birth of Christ, but we do so from the darkness of this present moment, a darkness we have become so used to, we think it is just how things are – it is what it is, in that voguish and complacent phrase – which is why that theme of judgement is so important, to wake us up from complacency and make us ready to greet the light when it comes.

As a child, I was so excited by the coming of the light of Christmas that I used to preview Christmas Eve on my calendar, its picture lying enticingly beyond double doors, which opened at my premature bidding to reveal the crib scene. I can still see it now, a coloured patch of paper, no bigger than a stamp, not much to look at until I held it up to my bedside lamp so the light shone through – the baby in the manger, his earthly parents looking on, provoking in me paradoxical feelings of both disappointment and anticipation.

Advent is a particularly busy time for media vicars, as the secular world's appetite for what we do spikes. I have a piece to finish for the Christmas edition of the *New Statesman*, another for *Women's Weekly*, a radio round-up of the year, and a piece for a topical political television programme. At least it *is* topical. Christmas for me actually began earlier than this, even earlier than on the High Street, when I appeared on a television Christmas special, recorded in the early autumn. There was an odd time-travelling feel to it, stepping out of a sunny London street into a studio frosted with white and planted with Christmas trees. The other guests in their Christmas jumpers were full of cheer, but I was there untinselled in a dog collar as a representative of the *version originale*. Trying to stand up for Christmas as a custodian of the Church's tradition sometimes feel like shouting into the wind, and trying to find a connection to what the mainstream is doing does not get easier – until you hear people's stories and realise that even now when the *magnum mysterium* could not be more mysterious, there is something very durable about drawing in those closest to you as the year grows darker and feasting in firelight or by a flickering TV.

Behind it, gathering force through Advent and the year's end, is the possibility of renewal, especially paradoxical now with the slap of a few remaining leaves falling from the trees onto the pavements, and the radiators creaking and clicking as the central heating comes on. Nature and our own affairs speak of a winding down as we approach the year's midnight, and the promise of spring and new birth lies far off. The paradoxical weirdness of Christianity, a reliable sign of its authentic presence, is expressed in the insistence that, in spite of everything, we look forward in hope. John the Baptist, looking like a battle-hardened eco-warrior, stands at the River Jordan announcing that the Lord is nigh, setting the mood of expectation and building excitement.

But churches seem so bad at doing that. Declining numbers, ageing congregations, a sense that we're moving further from the centre of most people's concerns, can make us very inward-looking and gloomy and hopeless.

The Free Church of Scotland – the Wee Frees as they're known – is sometimes caricatured as the very soul of dour Christianity. Unyielding as granite, in doctrine and custom, it is hard to think of a Christian denomination which appears more resistant to change. A friend of mine whose father was a Wee Free minister in the Highlands in the seventies was not allowed to read novels when she was growing up, lest they inflame unholy passions. Their church was so strict that upholstery was frowned on; thrift was the rule of the day and God forbid you should ever stray from the ways of the elders and forefathers. She went on to marry a German Roman Catholic, work in the City of London, and fill her house with lavishly overstuffed cushions, which tells you something about how children of clergy survive their upbringings.

This was back in the seventies, of course, but even today, the Wee Frees remain strictly Sabbatarian, Calvinist, with a remarkably austere liturgy to match. Hymns, until recently, were as unlikely as rugby songs; you won't find any musical instruments in their churches, where traditionally only the unaccompanied singing of psalms is permitted. I once heard a Gaelic congregation doing this on the Isle of Lewis, and while they were unlikely to be signed up by Simon Cowell, it was very moving in a strange sort of way, and very durable, surviving centuries of change, emigration, erosion and dilution. So when the Free Church's plenary general assembly voted to permit the singing of hymns and instrumental accompaniment in their churches for those congregations wishing to have them, it came as a surprise. Hard to overstate how startling that would be, like sending out One Direction to entertain a crowd that had turned up for Handel's *Messiah*.

A cynic might observe that permitting Gaelic-speaking crofters on Raasay to sing 'Kumbaya' may not universally be construed as progress. Nevertheless, it should make those who think the Church is dead pause for thought. Even this most conservative of denominations realises that it is not enough to survive – we must also allow ourselves to be renewed, with all the anxiety and uncertainty and discomfort that might entail.

David and I are in Wellingborough for a bit of desperate Christmas shopping. I buy myself some origami paper – and discover the brilliant Vietnamese restaurant jarringly sited in a thatched cottage has closed, so we go to McDonald's, which is packed, and my order is 'fulfilled' before David's, so I wedge myself into the seat by the lavatory waiting for him to appear as the 'smoky mayo' congeals on my 'patty'. But no David. Assuming he's gone for one of the 'crafty fags' six years of my nagging has failed to extinguish, I sit getting grumpier and grumpier until a member of staff approaches and tells me David is in fact upstairs and can I join him? Full of chips and indignation, I am mollified to discover that he's not been smoking, but attending to a lady who'd had the good fortune to collapse in front of a clergyman with ten years' experience in A&E. I think he may have saved her life. I, however, did not save his chips.

Advent is like a slightly easier Lent, requiring not only a decrease in indulgence but also an increase in giving. My generous gift for Advent when I was at theological college in Mirfield, and relatively zealous, was to offer to look after two Romanian theological students, Dan and Cristian, before they headed home for Christmas. Dan was from Transylvania but looked most unvampiric, blue-eyed and blond-haired, an inheritance from his ethnic German ancestors. Cristian was from Maramureş, Romania's Brigadoon, where ancient wooden churches and present-day horses and carts are unremarkable. I took them to London, which was completely new to them. We arrived at King's Cross to find the Underground closed, so we ended up pulling Eastern European suitcases full of swag along a grid-locked Euston Road, finally dumping our bags at left luggage in Victoria. Then we did Westminster Cathedral, Westminster Abbey, the Houses of Parliament, Madame Tussaud's, Marylebone High Street, Oxford Street, New Bond Street, the Burlington Arcade, Piccadilly and Trafalgar Square, getting soaked to the skin in the frequent bursts of slimy London rain. I had a hole in my shoe, so my feet were perpetually wet. In the evening I took them to the Christmas knees-up at a friend's church. One of the ladies did her annual turn with Fred, a rather unsettling life-size dummy with a mannequin's head dressed in clothes she made specially for him, attached to her at hands and feet by loops of string. She did the foxtrot, her replica partner following like a Fuseli incubus. The Romanians did their party piece too, singing a carol, which sounded like a funeral dirge and went on for very many verses. And then we all ended up singing Ivor Novello songs with Glyn at the piano: 'Waltz of My Heart', 'We'll Gather Lilacs' . . .

The next day I took them to the British Library, where I showed them the *Codex Sinaiticus* and the first draft of the lyrics for 'Yesterday', then on to the mummies in the British Museum and Karl Marx's place in the Reading Room – and we lunched at the Groucho Club. Cristian told me: 'I have been with my girlfriend for five years and we have never had sexual intercourses. Why you not resign homosexuality and marry a lady?' The waitress brought the tray of bread. 'May I take some?' asked Cristian. 'Have as much as you like,' I replied. He took six slices. When the bill was set on the table, he asked to see it. It came to £104, which made him laugh.

Then we walked through town and I bought Cristian a cheap camera to replace the one left on the train to London, and Dan a Game Boy to give to his orphaned cousin; and then, as dusk fell, we made our way through Hyde Park to the Serpentine, where an old woman, posh and genteelly shabby, took me to see an American Sweet Gum tree still in leaf. She gave me three of its gorgeously coloured leaves in a Boots bag to take home.

After a day on the town, I took them to Victoria coach station and Continental Departures (not yet 'International Departures'), to board the bus for Bucharest. The station was full of men in moustaches with huge bags in red-and-white nylon gingham, about the size of a hatchback, which the poor take back, full of swag, from West to East. I said goodbye and Happy Christmas to Dan and Cristian. Dan hugged me, then Cristian hugged me nervously and said, 'Not too close!' which made us all laugh. Then he hugged me again, which was nice of him.

There was a man sent from God, whose name was John, wearing not a garment made of camel hair with a leather belt around his waist but an old Rushden and Diamonds shirt with a cross round his neck. For this was not John the Baptist, centre stage in Advent; this was John the Bishop of Brixworth at our Diocesan Conference, which is held in a converted country house in Derbyshire. There, sooner or later, every ordained person in the C of E will come. And we came, in all our differences, bishops and readers and deacons and rectors and canons and lay ministers, from posh villages bordering Oxfordshire, from the battered former shoe towns of the central belt, where I live, from Peterborough and Northampton, with their city and county town dignity. All different, yet there are certain constants, certain hallmarks of the authentic C of E experience:

You will know them by their knitwear: the Anglican clergy
   between them must have more jumpers than the Baltic
   Fleet.
Thank you, Jesus, for the loaves and fishes, but is there a
   gluten-free alternative?
Very soon someone will play the flute, very slightly flat.

Wandering from seminar to workshop, from book stall to dining
hall, I wondered what we must look like to others. I was in Waitrose
the other day, in mufti on my day off, to order things for Christmas, and the lady taking my details said, 'It's Rev, isn't it?' I said,
yes, have we met? And she replied, 'No, but you look like one. And
you sound like one. In the nicest possible way.'

We are all called to be bearers of divine glory but we are, to use St
Paul's image, cracked pots, broken vessels, which hold that glory
haphazardly, if at all. Paul developed that image writing to the
church at Corinth, famous for its pottery, highly prized, with a
glossy black glaze decorated with figures in a reddish colour. They
made another kind of pottery also, an artefact they were famous for,
made by the dozen, from the cheapest materials, full of flaws and
imperfections and cracks. Household lamps. You placed a burning
wick in one and the light shone through the cracks. Ten a penny,
easily broken.

The Church of England now looks even more cracked than
usual. Agonising about women bishops and equal marriage, trying
to have it both ways, saying encouraging words, doing discouraging
things, desperately trying to hold on to the privileges in national
life that come with our legal status – seats in the House of Lords,
a presence in every place, the right to marry and bury and baptise
– despite the decline in numbers, a more crowded marketplace for
religion and belief, and a more diverse world. Some proclaim that
as a nation we are haemorrhaging Christian believers faster than
printed newspapers are losing readers.

But these are the headlines, and they tell only part of the story. What remains unreported is the day-by-day building of the kingdom of God, the effort in this life to anticipate the life of heaven, unobserved, the faithful discipleship of people who may not want to offer definitive answers to the great controversies of the day, but do want to take care of their neighbours, and to take responsibility for maintaining the life of a community, and to offer their imagination and creativity and resources to support others doing the same, and discover in their lives what it means to let Christ in – not as an individual conquering hero, before whom the world quails and falls, but as the child in the manger, wrapped in swaddling bands, to whom very far away a star is beginning to turn, as the universe and everything in it switches course.

A pre-Christmas trip to Norway for Radio Four with producer Sarah Jane Hall. She has many gifts, among them a knack for thinking of titles commissioning editors will find irresistible. *The Music That Melted* will report on the Geilo Ice Music Festival, an annual gathering in the snowy mountains around Norway's equivalent to Gstaad, not of oil-rich Norwegian skiers, but fans of the more esoteric music festivals. It is run by the Norwegian percussionist Terje Isungset and the American sculptor Bill Covitz, both of them, unusually, working in the medium of ice. Terje makes instruments from ice, Bill makes sculptures from ice, the latter using a chainsaw and a blowtorch, the former using blocks cut from a glacier which formed hundreds of thousands of years ago. The nature of the medium means that performances are rare and inaccessible, and so we find ourselves in a group of people dressed in thermal long johns in a log cabin at midnight, thousands of feet up and dozens of degrees under. We drink mulled wine and try to make out languages and accents muffled by balaclavas and fur-fringed parkas as we are led in procession from the log cabin through drifts of snow so deep we struggle to stay upright, along an avenue of flares to a break in the rocks and a wall of ice with an arch cut in it. We pass through this arch and then through an ice tunnel, with niches holding tea lights in coloured jam jars, turn a corner and emerge in a natural amphitheatre in the snow. On a slope are laid dozens of reindeer hides which we sit on. Someone brings us more mulled wine. Above us the sky is full of stars, the air so clear they look like diamonds thrown onto a black cloth.

In front of us is the stage, with an ice backdrop, lit from behind so it glows with a cold blue then a hot red. Sarah Jane lights a fag and I worry for a moment that she will burn a hole in the reindeer-skin hide, then she takes off with a digital recorder as Bill arrives on stage with a chainsaw. With this he turns a block of ice into a dolphin, or a porpoise, or maybe an ice creature of Norwegian mythology – it is difficult to tell. Then Terje and his band appear with a collection of instruments made from ice: horns that look like they've been wrenched off giant ice gramophones, a marimba made with tuned frozen slats, and then our soloist, a guitarist, carrying an instrument made also from ice, with an electric pick-up embedded underneath steel strings drawn across a fretted ice fingerboard. The horns sound, the marimba is struck with padded sticks, and the guitarist does his best to play, but as soon as his finger presses a string on the fingerboard it melts under the warmth and pressure and the note begins to slide away almost as soon as it is sounded. The whole performance lasts twenty minutes, which is as long as they can play and we can listen. Then we retreat down the mountain and back to the hotel where we find a bottle of whisky and sit up, getting drunk, telling stories about the awfulness of the BBC.

The next day we take a train to Bergen and then a plane to the Lofoten Islands up in the far north, where Sarah Jane has found a colony of artists who moved there for the 'blue hour', the sixty minutes of half-light that is all you get of the day at that latitude in winter. That may have been the original reason, but by the time they had spent a year or two there they'd adapted to their environment so thoroughly it was difficult to think of them adapting back to a kinder calendar. We visit one artist who lives with his wife in a cabin on a lake surrounded by huge A-frames on which drying cod are hung. Every day he goes for an early-morning swim in water so cold and vice-like I would have thought it impossible to take a breath. The cabin is filled with preparatory models and some finished pieces of work that seem obsessed by the Cold War, a conflict both political and literal. He shows us the remains of a model for a huge piece involving decommissioned Russian T34 tanks which, if it came off, would have been on the scale of the Battle of Stalingrad. It is difficult to take this entirely seriously, so remote from the geopolitical frontiers of the 1980s, but then he mentions that he has been visited by Mikhail and Raisa Gorbachev, who perched on the same uncomfortable sofa we are sitting on, drinking tea and talking Perestroika – an anecdote so implausible I thought it must be true.

It is Gaudete Sunday, the third Sunday of Advent, which the traditional end of the Catholic spectrum marks by wearing rose-pink vestments, one of only two occasions each year they are worn. It is derived from the Introit to the Mass, which comes from Paul's letter to the Philippians: 'Rejoice in the Lord always; again I say, rejoice!' This has always struck me as being interestingly at odds with the Gospel for the day, which focuses on John the Baptist, such a troubling figure, whose shaggy presence on the edge of consciousness, with bits of locust in his beard, seems to point not to rejoicing but something far darker and ambiguous. Does what we rejoice in stand beyond the horizon of all human experience, its darkness as well as its light?

When I was curate at St Paul's, Knightsbridge, some years ago, every Advent we hosted carol services for the big charities, twenty or thirty of them, all looking for a central London 'venue' for their annually inflated do, ticketed and aimed at the great and the good. The bigger they got, and they had to grow year by year, the likelier it was we would have to deal with event planners, hired to sort out the lighting and catering and celebrity readers, and roving women with Alice bands and clipboards bossing everyone around. Our job as hosting clergy was to try to maintain the lineaments of a liturgy while all around snow machines were blowing, and an *X Factor* finalist rose towards the ceiling on a hydraulic platform singing 'O Holy Night' so loudly Herod could have heard it from Jerusalem. The celebrities arrived early to run through their readings and my job was to take them to the vicarage for a glass of champagne and a pee before they were shown to the front pew. One of them cornered me and complained that his reading was not the 'King James Version' that he preferred and expressed his dismay at the dereliction of the Church, embodied by me, in giving up the time-honoured and traditional forms the nation has grown to love. What we had given him to read actually was the 'King James Version', or Authorised Version as it is properly known here, but I just adopted my 'how interesting' face, partly because there were more pressing matters, partly because he and I had form, which I had remembered and he had forgotten, form which had for an inglorious period exposed him to public ridicule and in which I was involved. Did any memory of that stir within him? I do not think so, and he read, sonorously, the 'King James Version' which I pretended to have photocopied but in fact merely handed him back the page he had given me to change.

I ran into a bishop who told me about a postcard he'd received from one of his clergy, in trouble and struggling, and feeling rather let down by the Church. The postcard, sent from a retreat house on a far Scottish island, read:

Dear Bishop; if you would walk with me, do not walk behind me for I may not lead. Do not walk in front of me, for I may not follow. Do not walk beside me, for the way may be narrow. In fact, why don't you just fuck off and leave me alone?

Sometimes we long for the wilderness, to be free from company that might be unwelcome or unbearable. I remember once asking a monk if the community he lived in had a hermitage to which they could retreat, away from all the others, if they felt the need. 'No,' he said, 'but if we did there'd be a very long queue.' For those it suits, it suits, but others have wilderness forced on them. A friend of mine, an MP, was asked by a widowed elderly constituent for help with housing, and she tried but there was nothing much she could do. When she delivered the bad news, she gave her a hug and the old lady burst into tears, not because of her housing problem but because she said it was the first time anyone had touched her since her husband died.

Advent is itself a wilderness. In the Orthodox Churches they fast just as rigorously in the run-up to Christmas as in the run-up to Easter. We've lost that, anticipating the feast of Christmas six weeks before it actually arrives. But fast precedes feast – otherwise it's just pointless self-indulgence – and if we don't admit the darkness we won't appreciate the light when it comes.

For it will come, heralded by the star, a tiny pinprick of light in the night sky, pointing to a cold and dirty stable in the back of beyond, and the arrival in a simple straw-filled manger of God in-carnate, nothing like what we expected, unimaginably greater than anything we could hope for, so the desert blooms, the blind can see, the prisoners are set free, and the lonely and the battered and the bruised join together with the angels in songs of joy.

My first Nativity in Finedon. In London, it was a decorous affair, angelic-looking children dressed like minor royals of the 1930s lis-tening quietly to Renaissance polyphony while the antique bam-bino was placed by a coped cleric in the manger. In Finedon it is a less orderly affair and whoever turns up gets a go, so we have two Marys sitting side by side at the manger, unsure as to who gets first go with a slightly chipped Tiny Tears depping for our Incarnate Lord. My favourite moment comes with the arrival of the Three Kings, Caspar, Balthasar and Melchior, in dishcloth robes and sweet-wrapper crowns. We actually have a Caspar and Balthasar living in the parish, thanks to immigration from the EU accession nations, but as far as I know no Melchior. No matter, for we have not three kings but four, with Charlie bringing up the rear in his Darth Vader costume, laying down his light sabre with the gold, frankincense and myrrh. It is not quite swords into ploughshares, as Isaiah, so clamorous at this time of year, prophesies, but I am moved nonetheless by this demilitarised gesture.

Alfred Delp was a Jesuit priest who stood up to the Nazis in Germany in the thirties and forties, and for this was arrested and eventually hanged. He wrote:

Advent is the time of promise; it is not yet the time of fulfilment. We are still in the midst of everything and in the logical inexorability and relentlessness of destiny . . . Space is still filled with the noise of destruction and annihilation, the shouts of self-assurance and arrogance, the weeping of despair and helplessness. But round about the horizon the eternal realities stand silent in their age-old longing. There shines on them already the first mild light of the radiant fulfilment to come. From afar sound the first notes as of pipes and voices, not yet discernible as a song or melody. It is all far off still, and only just announced and foretold. But it is happening, today.

CHRISTMAS

Teach, O teach us, Holy Child,
By Thy face so meek and mild,
Teach us to resemble Thee,
In Thy sweet humility.

I once saw a fight between two women on the tube in the week before Christmas. The train was packed until an interchange, when lots of people get off, and both women set their sights on the same vacated seat. The one standing further away was quicker off the mark and managed to insert herself into it just as the other tried to sit down. There was an unChristmassy exchange of views, and another. Handbags by Tottenham Court Road, I thought, if there were room to swing them, and I tightened the scarf obscuring my dog collar round my neck for fear I might be called on to arbitrate. But there was no need, for just as it got really nasty, the woman who'd failed to get the seat stopped, took a breath, and said, 'Shall we start again?'

The offer took her opponent completely by surprise; abandoning the insult on her lips, she paused, took a breath herself, and said, 'Yes.' The rest of us all breathed our sighs of relief, and by the time we got to Oxford Circus, we were practically exchanging telephone numbers. Peace had broken out.

Peace would falter, a little, at Knightsbridge during that month of carol services we hosted in the run-up to Christmas. The season of peace and goodwill, in the hands of experts, could be made a medium for the continuation of war by other means. Two great ladies, who had fallen out on Shrove Tuesday over the provision of pancakes – rolled or folded? – fell out again over mince pies. Should they be traditional mince pies, for which crumb-catching napkins (*'never* serviette') were necessary, or should they be mini one-bite mince pies, sparing the carpet from ground-in pastry and currants? I watched them prowl and strike, thinking of the great controversies of the early Church, and the synods and councils convened to settle the infinitesimally small yet infinitely import-ant matters around which churches align and fall apart. I thought too of the whole show beginning with a baby in a manger, miles from anywhere important, bawling in straw in the cold night air, as insignificant as a pet-shop hamster and yet the power that lit the stars.

Teach, O teach us, Holy Child . . .

Waiting for a plane to Edinburgh for Hogmanay and it is delayed so we finally board at half past nine instead of seven o'clock on a cold, dark night. The last two passengers have taken advantage of the delay to get drunk. One of them, naturally, is seated next to me. He says, 'Shleuur wurrgh eyaaargh the noo, big man?' So I say, Are you with a pal? And he says, 'Aye.' To the dismay of my neigh-bours, I offer to exchange my seat with his even drunker friend. From take-off to landing I can hear their commotion four rows behind, and when we get to the stand at Edinburgh the one I'd been sitting next to is having a fight with the couple sitting behind him, the girl losing her rag and telling him to fuck off. I tell this to my friend, who was working on the floor at Marks and Spen-cer on Princes Street on Christmas Eve, spreading peace and good cheer to the customers, when a fight broke out between two men in a queue. They were both pensioners. One had one leg, the other one arm.

*

To the hospital, where a parishioner has heralded Christmas by having a very premature baby girl, weighing under two pounds. The doctors have taken her off to intensive care where she lies in an incubator struggling for life. Her mum is there, by her side, but cannot touch her. When the nurses aren't looking, she tells me, she reaches into the incubator and lays her forearm under her baby's tiny feet, hoping that her pulse will transmit strength to her.

One of the things I love most about clerical life is the range of experience we come across, in parishes that cover everywhere from the Scillies to Lindisfarne. My clerical life so far has been a sandwich of privilege and deprivation, of joy and agony, with heroin-wrecked lives in remote Lincolnshire and that premature baby in an incubator in Kettering wrapped round perhaps the richest parish in the richest city in the world. When I was there we had a parishioner who bought a house in one of Belgravia's grandest streets and had it completely remodelled. He hoped to be in at Christmas, but the building work got delayed, so he booked himself into a suite at the Berkeley while a team of crack decorators went in to do up the house so he could spend Christmas Day there. He did, with his family, and on Boxing Day moved back into the suite and the builders returned, tore out all the temporary decorations, and got on with their job.

An urgent message in my inbox from a correspondent anxious to impress on me the significance of John 14:6, which asserts that the only way to God is through Jesus:

> NOT by the Pope – NOT by Mary – NOT by Mohamed – NOT by Allah – NOT by Buddha – NOT by Krishna – NOT by an Old Covenant Jew Rabbi – NOT by the Mason's Great Architect of the Universe AKA Satan AKA Lucifer the mason's god of 'light' – AKA – JAH-BUL-ON, the mason's Triune god Jehovah – Baal – Onasis/Osiris,

the brother/husband of the Eygptian SUN goddess Isis,
who gave a virgin birth to her Sun god son Horus on the
25th December! As do the masons, also worship their
Roman rooted, masonic rituals and degrees, held in secret,
to selected Romans, their Sun god Mithra, also born of a
virgin, on the 25th December, who was worshipped by the
main CORRUPT Gospel culprit, the Satanic murdering,
Pagan, Roman King Constantine, who forced in his new,
counterfeit, anti-Messiah, SUN god, SUN day worshipping
religion, by changing the HOLY SABBATH DAY from
Saturday, to SUN day and merely changed the names of Isis
to Mary and Horus to Jesus, then gave Jesus/Iesus (NOT
YESHUA) a virgin birth, the same as Horus, on the 25th
December! Woe woe woe . . .

It continues in this vein for many paragraphs.

After very many carol services I have noticed a thing that divides
Low Church clergy from High Church clergy. The latter announce
the hymn number and off they go, leaving everyone behind. The
former announce the hymn number and then read out the whole
of the first verse in a holy voice.

Years ago, when I was on the road to ordination but had not yet
arrived, I got up early on Christmas morning in the village where I
have a cottage and went with my guests to the lovely little church
for Book of Common Prayer Holy Communion, for which I had
volunteered to play the organ. I was playing the organ and one
of them, John, a critical theorist from Valencia, in the same spirit
volunteered to be my page-turner and stop-puller. To mark this
high and holy day I played for the voluntary my own fancy arrange-
ment of 'Ding Dong Merrily on High' and John discovered that if
he pushed some stops in and others out he could make different
noises. He got a bit carried away with this and when the angels

bent near the earth to touch their harps of gold they did so with an unexpected and ear-splitting trumpet blast, which made the congregation jump, and at the end applaud.

After church we went over to my parents' house in a nearby village for lunch, stopped for the Queen, had a flaming pudding, went for a walk. When we got back, Dad was so tired he had to go and lie down. Ominously he was lying down for longer than usual, and when I put my head round the door to check he was OK, I thought for a moment he'd died. I mentioned it to my brother Will and he said whenever he passes Dad asleep on a chair or in bed he checks to see if he's still breathing. Later, Dad appeared in the doorway with a tea tray, looking surprised to see us, and we all made to help him because we thought he was about to drop it. He looked terrible, grey and agonised, as if he was making an effort of endurance so great anything extra was impossible. We took him back to bed where he immediately fell asleep, covered with a rug which Mum tenderly laid over him. The cause of the agony, I know now, was Parkinson's, so debilitating not only physically, but of composure. I can only remember my father losing it once or twice, so to see him reduced that Christmas was troubling, and made me slightly ashamed of my own Christmas habit of bailing out, seeking amusement elsewhere, or going to bed after the pudding, usually with the first intimations of a hangover, in retreat from the compulsoriness of Christmas Day, unable or unwilling to summon the necessary bonhomie and patience.

The irony of being now its Master of Ceremonies I would not deny, although perhaps it is akin to finding the best way of coping with the awfulness of parties is by throwing them, hosting rather than guesting. I enjoyed hosting at home, and enjoyed seeing Christmas through the eyes of John's Spanish partner, now husband, Ramon. He loved it and said it was exactly what he had expected, which turned out to have been largely conditioned by the novels of Agatha Christie, read in translation. He would have been surprised had Christmas not involved thatched cottages, eccentric vicars and

Charades. In Spanish, I discovered, Miss Marple is Señorita Marr-play, which makes her sound like a siren; Carmen Miranda, not Margaret Rutherford.

Now, ten years into ordained ministry, I tend to associate Christmas with hospitals. There is a small surge of death in December and January, some say because of the uneven efficacy of the 'flu vaccine, or perhaps because people try to hold on for the gathered family, or the familiar things of Christmas, or the *X Factor* single. They try to hold on but fail, and I cannot remember a Christmas when I haven't been summoned to a hospital or a bedside or a grief-stricken household with unopened presents round an unlit tree. Once I was called out on Christmas Eve to the deathbed of a woman who lived above a pub. She was struggling for breath, surrounded by life-support equipment and looked after by a uniformed nurse, incongruous among the Christmas cards that covered every shelf. Even more incongruous was the din from downstairs, Slade's 'Merry Christmas', and a ragged karaoke singalong bellowing 'EVERYBODY'S HAVING FUN', as she took and released her last breath. I walked back to church for Midnight Mass, to take the death I had just witnessed to the crib in its patch of light.

I visit a parishioner who recalls one morning in September 1939 when she was a girl, having to take a case and her teddy to school and not knowing why, then being put on a train and sent away as an evacuee – but she didn't know that's what she was because no one told her what was happening. And then, three months later, the same thing but in reverse, and again not knowing what was happening, she was dropped off outside her front door and walked into her own house and the arms of her mother and father on Christmas Eve. The only thing she remembers clearly is the Christmas tree standing in the front room and everyone crying. She never went away again, but stayed at home through the Blitz and vividly recalls the swish-swish of an aerial mine coming down on its parachute and her brother coming home on leave silent and shaky instead of laughing and full of gusto. Christmas trees still make her cry.

A report in the paper from Heathrow, where passengers have been stranded for three days and the terminals have overflowed so people have been queuing in makeshift tents outside the buildings. There is a picture of a Santa going down the queue distributing gloves and scarves; a man looks at him with undisguised malevolence.

With an irony which suggests to me the lively intervention of divine grace, I, who dislike Christmas, elected to spend my life with someone who would put the crib up in September if I let him, someone who puts up individual stockings for the dogs and who diligently fills them with little presents after Midnight Mass, but not in front of them lest it spoil the surprise. David's Christmas rituals, however, are home-based, an effort I think to ensure we are not given over entirely to the demands of church and parish. This can produce a familiar tension, having grown up in a household where Christmas did not begin until my parents had the one and only row of the year.

After Midnight Mass and locking up, we have a whisky in the sitting room and the dogs' Advent calendars are updated. It is two by the time we get to bed and I have to be up at six for the early shift, even earlier than usual because David insists on smoked salmon, caviar and champagne for breakfast. Then church, always an anti-climax after Midnight Mass, with half the usual attendance on Christmas morning, bolstered only by the outlying farmers, who still come *en famille* this one day of the year, the men in those tweedy suits and check shirts that farmers and aristocrats and Eurosceptics wear.

And then we are done for the day, off duty, and back at the vicarage the dogs have their presents and we have ours. I bought David a chainsaw, at his request, and had it not been for the fortunate intervention of an American neighbour, who grew up in thickly wooded Maine, it might have been me on the bereaved list that year. As he went through the safety protocols with David in a borrowed skirt of chain mail, I opened mine. Being a bookish parson, when asked what I would like for Christmas or birthday, I can think only of whisky or books. I got a bottle of whisky, the Macallan, my favourite, and two books so marvellously ill-suited to the season I started reading them at once. One, from a parishioner, was a history of homosexuality in early modern Europe by a man called, wonderfully, Helmut Puff, the other, from my mother, was a nice edition of *Paradise Lost*, which I had skimmed in the days when I read for reasons of virtue; but for some reason, at a time when I find it very difficult to read anything and impossible to finish anything, I became completely absorbed by this least Christmassy of books. Nothing dispels the dread shade of Santa for me more efficiently than Milton:

> *Is this the Region, this the Soil, the Clime,*
> *Said then the lost Arch-Angel, this the seat*
> *That we must change for Heav'n; this mournful gloom*
> *For that celestial light? Be it so! since he,*
> *Who now is Sovran, can dispose and bid*
> *What shall be right: farthest from him is best*
> *Whom reason hath equalled, force hath made supreme*
> *Above his equals. Farewell, happy fields,*
> *Where joy for ever dwells! Hail, horrours, hail,*
> *Infernal world! And thou, profoundest Hell,*
> *Receive thy new Possessour! One who brings*
> *A mind not to be chang'd by Place or Time.*
> *The mind is its own place, and in itself*
> *Can make a Heav'n of Hell, a Hell of Heav'n.*
> *What matter where, if I be still the same,*
> *And what I should be, all but less then he*
> *Whom Thunder hath made greater? Here at least*
> *We shall be free; the Almighty hath not built*

Here for his envy, will not drive us hence:
Here we may reign secure, and, in my choyce,
To reign is worth ambition, though in Hell:
Better to reign in Hell, than serve in Heav'n!

On the strength of this, who wouldn't choose Satan?

I called Mum to thank her for the present and to ask when she wanted me to come and pick her up. The phone rang a dozen times and then the answering machine kicked in. After the beep, I'd just begun to leave a message when she picked the phone up. *Hello . . . I must be going deaf. I didn't hear it ringing,* she said. *Where were you?* I asked. *In the kitchen . . . can you hold on? . . . my hands are full of hot cranberries . . .*

My theme at Midnight Mass was bureaucracy – a registration, or census, at the time of Jesus' birth by the Roman authorities, who needed to know who was where, and doing what, in their province of Palestine. Mary and Joseph were making their way to Bethlehem for this reason, so the story goes, or perhaps the Gospel writers wanted to show the birth of Jesus of Nazareth fulfilled a prophecy about the coming of the Messiah. Either way, we end up with Mary and Joseph far from home and a birth in a stable.

Christmas, with its emphasis on families gathered round a blazing hearth, rather elides these details, of a stranger travelling with a pregnant teenager to whom he isn't married, with no suitable accommodation, and a highly implausible story about hallucinating shepherds, royal visitors, and a chest of gold in their saddlebag which somebody 'gave' them. What did the registrar make of them? Nothing, probably, just a mark on a census roll and off they went.

I looked up the last time I made my mark on a census roll, the national census of 2011. In some ways, it revealed a place not unlike the Roman Empire in the first century. It too had a very mixed population, including many who were born in foreign countries, living in households just as complex as ours, in relationships just as complex as ours. One really significant difference between 2011 and AD 0 is the importance of religion. In Ancient Rome there were followers of Mithras and Zoroaster, there were Samaritans and Druids, there were those who worshipped the Emperor, those who worshipped their great aunts, and Jews, like Joseph and Mary; but everyone would be something, everyone would tick a box marked 'religion'. In the Britain of 2011 the number of people who described themselves as having no religion doubled in a decade, and the number of people who described themselves as Christians in that same decade fell sharply. Is it that more and more are waking up from the sleep of religion into the wakefulness of reality? Is there a general decline in our willingness to be part of anything? In the Church we worry that our awfulness, however construed, has made us look laughably irrelevant or downright hostile to those outside.

But nothing in that, or in the census, captures what we captured gathered at the crib at midnight, in all our difference: *O magnum mysterium*, O great mystery, that animals should see the new-born Lord, lying in a manger! It is so wonderfully unlikely, so utterly unexpected, so unfathomably weird, that it makes Biblical scholars disputing the dating, or sceptics disputing the mechanics, or atheists wondering how anyone could take this seriously at all, sound like spinning the dial on an old radio, the static fading in and out and in again.

St Stephen's Day, when Good King Wenceslaus looked out, is Boxing Day, 26 December. The Sales, turkey sandwiches, football and hounds fill it now, but its original character endures in the carol, whose words are at once completely familiar and utterly strange. You will remember that the good king, out walking in bitter weather on this day with a page, sees yonder a peasant and is moved to pity. Flesh and wine and pine logs are donated to the fortunate serf, and page and monarch go forth together, but lest the page experience frostbite the good king generates miraculous heating to spare his toes: *heat was in the very sod that the saint had printed.*

This line, with its faintly rude double entendre so loved by choirboys, came into my mind when someone I met told me about a trip to Iceland. She had gone there to look at geological formations – in winter, which was ill advised – and had decided to drive over a mountain range to get to a little town and harbour on an inaccessible tongue of land. She drove and the night drew in and the road, little better than track, grew indistinct in fading light and falling snow and suddenly she was completely lost in a wild blizzard. This is how I die, she thought, frozen to death in a car buried under a snowdrift, all because I was too stupid to check the weather. And then she saw some lights just visible through the driving snow, and they got closer and it was a snow plough and her deliverance. She followed it all the way to town, her tyres finding grip in the very sod that its caterpillar tracks had printed.

After St Stephen's Day, a local festival follows in the English calendar, the Feast of St Egwin of Evesham. He was born in the seventh century in Worcester, a nephew of King Æthelred of Mercia. After entering a Benedictine monastery, he was fast-tracked to the bishopric of Worcester, where, in common with many saints of the period (or any period), he alienated the clergy by insisting they behave themselves. This caused so much resentment he was eventually ordered to Rome to give an account of himself to the Pope. In pique, he shackled his legs in irons and threw the key into the River Avon as a rather showy sign of his obedience. It must have made his journey all the more difficult, and crossing the Alps he also had to deal with a water shortage by making a cataract spring forth from a rock to slake his and his companions' thirst. Things improved on their arrival in Rome. Egwin prayed at the tomb of the Apostles and the prayer was answered, in a way, when he went fishing for his supper and caught a fish in the Tiber.

It spat out the very key he had thrown into the Avon when he set off. His shackles were loosed, the Pope adjudicated in his favour, and Egwin returned to Worcestershire where he founded Evesham Abbey after the Virgin Mary told a swineherd called Eof where to build it.

I went to give a talk in Evesham some time ago at the invitation of its congenial vicar, and came across the ruins of the abbey Egwin founded on a tour of the town. More delightful even than the ruins was the Evesham Hotel, my favourite in the world, run by Mr Jenkinson, a sort of benign(ish) Basil Fawlty, who serves vodka made from rats and offers guests the use of a Sinclair C5 which is parked in a corridor. In the Gents next to its excellent restaurant a giant motorised rag doll performs a sinister dance when you stand at the urinal, which can quite put you off your stride if you are unprepared for it.

Lunch with a bishop who remarks that he went into a bookshop the other day and found the Theology Section no longer there. When he enquired about it at the desk, he was told it had been 'moved for Christmas'.

Vivid dream last night: arriving at Westminster Abbey for a coronation dressed in a cope; not to officiate but because, as I said to the gentleman on the door, 'I am engaged to the Duchess of Cambridge's sister.' With this, I was joined by Kate, who practised her descent from the triforium to the nave on a wire, singing 'I'm the Queen of England' (her, not me), and then I made my way to the choir, where I said to the lady usher, 'I am engaged to the Duchess of Cambridge's sister,' and she replied, sourly, 'I think we all knew that.' I then saw two friendly prelates in red copes look a bit funnily at me and I realised that my cope was actually a Santa suit.

David and I were staying one New Year's Eve in a wooden bungalow, built from a kit in the 1930s, deep in the woods on the coast of

North Devon. It had been restored by a heritage charity, repainted in a livery of brown and cream, and inside was wonderfully snug. It needed to be that night, because the weather was foul. The rain was lashing down, the wind howled, and the sea crashed onto the rocks at the foot of the cliffs. It was the dark and stormy night ghost stories begin with and we were sitting in firelight reading M. R. James ghost stories out loud, when suddenly Daisy, the most diligent of the dogs, started and looked to the French windows. She barked and I could swear I heard someone tap on the glass. The dogs ran to the French windows. There was another tap and I thought of the tales we would tell each other when we were kids of escaped psychopaths picking off careless teens one by one in a wooden hut on a beach.

The tapping came again, no mistaking it, so I went to the French windows, pulled back the curtain, and saw two faces, strange faces, looking at me through the glass, blurry with rain.

There were two young Japanese men standing on the verandah, soaking wet, freezing, dressed for a nightclub rather than a foul, wintry night. We let them in and tried to discover who they were and what they wanted, but they did not speak English very well and all I could work out was where they needed to go. It turned out to be not far away, so – idiotically – we gave them directions and off they went, into the terrible night, until David said, 'We're going to have to take them.' We found them a little further up the path, shivering and dripping, and drove them to where they were staying, with the potter Sandy Brown, where one, from the Japanese ceramic centre of Mashiko, had just started his apprenticeship. She was so delighted to see them, and so delighted, she said, that she wasn't going to have to phone his mother to explain his death from exposure, that she gave us a tour of the studio and a vastly discounted price on a gorgeous painted plate.

In Finland they mark the feast of St Sylvester, which falls on New Year's Eve, by looking forward to the coming year with the medium of molybdomancy. A chunk of tin or lead is melted over the fire and then thrown in a bucket of cold water. The resulting blob of metal is held up to candlelight and its shadows analysed for prophetic meaning.

EPIPHANY

Vicars always complain about the world starting Christmas in November, but worse, I think, is ending it on Boxing Day. For us, the feast goes up to Epiphany, or Twelfth Night as English tradition obstinately calls it, which falls on 6 January. It is just as important as the Nativity, which marked Christ's birth, but marking now the manifestation of God to the world in that child. So following a star which rises in the east, the Magi, or wise men, or three kings, or three nutty professors as a rather insistently secularist director of a Nativity play I once met had it, arrive at the crib. Unfortunately, everyone else has gone home by now, back at work after the New Year, and the slightly desperate effort we clergy who care about such things make in stressing the point is lost. I normally place the three kings at the back of the church at Advent, moving them, service by service, towards the crib where they finally appear on the Feast of the Epiphany, offering their gifts, on time liturgically, but so late to the party everyone else is having they might as well have not bothered.

When I was pastoral assistant at Stamford, that lovely stony town where Northamptonshire and Lincolnshire and Cambridge-shire and Rutland meet, the Rector, Fr Michael Thompson, did not give up such things without a fight and Epiphany at St Mary's was especially splendid. The church has a massive tower and broach spire, which, perched on its hill, looks enormous. Inside, it isn't big at all, certainly not big enough for all the clergy Michael had mustered for the Feast. There were, as well as the rector, eleven assistant priests, retired from duty, including canons of both West-minster and Windsor, for the grander clergy, in the days when it was affordable, liked to see out their days in places like Stamford, so perfectly, antiquely English it seemed to be permanently standing in for Middlemarch or Cranford or Casterbridge, and every now and then you see in the background of a BBC costume drama a familiar street corner with the Pay and Display sign taken down. With servers, that made fifteen in the crowded Sanctuary, most dressed in that grandest of vestments, the cope, a huge semicircle of gorgeous textile, clanking with bullion, draped round the shoulders and worn as a floor-length cloak.

We sang 'We Three Kings of Orient Are' and set off in proces-sion, led by me swinging a thurible, but gingerly – for the church was too small for our smoky, glittering pageant, and copes heavy with bullion are a notorious trip hazard – bearing our gifts to the crib. Gold, a sign of the child's kingship; frankincense, anticipat-ing in this world the kingdom that is not of it; and myrrh, for the tomb.

My grandmother, born in 1901, lost three of her twelve siblings in infancy, and used to say, a century later, that whenever she was tempted to indulge a feeling of nostalgia for times past she remem-bered the frequency with which she and her sisters and brothers would gather at a tiny graveside in rustling black crepe. Today, the death of a child is so unusual that most of us will be spared that excruciating grief – so unusual, that the few who do suffer it feel they live thereafter in a parallel universe. A friend of mine lost his teenage son to meningitis a few years ago. The night after, he took the rubbish out and at the dustbins encountered his next-door neighbour, a friend, lost for words, who said with witless precision, 'Sooner you than me.'

In the Middle Ages, when the infant mortality rate was roughly 50 per cent, the Feast of Holy Innocents, which falls as a kind of fulcrum between Christmas and Epiphany, was exactly that, a feast, and one of the jolliest in the Church's calendar. This is rather a surprise, because it commemorates Herod's murder of the baby boys of Bethlehem after he was warned that one, Jesus, would be his undoing. In Alicante, in the town of Ibi, Holy Innocents is marked by the festival of Els Enfarinats, when the townsfolk dress in mock military uniform and stage a coup d'état. There is a procession with a special band and the Enfarinats then meet in front of the church for the Aixavegó, when fines are levied on those who have refused to pay them tax; those who refuse to pay are marched off to jail. The procession ends at the St Joaquim Sanctuary where there is an enormous fight and flour and eggs are thrown with tremendous gusto. At five in the afternoon the Enfarinats' authority ends, the status quo is restored, and there are fireworks and a dance.

In England, until the Reformation, Holy Innocents was known as the Childermass, or Children's Mass, and in cathedrals it marked the end of the reign of the boy bishop. He was a child, a chorister usually, elected on 6 December, the feast of St Nicholas, the patron of children, and whose authority lasted till Holy Innocents' day, twenty-two days later. To mark this spectacular reversal of roles on the eve of the feast, at Vespers, the real bishop would step down from his throne during the singing of the Magnificat, at the words 'He hath put down the mighty from their seat', and the boy would take his place at the phrase 'and hath exalted the humble and meek'. After his election, the boy was dressed in cope and mitre and pectoral cross, given a crook; attended by schoolmates dressed as priests, he would make a circuit of the city to bestow his blessing on the people. This was not merely picturesque – the boy bishop and his colleagues then took possession of the cathedral and performed all the ceremonies and offices, except Mass, until the Childermass. The custom was banned, boringly, by Henry VIII in 1542, revived by Mary in 1552 and finally abolished by Elizabeth in the Protestant shakedown of her reign. Although it has since been revived in our time in places like Hereford and Winchester and in Peterborough, it is a revival only of the panto aspects of the tradition, the dressing up rather than the wielding of authority, which is rather a shame, for some have observed that a ten-year-old is no more likely to mess things up than a Right Reverend Father in God.

Why jolly? Herod, in his raging, slew the little childer, we sing in the Coventry Carol, one of the dark minor-key carols that fall like rain in the desert of the ding-dong merrily on highs. We rejoice because beyond the furthest horizon of cruelty, limitless light breaks. That paradox of hope wrenched from abandonment resounds in the Kontakion for the Dead, the Russian funeral hymn: 'All we go down to the dust; and weeping o'er the grave we make our song: Alleluia, alleluia, alleluia.'

Epiphany is a time of gifts, of gold, frankincense and myrrh, but in continental Europe the theme is expanded. In Italy, La Befana comes on this day, a witch with presents for the good children and lumps of coal for the could-do-betters. In France it is celebrated as Les Rois, and a special galette is served in which a bean is concealed, and whoever finds the bean gets to wear a crown.

An unexpected gift came to me from the kingly generosity of an eccentric millionaire who I interviewed on *Saturday Live*, on Radio Four, which I then occasionally presented when the incumbent, Fi Glover, was on maternity leave. James, a tycoon and a writer, was especially congenial and after the programme, standing outside Broadcasting House, he asked me where I lived. I was curate at Knightsbridge at the time, which was on his way home, so he offered me a lift. A black car slid silently to a halt beside us and as we glided past Hyde Park I settled into its mocha leather interior and he said, 'I walk my dogs there every day. Do you like dogs?' I said I did and had always had dachshunds, but a dog would not be practical now. 'Why?' he asked. I burbled something about living in central London and he said, 'So do I. It's not a problem.' When he dropped me off, he said, 'I think I'm going to get you a dachshund. Someone will be in touch.' I laughed and said goodbye.

The following Monday his PA called. 'We have arranged a dachshund for you. Her name is Daisy. A car will come and pick you up and take you to the Randolph Hotel in Oxford where you will meet the breeder and then take you to Harrods, where James will meet you at Pet Kingdom and make sure you have everything you need.' I said, 'Thank you very much.' David was on holiday from theological college at the time, and staying with me in London. When I got in I told him what had happened and said, 'It is a bit overwhelming, isn't it? I don't know if we should accept.' He said, 'Shut up – I'm going to Oxford.' I couldn't go, so David was picked up and driven to Oxford, and I arranged to meet him and James and the dog at Harrods. When I got there, James was holding the tiniest, prettiest puppy I had ever seen, white and tan markings, like a cow's, with blue eyes, exhausted, David said, from crying all the way from Oxford to London. We were escorted by a Harrods minder to Pet Kingdom, where David and I made a beeline for a smart dog-boutique, where James commanded us to get whatever we wanted. I had, I confessed, already checked out the website, but it was so expensive I had called his PA and said, 'Does he really want to do this? It's terribly dear.' She just laughed. So we arrived home with a pile of organic dog-bed linen, almond shampoo which cost more than my shampoo, and Daisy, who was to change our lives and bring us joy. Daisy was followed by Pongo. Then Audrey and H. Now we have four sausage dogs, which does nothing to challenge the stereotype of gay couples falling for tiny little dogs and doting on them as if they were their children.

How can you believe that your God is the right God? people ask. And I admit, if I had been born in Tibet, or Baghdad, or Kyoto I would probably not be doing what I am doing now. But I was born in Northampton in 1962, in Christendom, however faded, and had just enough exposure to the Church to know how to find my way back there when I needed to.

But that is not the reason why I am a Christian. I am a Christian because I believe God became man, or rather *a* man, in a particular place at a particular time, and that same conviction in others spread out unevenly from first-century Palestine to me, here and now. It is the unlikeliest thing, which is one reason to find it persuasive, I think. There is never a good time to get a dog, never a good time to have a child. There is never a good time for God to become incarnate.

After Christmas I went to stay with a friend in Staffordshire. One afternoon we visited the Wedgwood factory at Barlaston, partly because Josiah Wedgwood is a hero of mine, partly because Epiphany, with its giving of gifts, always makes me want to go shopping (bad vicar). The factory, which moved from Etruria in the nineteenth century, is based in a park where Wedgwood's house still stands, more a Palladian villa than a mansion. It was a cold bright morning, with no one around when I'd expected it to be busy; we had some soup and a sandwich in the cafeteria, then I asked the two funny and I expect slightly bored ladies at Reception for a discount; they were game, letting us in at half-price because the factory was closed. The exhibition itself was quite good, only there was too much information (audio guide, video, exhibits, interpretation panels, commentary). Eventually we came to the demonstration room, where craftsmen and women sat at work-tables throwing pots, lathing pots, painting pots and so on. I talked to a man patiently painting figurines, ladies in extravagant hats and dresses who looked like they'd just stepped out of a Fragonard painting. The figurine he was painting was called 'Nina', and he hated Nina because she wears red, which needs two coats, so she takes twice as long to do as the others, and seeing as he is paid pro rata, it means he is paid less. 'I hate a row of Ninas,' he sighed . . . Which did he like? 'Jeanne: she's a doddle.'

I talked to a lady who painted the dinner services, the grandest the pottery produces. There was one in black and gold that looked a bit blingy to me, but sold well to the kind of clients who throw banquets. One of these dinner services cost sixty thousand pounds – double that, I should think, today – and was a favourite of the Queen, the Sultan of Brunei and Frank Sinatra. I watched her work, filling the gaps between some complicated gilt scrolling on a teacup. She put a blob of blue pigment, which looked like a lump of dissolving blue jasper, on a slate, and loosened it with some solvent from a china pot to her right. Then she dipped a paintbrush in the pigment until the head was wobbly and fat and, instead of taking the brush to the cup, she took the cup to the brush and, with great skill, turned it this way and that, allowing the cup, it seemed, to take the pigment.

They had some one-offs for sale in the shop, but they were amazingly expensive – a bowl in black basalt with white moulded reliefs was £3,000 – but in the factory shop I bought a big and very elegant bowl by Jasper Conran for forty quid, a second.

At dinner that evening we were talking about the glitter of bling, and the glamour of power, and the mystique of royalty, and how that works today, if at all. Princess Diana came up, who seemed to me to manage to be both self-deprecating and almost embarrassed by her status and yet use it to the full when it suited her. I had known her slightly (our acquaintanceship couldn't have been much slighter) and went on to say something about the *Panorama* interview she gave as her marriage to the Prince of Wales disintegrated. Then my friend said, 'I know so many people who claim to have known her, people who met her on the charity circuit . . . of course, they didn't know her at all.' I said, evenly, 'Yes, that's how I knew her,' and he said, evenly, 'I guess she had a knack for making you feel that she was sharing intimacies with you, when they weren't really intimacies at all.'

He's right about the Princess Diana thing. I met her, precisely, twice: once with a semicircle of others at a charity auction at Christie's, and once at the London Lighthouse, of which we were both patrons, when I was talking to her step-brother and she came over to say hello. Funny, friendly, but covered in diamonds, which flashed like tiny strobes as she entered the room.

On the way home, I turned off and found myself in Walsall. I decided to revisit the New Gallery and parked in another of those retail parks on the outskirts of town, then crossed an unlovely stretch of ring road to where the New Gallery stands.

The permanent collection is hung thematically, the best way to display so idiosyncratic a collection. The haphazardness of the hang makes the gems shine with more lustre, for being unexpected. I loved a twelfth-century French carved wooden bust of Christ, very beautiful, wearing the crown of thorns; the man of sorrows, wide-eyed and distressed. The drapery of the robe over Jesus' shoulders followed the grain of the wood, which had cracked over the centuries, and two deep fissures ran from Christ's breast to his face, the splitting king crowned with thorns.

I also loved a Dürer woodcut, from the end of the fifteenth century, of a men's bathhouse, in Nuremberg, I presume. If you ever thought the homoerotic was invented only with homosexuality in the nineteenth century, look at this and you'll think again. A consort (interesting word) stand naked but for negligible cache-sexes, serenading bathers (and each other) in a bathhouse. The younger men stare knowingly, erotically, out of the picture, while an old man stands slightly apart, in profile, edged out of the centre by the unanswerable, irresistible allure of the young and the beautiful and the naked.

I picked up a couple of Galettes des Rois from Patisserie Valerie in London on my way home to donate to the church where I was preaching that Epiphany Sunday. It was, of course, more expensive and more trouble than I'd expected, so I was in a bad mood by the time I got there. My mood was not sweetened by the lady of the parish on catering duty that day, who relieved me of them brusquely and without thanks. I went to the vestry and there talked to my fellow clergy, one of whom pointed to a mark on the gold cope I had been given to wear and said without embellishment, 'That's a bloodstain from my daughter's wedding.' Prayers were said at crib and font, the altar was incensed, and then Mass, with me preaching. They seemed to like the sermon. Galettes des Rois were distributed afterwards, but when I went for a second piece the plate was snatched from my fingers for the catering lady wasn't sure there was enough to go round. She came back later with another slice.

The Queen is coming on a visit to Broadcasting House, and even in the BBC, where monarchist sympathies do not always run high, people are finding excuses to watch her come and go. She is preceded by outriders, and I suppose her security detail, which has obliged a stricter observance of our everyday routines and main reception is unusually thronged with senior management.

I, with no ambivalence about the monarchy, watch her arrive from the steps of All Souls, Langham Place, a vantage point to which I feel I have a right as an incumbent of the Church of England. I have not seen the Queen arrive somewhere for a while now and I am struck by the eerie silence when she does. The last time I saw her arrive somewhere was at the Royal Academy of Music, when I was Chaplain, and everyone clapped and cheered as she emerged, in searing lemon, from the royal car. The silence now does not indicate the decline of popularity, but the rise of new technology: smartphones, which people hold up, making clapping impossible. It is more important to capture the moment on your phone than to greet the Lord's anointed. I wonder if she notices?

Inside, the Queen sits inscrutably while a band performs for her at Radio One. Political interviewers, noted for their iron indifference to the great and the good, now bow and smile as she is led down the line by the Director-General, and then she is gone and things return to normal.

Later that day another security detail arrives, more rigorous, I think, even than hers, for thanks to Sian Williams, my co-host on *Saturday Live*, we are to have a special guest on the programme. Bill Gates, founder of Microsoft, at various times the richest man in the world, had a member of staff who is a friend of Sian's and he's offered his boss to the programme to be interviewed about the work of the Gates Foundation. The team assess not only the security risks but also the precise time he needs to be where we need him to be. This choreography is so well worked out that he will step out of his car, through a normally closed door, into a lift, along a corridor, and into our studio at precisely the moment we go to an item on tape, giving him two minutes to settle before the interview begins.

The day dawns, the guest arrives, and the atmosphere changes when he enters the studio. It is Bill Gates, more powerful, some would say, than many politicians and rulers and potentates. For some reason, we talk a bit about the sound various early computers made when they were loading data, a moment of IT nostalgia, and then we are on air. He talks about what he wants to talk about in a very measured way, and says no more than he wants to say.

Afterwards, I don't remember what he said, apart from thinking it sounded like a good idea, but I remember the other guest with us round the table called him, respectfully, Mr Gates, while we called him, in line with the programme's temper and our correspondence with his office, Bill. Once, when his fellow guest's 'Mr Gates' was followed by my 'Bill', he looked up, for a second, and I felt a frisson of lese-majesty.

A poem for the Epiphany, 'Bethlehem Down', written by Bruce Blunt for his friend the composer Peter Warlock to set to music. I'd like to say they did it in a surge of piety, but it was actually written to pay for a drinking bout when they were both stony broke – on Christmas Eve 1927. Warlock, when he'd recovered from the hangover, described it as an 'immortal carouse'. Worth remembering,

if you find yourself as I did once at a Midnight Mass with half
the congregation so drunk they could barely stand, let alone sing,
that something so hauntingly lovely, so theologically profound, was
written on the back of a fag packet down the pub.

'When He is King we will give Him a King's gifts,
Myrrh for its sweetness, and gold for a crown,
Beautiful robes,' said the young girl to Joseph,
Fair with her firstborn on Bethlehem Down.

Bethlehem Down is full of the starlight,
Winds for the spices, and stars for the gold,
Mary for sleep, and for lullaby music
Songs of a shepherd by Bethlehem fold.

When He is King, they will clothe Him in grave sheets,
Myrrh for embalming, and wood for a crown,
He that lies now in the white arms of Mary
Sleeping so lightly on Bethlehem Down.

Here He has peace and a short while for dreaming,
Close-huddled oxen to keep Him from cold,
Mary for love, and for lullaby music
Songs of a shepherd by Bethlehem fold.

*

When I was growing up, not far from my present parish of Finedon,
in the 1970s, the main road between Kettering and Thrapston was
the A604. I got to know it well, first as a passenger in my parents'
car, then on my purple moped, a Yamaha FS1E, or Yammy Fizzer,
with its 49cc of two-stroke power to enlarge my horizons. Fifteen
years later, I came up one weekend to look at a house for sale, a
house about a mile off that road. I drove from London, where I
was then living, but when I got to the turn-off for the A604, the
road I knew so well, it was no longer there. The towns and villages

were where they used to be, the topography hadn't changed, hills and streams and woods and farms were where I expected to find them; but the A604 had been superseded by the A14, a wider road which more or less followed the old one, but gave a different view. A journey I'd taken often through country I knew well was suddenly different, and I felt that odd sensation of finding myself a stranger in familiar territory.

On *Saturday Live*, I interviewed a film director who told me two interesting things, both off air, which is when the most interesting things are often said. First, 20 per cent of the photographs ever taken were taken last year, smartphones with inbuilt cameras exponentially expanding the archive. Second, how important it is to get the architecture of a script right. Not dialogue, not setting, but the outline of the story. This, he told me, was the critical stage in the process of making a film: 'The most important thing to get right is the narrative arc.' Every story has an arc, a line, if you like, which you can plot, beginning at the beginning, rising at the middle and declining at the end; how steeply or how gently it falls gives the story its shape.

I thought of this arc when I thought of the Epiphany, and the Wise Men's encounter with the infant Jesus. It wasn't simply because of the star, itself describing an arc through the skies to Bethlehem, but rather the story itself that provoked the question: what kind of an arc does it have? It begins clearly enough, rising out of the hope of the Jewish people. We know from the Old Testament that certain things will happen when the Saviour is born; a star will rise and kings will travel to his brightness, bringing gifts of treasure and spices. So that's where the arc begins to rise, in the East, and along its course come the Magi, with gold, frankincense and myrrh. Arriving at Bethlehem, they complete the ensemble around the crib, worshipping the Christ child, the arc at its high point. But then, as Matthew's account concludes, instead of declining with their return journey the arc takes off in a new direction, as they do, by another road.

Bad technique, my interviewee would say, and he's right. But this is not a screenplay, and our heroes are not riding off into the sunset. For the arc of this story is not what we thought it was, any more than their journey was what they thought it was.

My last service at Boston Stump, where I was ordained and served as curate, marked the end of the formal training that began in theological college, where I learned about the importance of the inward journey, through the disciplines of silence and stillness and self-examination. At Boston I learned the importance of the outward journey, to take God to the world and to try to be patient, gentle and steadfast, especially when the likeness of Christ is hard to discern in those I meet, let alone in one's reflection. And to try to look like I mean it, to give Christian faith sharpness, focus, contour, to make it visible again.

We do this, if we do it at all, by not going where the arc leads us, for the arc that rises from our expectations does not lead us very far at all. The impossible arc of the star of Bethlehem, which some say was really a supernova, or an alignment of the planets, or a comet, the impossible arc which does not even work within the context of the story itself, leading the Wise Men in entirely the wrong direction; the star that is only there to show the child, the fulfilment of Old Testament prophecy, is the one we must follow to take us beyond our expectations to a place we do not want to go.

HATCHING

A young woman comes into church to arrange a baptism for her baby daughter. She is asked to fill in the form for the registers and under 'father's occupation' she writes 'alcoholic'.

I am not sure if you can renew a baptismal vow, but that is what David and I did when we took our party of pilgrims from Finedon to the Holy Land, to a bend in the River Jordan, in the waters where Jesus received the baptism of John two thousand years ago. I had no idea if it was the right bend, but it brought with it its own drama: on our side, teenagers from the Israeli Defense Force with M16s looking across thirty feet of muddy water at teenagers from the Jordanian army with Kalashnikovs, post-modern hatreds down by the riverside. This all happened in the desert, not far from Jericho, where the water came as such a surprise I suddenly thought of Isaiah and the prophet foretelling the stupendous irrigation God will bring when the time is right. That time came, Christians believe, when Jesus Christ, down from Galilee, arrived to receive baptism from John the Baptist, whom the tradition treats as the herald of the one who comes.

Some people say John was an Essene, a member of a radical Jewish sect based in a sort of monastery at Qumran, best known now for having produced and preserved the Dead Sea Scrolls. Archaeologists have shown that their community had formidable plumbing, with cisterns and ducts and basins, and surmise that they must have taken ritual bathing very seriously; holy lustrations to wash away sins, not only theirs but all Israel's. So what was Jesus, the only person ever to have had no need of being cleansed, doing there?

At the riverside, where the Israeli tourist board had erected a handy H&S compliant platform, we could splash ourselves with water and fill a bottle to take home, the Anglican and RC way, but some enthusiastic Americans were robing in white and undergoing total immersion. They belonged to that branch of Christianity which subscribes to a version of Zionism, believing that Israel's occupation of the Holy Land will herald the Second Coming, when Christ will return in a final reckoning, delighting those with the peculiar appetite for catastrophe religion can engender. They also brought redneck enthusiasm for guns and God and gewgaws to the complex politics of the Holy Land and at the gift shop where we bought ice creams, they bought T-shirts with what looked like jokey slogans until you saw them close up. I saw one young man wearing one which showed a pregnant woman in a hijab in a rifle's sights, the cross hairs meeting over her pregnant belly. The slogan read: *One shot, two kills.*

Two young men come into church. One is silent and looks put upon, the other, rough and tough, looks like he has just got out of prison. They are neither spick nor span, and both shine with a muck sweat that makes me think they are speeding or on coke – and both are wearing rosaries, which in prison are sometimes used to signify an interest in drug dealing. The tough one comes over and asks if they could talk to me. We sit in the side chapel, under a stained-glass window showing one of my predecessors baptising babies on a Victorian mission to China. The tougher one does the talking; the silent one says nothing, but is clearly under his thumb. They are desperate to be baptised. Why? 'Because our flat is haunted by something evil.' I ask what has happened and they describe a scenario which sounds to me like a précis of a horror film amplified by amphetamine and fatigue hallucinations. I say I will go round and bless it later, and they ask me to bless them first. I take them to the font and they splash themselves with its water, like overheating beasts at a water hole.

Later, I arrive at their flat, one room plus bedroom, the curtains closed, overflowing ashtrays, a stink of cigarette smoke and dogs, and that hot sweetish smell of something nameless that sticks in the back of your throat and up your nostrils. The tougher one is there alone, in jeans and a singlet, with prison-bulked muscles and terrible tattoos. It is the other man's flat, but he has moved in and turned the living room into his own, where he does his methadone, leaving the tenant practically a prisoner in the bedroom, which has no independent access to the bathroom or kitchen. If he wants to go for a pee or a cup of tea he has to step over his friend, who has a complicated love life, which he vigorously pursues in spite of the amounts of psychoactive drugs he has on board. Why does he put up with this? He is smitten, I think, by this bad boy, who does what the hell he wants and fucks a lot, and gets into fights. He looks at him not quite adoringly, but like a dog with a bad master.

He makes me a cup of tea which I do not drink, rolls fags, and tells me a bit of his story, a mixture of escapades with the police, boasting of his immunity to the effects of a taser, and terrible neglect, and he gets angrier as he talks. I notice on the wall behind him a magnetic kitchen-knife holder with a butcher's knife and a cleaver stuck to it. I begin to wonder: Have I got enough time to get to the door and out of here if I need to? But I am not in the least scared – unusually for me, a physical coward who's never hit anyone in his life. Perhaps that is the Grace of Orders, God giving us the means to deal with the challenges sent our way? My brother, who used to be a cop, says the same thing about facing down criminals when he was on duty. It's the uniform.

Perhaps he sees I am not frightened, he begins to calm down and his tone changes. He boasts some more about the run-ins he's had with the police: falling off a roof legging it from a robbery, and 'breaking my back in six places'. He's been hit so hard they've had to put 'metal plates in my cheeks' – and suddenly he stands up and takes off his singlet and invites me to run my hand down his spine to feel where the fractures were, and then to feel the side of his face. Why does he want me to stroke his back and his cheek? Why does he want me to touch him? I'm not falling for this, I think, and am about to make my excuses and leave when the flatmate turns up with a cut over his eye, thanks to some 'foreigners' who'd beaten him up in town.

In the end they are both baptised by me, in one of our Saturday-afternoon baptismathons, when a dozen candidates queue by the font as I take them through the service as best I can, trying to explain the dense mysteries of the liturgy and theology without being completely incomprehensible or completely facetious. This is difficult, even with the most diligent and attentive of candidates, but most of our candidates, like these two young men, just want to 'get done' as a way of marking the arrival of a baby, or as a talisman against evil, or to make the baby thrive ('Do you do babbies?' I was once asked). Once a young woman approached the saving waters and, in a gesture I found touching, to mark the solemnity of the occasion took out her chewing gum and stuck it on the side of the font before I splashed her head. Sometimes that gap between what I think I am doing and what they think I am doing is so egregious I could be demoralised, but then I remember the story from the Acts of the Apostles of St Philip and the African eunuch.

A Palestinian peasant, on foot, accosts the entourage of a high-ranking royal official, an African, a eunuch, who is reading the prophecy of Isaiah in his government chariot as it makes its way along a desert road. Philip offers to help him interpret the scripture he is reading. The eunuch invites him to jump in and off they go, but before they've gone very far so persuasive is Philip that the eunuch commands the chariot to stop at a stream of water so that this stranger may baptise him into the faith he knew nothing of when he'd left town that morning. A vivid story, in which baptism is something that makes the rich poor and the poor rich, something that brings forth life in the desert, something that's available to all, even those who fall outside the assembly of Israel. In some versions of the Bible, before Philip baptises him, the eunuch says, 'I believe that Jesus Christ is the Son of God.' In others, that sentence is missing; a later addition, I guess, inserted by scribes who wished to show that baptism is not freely available to all, it is available only to those who confess that Jesus Christ is the Son of God. In other words, you can only be baptised once you've passed the test of orthodox faith. Baptism is for those in the know.

But in the original version it appears that this was not the case. You didn't need to pass any test of orthodox faith to receive it, you needed simply to want it, to want it without knowing exactly what it was. And God, in answer to that want, provides, and the story ends with the baptised eunuch going on his way, rejoicing.

I lost track of the tough guy until a policeman told me that he'd been felled by a concerted fusillade of tasers outside the shop he had been burgling and had eventually been sent to prison. I went to see him there and thought he would be lost to the depressingly common cycle of prison, probation, methadone, crime and prison. Actually, the very last time I saw him, he and his girlfriend were walking down the street pushing a pram.

Discovered that the 1662 prayer book baptism rite addressed to those of riper years was not intended for late vocations, as I thought, but for the growing populations of slaves on English-owned plantations. Not a pastoral effort to gather converts to the congregation of the Lord, but for those forced into it against their will. I have not baptised adults against their will, I think, but I have baptised those whose understanding of the solemn purpose they were undertaking was perhaps not firm. I have baptised babies, who blinked unknowingly as they were held over the font, I have baptised toddlers who certainly did not want to be held over the font at all. I once baptised a child who turned over in my arms and dived into the font, like a tiny Tom Daley.

Sarah the Martyr, venerated in the Coptic Church of Egypt, was a fourth-century saint whose vivid life bore witness to the soundness of an orthodox theology of baptism. She lived in Antioch but was unable to baptise her twin boys due to the persecution of Christians there by the Roman Emperor Diocletian, so they escaped to Egypt in a boat. Unfortunately, en route a terrible storm blew up; worried that if they drowned unbaptised her boys would be damned, Sarah baptised them herself in her own blood. She slashed her breast, marked the foreheads and breasts with the sign of the cross in her blood, then dipped them three times in the sea, invoking the Trinitarian formula of Father, Son and Holy Spirit. The ship, happily, survived the storm and when they got to Alexandria, Sarah took her sons to Pope Peter I for their official baptism. He tried three times to baptise them, but each time the water in the font froze. 'It is, indeed, one baptism,' the Pope thoughtfully pronounced, and gave up. Sarah and her sons returned to Antioch where, unfortunately, she was accused of adultery and all three were burned alive.

I have been invited to the baptism of a Romanian baby at their temporary parish down the road, set up to provide for the needs of an arriving community now that citizens of the EU accession nations are admitted to the UK. There are about twenty Romanians there, including one enormous man, about six foot five and built like a tank, a rugby player originally from Bucharest. The baby boy being baptised is called Vladek and his parents are from Bessarabia, ethnically Romanian but absorbed into the Soviet Union after the war. They are young and shy and very poor, and I meet them in the porch where the priest is performing a rite of exorcism over the baby and his godmother. It goes on and on, very wordy like the Book of Common Prayer, but with interesting cultic elements. The priest blows the sign of the cross over the baby three times, the godmother says the creed three times facing different directions, someone spits. The deacon is very bossy, telling the worshippers to be quiet (when they want you to shut up, Romanians go *sssss!* not *ssssh!*). Then we go – processed is too formal an expression – into a side chapel where they've filled a fibreglass pond with water and tried to prettify it with vases of flowers. They strip the baby and then the priest anoints him, a dab on the ears, the nose, the mouth, and then rubs him all over with oils until he's as slippery as an eel. Then we proceed to the font, in which he is immersed three times, provoking an outraged wail. I am suddenly so moved – at the liturgy, the baby's distress, the delight of the congregation – that my eyes fill with tears.

When the baptism is over, I stay to have a drink with the family and friends. Afterwards, taking a shortcut through the church, I run into a friend who is excited to see me and invites me to supper. Just then a regular, red in the face, snaps, 'We do NOT TALK in the church!' in an outraged voice, like Mrs Bridges to Ruby. I say sorry to his retreating back, but as I walk away I think of the pleasant and polite Romanians and their joy in the baptism of Vladek and how much I've been moved by it, and then I think of him and say out loud, 'You nasty old git.' So much for the negotiation of wrath.

In Finedon the font, at first sight, rather lets us down. St Mary's is grand and handsome, built unusually in one effort in the fourteenth century between the decision by the monks of Peterborough, who had the power and the prestige in these parts, to make a statement and the arrival of the Black Death, which caused a halt to be called before the chancel could be vaulted. But the builders retained the Norman font from the church that had been pulled down to make way for this one. Rather like city banks in their glittering skyscrapers that retain a reminder of their seventeenth-century origins in the atrium, so our ancestors decided to keep this. It is four-sided, each panel carved with scenes from the life of Christ – an Annunciation, his baptism by John in the Jordan – threshold narratives on the threshold of entry into the faith. Nothing very unusual in that, but the corners have been chamfered, so heavily, so crudely, that it looks like a block of cheese from which someone has selfishly sliced off the corners. And then you see that the carvings have been smashed, defaced, scarred with a deliberation which makes you wonder about the intentions of the vandals.

It is the work of reformers, in the sixteenth or seventeenth centuries, inflamed with righteous indignation at the apostasy of gewgaws and fanciness, in a period of regime change. They came to church in a gang, intent on tearing down the statues, whitewashing the paintings, trashing the relics and smashing up the font. They seem so distant from us now, with our piles of cans for the foodbank, our windfalls and allotment surpluses left for whoever wants them, our slightly over-reaching offers of welcome to 'all', these days of intensity of feeling and violence. And then you see on the news a bearded idiot in Iraq, swinging a sledgehammer at a two-thousand-year-old frieze, men in medieval costumes filming themselves in HD laying Semtex round the pillars of an ancient temple, beheading an octogenarian keeper of antiquities because of a religious zealotry that dresses in vestments their desire to demonise and subjugate their opponents. Sometimes I loathe religion. I loathe it when it is adopted as a cosmic justification for a political agenda that needs to turn its vices into virtues and its violence into crusade or jihad.

You may see that righteous paradoxical rage burning in Mrs Carry A. Nation, the most violent advocate of Temperance in the history of that movement in the United States. She was born to bewildered and delusional parents in Kentucky, and during the Civil War married a drunken doctor who abandoned her before the birth of their daughter and then died of alcoholism. She became a firm advocate of Temperance, understandably, trained as a school teacher and found herself a second husband, a minister called David A. Nation. The couple moved to Medicine Lodge, Kansas, where she opened a dry hotel and formed a branch of the Woman's Christian

Temperance Union. At first her methods were relatively mild. She would take a choir to bars and sing hymns at people trying to drink, and she'd denounce bartenders in the street as 'Destroyers of Men's Souls'. However, one morning in 1900 she was woken by an eerie voice saying, 'Carry A. Nation! Go to Kiowa! I'll stand by you! Take something in your hands, and throw it at these places in Kiowa and smash them!' So on 7 June 1900 she gathered a band of women who armed themselves with stones and went to Dobson's Saloon in the town of Kiowa, where she shouted, 'Men, I have come to save you from a drunkard's fate', and then proceeded to smash the bartender's entire stock. Two other saloons in Kiowa were also destroyed, and the state was then hit by a dreadful tornado which Mrs Nation took to be a sign of divine approval.

She continued smashing up bars in Kansas, then Wichita, and her long record of arrest began. This irritated her husband, who one day rather snippily said, 'Why not take a hatchet with you next time?' so she did, divorcing him soon after. Mrs Nation and her band of hymn-singing supporters continued their 'hatchetations' spree, smashing up bars in Kansas City, Missouri, and many places in Minneapolis, Texas and Washington, DC. Arrested more than thirty times, she paid the fines courts imposed upon her by selling her hatchets as souvenirs. As her fame grew, she launched a newspaper, *The Smasher*, and undertook lecture tours of the United States and England, where she went down so badly someone threw an egg at her in Canterbury's Theatre of Varieties, which discouraged her and she returned to the United States to live in Arkansas in a house called Hatchet Hall. There she lost her reason entirely; after applauding the assassination of President McKinley on the grounds that as a drinker he had got what he deserved, she was confined in the Evergreen Place Hospital and Sanitarium in Leavenworth, Kansas, where she died, raving, in 1911. To mark her centenary a bar was opened in Boston, Massachusetts, called the Carry A. Nation.

*

Boston Stump, where the Reformation battles were played out on an epic scale, bears its scars too. The outside of that church, one of the grandest in the land, was once so thickly studded with saints, each in a niche, that it must have looked like a vision of heaven – until the reformers arrived. They came in several waves, the first led by John Taverner, the Tudor composer, who oversaw the music there, but in the heat of the moment personally oversaw the destruction of the rood screen, one of the finest in England. His bones lie under the tower, a plaque commemorates him, and I like to think a faint whirring may be heard under the flags as restored Medieval liturgies are performed on them with as much ceremony as congregants can muster.

There is, however, a strain to our ceremonial now, recovered imperfectly as a protest in the 1850s and thereabouts but forever self-conscious, an attempt to recreate the past under the noses of those who think the past should be left where it is. We all do it, of whichever churchmanship, on those rare occasions when the clergy of the diocese gather in church, those towards the High end of the spectrum vested in surplices and stoles, towards the Low end in black preaching scarves, minor differences that indicate major disagreements, but both as artificial in their way as the Sealed Knot's roundheads and cavaliers in bifocals pretending to refight Edgehill.

I preside at a posh baptism at St Paul's: a billionaire's baby, who arrives with a stylist and a make-up artist. His eighteen-month-old cheeks are flushed with rouge, his face airbrushed smooth for the photo call. Among the celebrity godparents are a famous footballer and a stadium-filling singer. One of the older members of the clergy who helps out at St Paul's told me there was an awkward scene at the same font years ago when the Duchess of York, later Queen Elizabeth then the Queen Mother, encountered Lillie Langtry, mistress of the Duchess's grandfather-in-law, Edward VII. The waters of salvation nearly froze.

People often ask about the difference in clientele between the rough parts of Boston and the posh enclave of Belgravia, but the real difference is between places like these and the middle-class, middle England parishes. The posh and the rough are alike unbothered by the opinion of people outside their own set, and alike unbothered by the opinion of the clergy. I quite like that, at least in theory. It is easier to disappoint someone with expectations than someone indifferent. But I get irritated when people have so little idea of what we do, or care so little about it, that they trespass on our territory. I did a posh wedding once and when I got there the ushers had taken it upon themselves to remove all the Gift Aid envelopes from the pews. When I asked them why, and insisted they put them back, they said they 'struck the wrong note'.

CANDLEMAS

Now there was a man in Jerusalem whose name was Simeon; this man was righteous and devout, looking forward to the consolation of Israel, and the Holy Spirit rested on him. It had been revealed to him by the Holy Spirit that he would not see death before he had seen the Lord's Messiah. Guided by the Spirit, Simeon came into the temple; and when the parents brought in the child Jesus, to do for him what was customary under the law, Simeon took him in his arms and praised God, saying,

> *Lord, now lettest thou thy servant depart in peace, according to thy word. For mine eyes have seen thy salvation; which thou hast prepared before the face of all people; to be a light to lighten the Gentiles and to be the glory of thy people Israel.*

Candlemas falls on 2 February, and in England once marked the end of Christmas proper. Decorations were taken down for Epiphany – Twelfth Night – but the greenery was kept in church until this date. I am not sure why; perhaps to keep the hope of greenness going until the first signs of spring? The Gospel set for the feast continues the theme of first signs. Simeon, the old priest, finally sees that salvation has arrived in the child Jesus and knows his time is done. It is a particularly lovely passage from Scripture, but you need not wait a year for it to come round again, for you can hear it every day, said or sung in monasteries, the last service of the day, and at Evensong in the Church of England, known by its Latin name the *Nunc dimittis*. To our worship, to our character it gives a characteristic dying fall, so end-of-empire, so time-for-bed.

We sang the *Nunc dimittis*, the Canticle of Simeon, every Choral Evensong at Boston Stump, but I always thought that dying fall was at odds with the assertiveness of the building. The parish church of St Botolph, Boston, has the highest tower in England – 272 feet – and you can see it for miles around. People often ask, 'Why is it called the Stump?' Phil and Tony, the stonemasons on the staff when I was curate there ten years ago, thought the name went back to the gap between the completion of the nave, in about 1400, and the completion of the tower in about 1550. A long gap, one hundred and fifty years, probably caused by the wool-rich citizens of the town running out of money after the Black Death. So for a long time the huge nave stood with only a stump at its west end, and this endured for so long that by the time the tower was finally capped with its magnificent octagonal lantern, the name stuck.

It is a long climb to the top of the lantern, the last two-thirds of it via a narrow, twisting staircase in pitch-darkness, and when you finally emerge, right by the weather vanes, your legs feel like you have run the marathon. Pity the boys who had to carry the wood to fuel the beacon up from ground level to the top of the tower, all 365 steps. But the view is wonderful: on a clear day you can see from Hunstanton to Lincoln Cathedral, across the Wash, across the Wolds. It is a view most people never get to see, because Boston Stump is more looked at than looked from, a landmark by day, a giant candle, lit with floodlights, by night.

I remember a day when the vicar was away and I was on duty, driving back to Boston by night through the thirty miles of cabbage fields that lie to the west, feeling more and more uneasy as I approached the town. I realised why I felt uneasy when it struck me that I could not see the Stump. That lit candle, the beacon for sailors out on the Wash, for travellers coming from Lincoln, had been snuffed out. For an awful moment I thought that I had accidentally left a votive candle unattended and its tiny flame had contrived to burn down this mighty church. In my mind, I rehearsed phoning the vicar to tell him what had happened on my watch. To my relief, it turned out the Stump was in darkness because the lights were being turned on later, for a civic event that I had forgotten about.

When I was training to be a priest, I came into college after Matins one Candlemas to find the Principal taking down the poster I had put up advertising the Blessing of Throats. Candlemas, at which the candles for use in the following year are blessed, is followed by the feast of St Blaise, patron of the sore-throated, and the custom arose for the new candles to be used as a prophylaxis, held in the shape of the cross over throats of the faithful to keep inflammation at bay. In parts of Catholic Europe this endures, but in the post-Reformation Church of England it is more likely to be seen as silliness. 'I presume this is a spoof,' the Principal said, breaking Greater Silence. 'No,' I said, 'it isn't.' 'Yes, it is,' he insisted, and walked off; then turned and said, 'It's not even in the calendar.'

Our resistance to the more picturesque elements in the Catholic tradition recalls, however faintly, the murderous animosities of the Reformation, when people like Latimer and Ridley and Cranmer lit candles of a different kind outside the colleges and churches of Oxford. In those days, burning of heretics was not a tactic reserved by one side: Protestants burned Catholics, Catholics burned Protestants. At the Stump's parish library, housed in a parvise – a chamber over the porch – Foxe's *Book of Martyrs* was always popular with visiting parties of schoolboys. Foxe, who came from Boston, was a Protestant and wrote this account of the lives and grisly deaths of his co-religionists, victims of Bloody Mary and her attempt to restore to England the Catholic faith of its fathers. The book, a first

edition, was popular for its exceptionally fine illustrations of the
martyr-bishops standing with remarkable composure in the burning pyres, Cranmer thrusting the hand which signed his recanta-
tion into the flames first, a scroll of speech spooling from Latimer's
mouth encouraging him to be of good cheer, for they shall that day
light such a candle as shall never be put out.

To Trinity College Dublin to preach for Candlemas, the guest of
the university Chaplain, who met me at the airport. We drove
to town and talked shop, then he showed me to my room in the
Georgian guest quarters overlooking a rugby field where a match
was just finishing as I unpacked. I walked up to the campanile –
campaneel, someone called it – and he took me to see the Book of
Kells, the illuminated Gospel manuscript that is Ireland's greatest
treasure, kept in the University Library. Gospel manuscripts are my
thing and I was excited as we crowded into a small, underground
chamber and round a glass case. There it was, the Book itself,
open at an indifferent page from Matthew with an illumination
showing Christ between two of the disciples, about to withdraw to
another place. It was beautiful, if slightly disappointing; like seeing
Beefeaters in their daily blue rather than the scarlet of high and
holy days.

   Beautiful and not disappointing at all was the library – the Long
Room – the oldest, biggest library in Ireland, built into soaring
alcoves guarded by busts of Shakespeare, Demosthenes, Cicero
and their peers. High above our heads, a wooden barrel-vault that
looked like a film set. It is a film set, George Lucas's Jedi Library,
and the subject of litigation. Apparently, he used the library's design
without permission.

   We went to the chapel, a long central aisle, lovely wood panelling, a lively acoustic, and the Chaplain walked me through the
service; meticulously, with firm instructions to follow the line of
yellow encaustic tiles to position one, then to move at the inton-
ation of the Credo with him to position two, ascending the altar

steps one at a time in a slow and even rhythm before taking my place at the lectern.

I was feeling a bit light-headed and asked if we could stop for tea and a bun, so he took me to the best tea shop in Dublin, which was closed, so I suggested we stop at the nearest one, because I was beginning to have one of those blood-sugar moments. Then on to drinks, first in the smallest bar in Dublin, where they pulled me a Guinness with a shamrock head. It was like drinking on the Northern Line at rush hour, so then we went to a new bar, where giant lampshades descended and ascended, like the Holy Spirit at Jesus' baptism, and waiters of many nations rushed a bit peremptorily between tables. Then dinner at Jaipur, a posh fusion Indian restaurant, and back to Trinity. I was up four times in the night to pee.

The radio woke me at a quarter to eight with a farming programme, a bizarre combination of mid-Atlantic voiceovers and stings, and then someone said, 'Now, Wicklow farmers did last week have a meeting about nitrate levels in fertilisers . . .' The news came on at eight and a rushed and slightly flustered young woman reported on the loss of the Space Shuttle *Columbia*, which had broken up on re-entry killing seven astronauts. She kept referring to 'NASA headquarters at Cape *Carnival* . . .'

I had breakfast with a slightly lugubrious but congenial professor of Safety Science from the University of Delft, and we talked about the Space Shuttle disaster, which he seemed curiously excited about. It turned out the first Space Shuttle disaster, when *Challenger* blew up on take-off, is a paradigm case for safety scientists. We talked a bit about the BBC and I told him about the Statement of Values, set forth in a gushy pamphlet, which we are all supposed to subscribe to. He said, 'Well, that *is* depressing.'

I walked over to the Blessed Sacrament Chapel and said Morning Prayer, then sat trying to empty the rubbish out of my head and make the most of the quiet. The Chaplain arrived and I went with him to get togged up in an academic gown that he'd laid out for me.

There were about forty people in church, not bad for a university chapel on a Sunday, most of them Roman Catholics off piste in an Anglican foundation. We left church to a recessional, played with amazing dash by an organ scholar. The tune sounded familiar but I could not place it, and then I realised I had written it. It was 'So Cold the Night', a minor hit from my eighties past.

In Victoria Olsen's biography of the pioneer photographer Julia Margaret Cameron, she recounts Henry Mayhew's interview with a London street photographer, *circa* 1860.

The street photographer was able to get away with all kinds of fraud because people didn't know what to expect from a photograph. When portraits turned out badly, he charged extra for 'brightening solutions' or 'American Air-Preserver' papers, or he would promise them the likenesses would 'come out' in a few hours. He charged them a penny to have their warts painfully removed by a photographic acid, two pence to be mesmerised by the camera, and a shilling to dye their hair and whiskers with nitrate of silver (though it stained their skin too). But the best scam was when he and his partner didn't have enough time or light to take a photograph at all . . . and they offered their sitter someone else's likeness.

When a young woman complained that 'this isn't me; it's got a widow's cap, and I was never married in all my life!', the photographer persuaded her that 'this ain't a cap, it's the shadow of the hair'. Another woman saw her picture and cried out, 'Bless me! there's a child: I haven't ne'er a child!' She was told, 'It's the way you sat; and what occasioned it was a child passing through the yard.'

The canny photographer concluded, 'People don't know their own faces. Half of 'em have never looked in a glass half a dozen times in their life, and directly they see a pair of eyes and a nose, they fancy they are their own.'

People have to learn to see themselves.

For mine eyes have seen thy salvation; which thou hast prepared before the face of all people; to be a light to lighten the Gentiles and to be the glory of thy people Israel.

It's locking-up time and I'm talking to Phil and Tony, the Stump's stonemasons, when three rough lads whom I haven't seen before come into church. They make some noise as they go round the building and the verger has to discourage them from getting too near the altar, and its candlesticks, in the Cotton Chapel. I go to check them out and we talk. They are wild-eyed, not too clean, and one is toothless; on methadone and homeless, I guess, and they ask if they can have something to eat. I take them to Captain Cod round the corner and buy them fish and chips. As they eat, the toothless one goes into his bag, and, mugging surprise, produces from it one of our candlesticks. He asks me what it is and I say it is one of our candlesticks and could I have it back? He returns it, without demur or embarrassment. I give them three pairs of socks each, bought from Poundstretcher.

Suburban Manchester, Monday morning, a sunny winter's day but chilly. Leaves fall from the trees, filling the gardens, front and back, in a street of handsome semi-detached houses. Outside one a people-carrier, warm from the school run, stands in the drive, as the sound of Radio Four and barking spaniels emerges from the opening front door. Who lives in a house like this?

The Poet Laureate, Carol Ann Duffy, lives here. Poets Laureate, like clergy, have come down in the world since the days Lord Tennyson held court in Belgravia. Even so, she, like him, is entitled to a 'butt of sherry sack', one of that post's peculiar perks, which translates into six hundred bottles of manzanilla. The first consignment has not yet arrived, so she offers me a cup of tea instead. I am there to interview her for *Songs of Praise*, a poetry special, and while the crew set up and she gets the dogs into the kitchen, I snoop around.

I'd interviewed the last Poet Laureate, Andrew Motion, at his house in North London, surrounded by knick-knacks with literary associations, including a monogrammed briefcase that Siegfried Sassoon had taken to the Western Front.

Carol Ann Duffy's house is more of a surprise; suburban and seemly, but with a hint of subversion. I note a fabric sculpture of a string quartet, the second violinist's music facing the wrong way; a cushion cover embroidered extravagantly with the face of Ella Fitzgerald; but most eye-catching is the kitchen door, on which is painted, in glittering gold letters, words I recognise but take a moment to place: *Softnesse, and peace, and joy, and love, and blisse, Exalted Manna, gladnesse of the best, Heaven in ordinarie, man well drest, The Milkie way, the bird of Paradise . . .* George Herbert's *Prayer*: rich imagery for a kitchen door.

The poem, she tells me, is one of her favourites, for its abundance and generosity and peculiar lack of a main verb, and for opening up a way to heaven from earth, a suburban Jacob's ladder, coming down from the ineffable to the fan-assisted. She reads for us her own poem of the same name, *Prayer*, a secular reply, I suppose, to Herbert's, but not, she says, *inspired* by it, although it was in the background when she wrote it, and in an interview I read in the paper she described it as a 'secular' prayer.

What is a secular prayer? For George Herbert, for me, what makes a prayer a prayer is its addressee. To whom, to what, is a secular prayer addressed? Is it like mailing a letter during a postal strike, wondering where, if anywhere, it will arrive? Is it like that installation at the Tate Modern a while ago, in which you walk into dense, black, light-absorbing nothingness, until you bump into the back wall? Is it like broadcasting a distress signal, not knowing if there's anyone there, but hoping there may be?

Duffy had been brought up as a Catholic and, although she left the Church, the Church has not entirely left her. Little bits of Latin, phrases from Scripture, dates from the Church's calendar appear in her poetry, like splinters, she says, rising to the surface;

and some of that poetry explicitly claims territory from Christian tradition. There is a very late Father Christmas hanging from the mantelpiece, and one of her best-known works is *The Manchester Carols*, a modern telling of the Christmas story. 'I love Christmas,' she tells me, 'and I believe in Father Christmas.' There are, however, limits to her belief, and when I ask if she ever sneaks off to Midnight Mass, she says, firmly, 'No.'

That disconnect, between form and content, seems to me to be characteristic of the way Christianity sits in our culture: we like the smells and bells, Evensong at Westminster Abbey, Spanish polychrome religious sculpture, but we treat them as if they float freely in the atmosphere, unattached to the commitments and contexts in which they took shape.

Of course we do. Church politics, the vicissitudes of living with others, rattling the poor box, erode the mystery and the magic. Jesus, observed Oscar Wilde, changed water into wine, and the Church has been trying to turn it back into water ever since.

But there is no wine without water, no transcendent mystery without earthly foundations, without walls and roofs and arches and buttresses and naves and chancels and towers.

Who lives in a house like this?

Caught up in its grammar of permanence, you'd think that congregations in churches would be, if not at home in eternity, then looking towards its horizon with this passing world. When the architects built St Paul's, Knightsbridge, they consciously used that grammar, looking back to the Gothic, with its soaring verticals, pointed arches, dazzling decoration, conspiring to realise on earth the heavenly city. Angels, apostles and Israelites look down on us and offer, in return, a vision of heaven. But the most arresting architectural feature in my old parish church is something that's not there: the gap between the end of the galleries, in which the servant class would sit, and the beginning of the chancel, where the choir and clergy operate. The galleries stop short, as if, in the middle of construction, the builders changed their minds.

St Paul's began, like so many churches of the mid-Victorian period, as a place for preaching, where the gathered community would meet to hear the Word. Look west from the chancel and that can be clearly seen; it looks more like a place for discussion and debate than a place of mysterious transcendence. Look east, beyond the galleries' abrupt end, and something completely different is revealed, as the eye is led, through incense and candlelight and ornament, to the High Altar and Christ crucified above it.

Very Anglican that, for a church to express in its architecture a tension between our two identities: a Church of the Reformation, and the Word supreme, and a Church of the faith Catholic, enthroning the Eucharist. The community this building served and shaped expresses that tension and still does. In the 1850s, churches founded by eager High Church curates from St Paul's ignited the Ritualist Riots, when Protestant heavies revolted in protest at scandalous Popish practices like having candles on the altar and wearing vestments. No one riots now, but the tensions remain, and for anyone trying to find an identity in the middle of those tensions the pilgrimage can be frustrating, the signposts unreliable, the way ahead unclear.

For some, that's an indictment of Anglicanism, so divided it cannot stand.

Who lives in a house like this?

Weirdly, I am half-awake in bed and hear myself on the *Today* programme, only it is Alistair McGowan doing an impression of me. I resolve at once to sound even more poncey so more impressionists will have a go at doing me, then I will be able vastly to inflate my fee for opening a supermarket, if anyone should ever ask me to open a supermarket.

Between the matinee and first night of the Finedon panto, in which I opened Act II with a dance routine in eerie ultraviolet, I nip into the Co-op for a bottle of wine. When I get home, I realise I hadn't taken my glitter make-up off and had stood there in the queue looking like Moses come down from the mountain, his face shining with the light of God.

I think again of Boston Stump and its lit lantern, symbolising the light of Christ shining in the darkness of the world, but conveniently also a beacon for shipping. Once I saw an old man there, walking around on his own, looking nostalgic, so I introduced myself and asked if he'd visited before. Not exactly, he replied, in accented English, but it was a place of happy memories. He'd been in the Luftwaffe during the war, a bomber pilot, and on the return leg of a raid when he saw the tower of the Stump he knew he was heading out to the North Sea and to safety.

I wondered what drew him back to Boston Stump, at ground-level this time. Was he, like the Jews of Jerusalem, drawn to the Temple for purification – as Candlemas is also called – to have his sins acknowledged and reckoned and made right with God? He never said anything about it, but during the war a German plane dropped a stick of bombs on Boston, causing death and mayhem, still remembered by many of the parishioners. Was he seeking forgiveness of some kind? And if he was, would we be capable of giving it?

Oh God of forgiveness, don't forgive, I heard a rabbi once pray at Auschwitz. I thought of this on Holocaust Memorial Day, when I talked to a woman who had survived the Nazi deportation of Jews from Hungary in 1944. Not all in her family were so lucky. Could she forgive? No, she couldn't. But who of us could, if we had suffered what she had suffered? If all we had to rely on was our own capacity for forgiveness, who would escape condemnation?

And that would be that, darkness, unending and eternal, were it not for the light come into the world. At Christmas and at Easter we hear the prologue to the Gospel of John, that great hymn to Christ the Incarnate Word: *the light shineth in darkness, and the darkness comprehended it not.* Note the difference in tenses here – the light shineth, continues to shine – the darkness comprehended it not – darkness's work is done.

This is not the eternal struggle between light and darkness, between good and evil, which the mystery religions of the ancient Near East proposed, and with which many creeds, ancient and modern, agree. Nor is it enough to describe Christ's light simply as a beacon to guide us through the treacherous waters of an unfamiliar coast or a stormy sea. It is much more than that.

It is something that the darkness of the world doesn't even begin to get, something before which darkness falls away and is overcome for ever. It is what Simeon saw in the child brought to the Temple: his own and ours and the world's salvation.

Years ago in the original Broadcasting House's reception there was a display showing what the proposed New Broadcasting House would look like, with a digital tour as the centrepiece. You could see the new building from Regent Street and from Riding House Street; we were taken round the side of the building, entering, virtually, via a glittering atrium, and given a short trip round this new palace of glass and steel and light. The building was inhabited by little digitised figures, walking around, chatting in corridors, sipping cappuccinos. Each one, male-female, black-white, young-old, was wearing a suit. In other words, no programme makers.

And now it is here, the new building, for which a 'coral'-coloured lanyard is essential, and we can only get one after we have attended an induction course for using the new building. It begins with a stirring address and then moves on to practical matters with a seminar on how to go in and out of the doors at the front. In summary, we learn that it is inadvisable to try to use a revolving door in the opposite direction from the one in which it is travelling.

I am just going to bed when the phone rings. It's a parishioner, unusually distracted, telling me that her husband, whom I had seen in hospital the day before, is not looking good and the family has been called in. 'Do you want me to come?' I ask. I take the things I need and drive to the hospital, so tired I nearly get hit by a lorry on the bypass. At the hospital, I say an unsuitable alleluia because the car park is empty, save for their son and his wife, with whom I converge. On the ward, nurses are worried by the readings from the monitors. As soon as we are ushered to his bedside, a doctor arrives and we are ushered out. We sit in one of those ominously feature-less rooms, with old colouring books and a box of tissues, and I say a prayer. A nurse comes in and says they are going to be some time, so I tell the family I will be back in a few minutes, then I go to see Dad, who is dying in the room directly opposite.

It is, by now, one in the morning, and he is fast asleep, breathing with what looks like more effort than usual, and he is unaware that I am there. I have my kit with me so I anoint him, making the sign of the cross on his forehead in holy oil, thinking that if he was conscious he would flinch with embarrassment at this 'palaver'. And then I kiss him on the forehead. I haven't kissed him since I was eight years old.

Back at my parishioner's bedside, the nurse is making him com-fortable. Then we notice that he has stopped breathing. He has no Do Not Resuscitate notice so we are shooed out again and a crash team arrives. I hope they won't resuscitate him because surely it is only delaying by a few minutes a death which is at hand. A young doctor comes in to tell us they have restarted his heart and here are the options . . . His wife looks at me and I say it is her call, but the doctor says, 'Actually, no, it isn't.' After he's finished setting out the medical scenario with a sort of tender impatience, she agrees to withdraw ventilation and let events take their course. At the bedside, the medics step back and I finally step in, anointing my parishioner and saying the appropriate prayers. Back home, David hands me a whisky and leaves me to decompress.

Two days later, just as I am about to give a speech to a WI meet-ing at the other end of the county, a text from David arrives to tell me that my father has just died. I go on stage and do my piece and at the end someone talks to me about her bereavement while I keep my own to myself until I'm driving home, on the coldest night of the year, worrying I might skid, and then I say out loud, 'Daddy, my daddy!' like Jenny Agutter in *The Railway Children*.

ASH WEDNESDAY

Ashing of penitents tonight in Finedon to mark the beginning of Lent. It starts with a technical challenge: how best to reduce to ashes the palm crosses we are given on Palm Sunday in the previous year which provide for our needs this evening. Nothing simpler, you might think, but like the Cardinals in Conclave struggling to get the puff of smoke the right colour to signify the election of a new Pope, we too struggle to get this right. Not only to reduce them to ash but to get the ash the right consistency to stick to the faithful's foreheads. I have my own method. I burn them in a wood burner until they are totally consumed and then tip the ash into a small lidded bowl by my favourite potter, Phil Rogers, and mix it with a drop or two of olive oil to make it viscous and sticky. 'Remember, you are dust, and to dust you shall return,' I say as I draw the outline of a cross in ash on my parishioners' foreheads. It is both intimate and awful, and sometimes they flinch and I wonder if we really need so unnuanced a reminder of our own mortality? I think we do, not because we seek to indulge a buried impulse of self-loathing, but because we need to get real.

Death will come to us all, no matter how much we try to dismiss it to the edges of our lives, in hospitals and nursing homes, and the fringes of our consciousness. In an age of miraculous medicine and relative wealth and ease, we have rather fallen out with death, and see it, if we can bear to look at it, as a dreadful enemy, to be kept at bay by intensifying our experience of life, with bungee-jumping or white-water rafting or having affairs. Sooner or later, however, we will have to make its acquaintance.

The complicated mechanisms of penance and self-mortification, just part of life for our ancestors, seem bizarre to the point of preposterous now. Expert in these disciplines was St Joseph of the Cross, an admirable friar in seventeenth-century Italy, notable for his calm and composed attitude to life. But he put tacks in his sandals, to prick him as he walked, and wore a spiked cross strapped to his back, causing a wound which never healed. If we knew someone was doing this today, we would inform social services or the Psychiatric Crisis Team, but in his day it was seen as a way of living more fully the life of Jesus Christ by sharing in his sufferings. The practice has dropped off now, though might still be found in some traditionalist Roman Catholic circles. A friend of mine, a Benedictine monk, entered the monastery in the days when this sort of self-mortification was commonly done, and on Fridays in Lent the novices were expected to kneel in their cells and whip themselves with a little scourge as they said the miserere. The novice master would stand at the end of each corridor to make sure they were fulfilling their duty, but actually they were all whipping their pillows as they chanted away.

Betty, who comes to Morning Prayer and looks like she wouldn't say boo to a goose, tells me that she was a nurse at the London Hospital during the war and lived in the East End, where she was adopted by a family who lived in the same street as her digs. They called her the Country Mouse and took good care of her, but she could never understand why the mother of the household never had to queue when she went to the butcher's or the greengrocer's, and why, in this time of austerity and fasting, this family never went without food, or why people went suddenly quiet when her twin boys, Ronnie and Reggie, turned up to help out with the shopping.

*

Five or so years ago, in the gap between Knightsbridge and Finedon, I was working at Broadcasting House on Ash Wednesday, so for the first time in years I sat in the pews for the Evening Liturgy and the imposition of ashes. It was at one of the great Anglo-Catholic shrines, the kind of place that once sent curates out around Europe to collect picturesque liturgical embellishments. Its liturgy, for all the leanness of Lent, was indeed picturesque, and so was the celebrant, a man of austere appearance and sonorous tone. When he marked my forehead with the sign of the cross and reminded me that I was dust, he sounded like he meant it personally, and after the Mass we all left church in chastened silence. Until we turned the corner, at which point everyone, safely out of sight, produced hankies and started dabbing at the smudge on their foreheads. I sometimes think it should be a rubric in the order of service on this day: *All depart in silence. Please help yourself to a Wet Wipe as you leave.*

For those of us pleased with ourselves for leaving the smudgy cross unwiped, Jesus has something to say: *Beware of practising your piety before others in order to be seen by them.* There is, inevitably, a tension between the gospel and what we make of it, but what do we think we're doing, heading out into the streets branded on our foreheads with the sign of the faith we proclaim, precisely *in order to be seen by others?*

It is difficult for us to imagine in the here and now just how religious the Jewish world of Jesus was, how cultic, how concerned with doing the right things in the right way. The meticulous observance of the Law, given to Moses by God, and handed on generation to generation, set the Jews apart for salvation. Abandoning the Law was their downfall, and in every Jew the memory of that hard lesson was deeply imprinted.

In uncertain times we all seek certainty. For the Jews, the Scribes and Pharisees, custodians and interpreters of the Law, offered exactly that: stick to the rules, in all their detail and complexity, in every jot and tittle, and you and Israel shall be saved. But the problem with such a scheme is that it can lapse very easily into mere legalism. This, I suspect, is a universal religious phenomenon.

How disconcerting for those upstanding Temple regulars, then, to be confronted by Jesus, who compares the respectable Pharisee, done up in the proper kit, saying the proper prayers, with the disreputable tax collector, who simply implores God for mercy – and asks which of these is justified? Or the Jesus who stands between the mob and the woman taken in adultery – and says, Let those among you without sin cast the first stone? Who teaches that the whole of the Law is summed up in the commandment to love God and one another?

They found him outrageous, for what he taught made the whole elaborate system seem mere spectacle.

What Jesus teaches is far more threatening than that. He doesn't say, I come to dismiss the Law; he says, I am its fulfilment. He says everything the Law seeks to preserve and strives to establish is now present, not in some future hope, or folk-memory, but in me: God is with us, Advent proclaimed, and now we begin to discover the consequences of that claim.

To be a Christian is to belong to Christ, to be willing to walk with him to our own Calvaries and to suffer the cross, that paradoxical symbol of life won through death, the symbol we smudge on our foreheads and wipe off as soon as is decently possible.

As the Arab world lit up with revolution, I went to Cairo while making a documentary for Radio Three with one of my favourite producers, Lawrence Grissell. We were making a global history of homosexuality and came in search of early evidence of the love that dare not speak its name. We had driven out to the tomb complex at Thebes with a young Egyptologist from the Department of Antiquities, and he took us to see a tomb occupied by two courtiers, a hairdresser and his 'brother', or perhaps lover – the meaning is not clear. Tempting though it is to see this as an early and honoured example of what we would call a same-sex couple, the Egyptologist was not persuaded. He did show us, however, something about which there is no doubt: a painting on a wall in another tomb, five thousand years old, in which a sailor calls another sailor a pouf.

Cairo was not thronged with tourists. The demonstrations in Tahrir Square were still live, and although the immediate crisis had passed there were army units just round the corner. Lawrence, with typical resourcefulness, managed to take advantage of this unstable time to secure us junior suites at a grand hotel, suites which came with butlers. This luxury had been secured for about eighty US dollars a night, so we returned at the end of a day's recording to a marble lobby and almost too attentive service from uniformed staff, looking to make up their vastly reduced income from tips. It was also Ramadan, and after sundown the hotel suddenly filled with prosperous and by now ravenous Egyptians who practically ran to the buffet. We had a local driver and fixer, and when we stopped for lunch in restaurants deserted for Ramadan by locals and for revolution by tourists, they did not join us. I talked to the driver later and discovered that he was a Copt, a Christian, unlike our fixer, a Muslim. 'But,' he said, and I feel a spurt of shame recalling it, 'I prefer not to eat in front of my Muslim colleagues while they are fasting.'

I am opening up the church and as I push against the unbolted doors, instead of swinging open they stick. This usually means we have a rough sleeper in the porch nestled up against the doors, as near to out of the rain as you can be.

I've learnt, in these circumstances, to push very gently; partly to encourage the rough sleeper to embrace the day, to open the doors wide enough to offer a cup of coffee and a bun, and because I once accidentally whacked a regular on the head, causing him to express his dismay with impressive fluency. Instead of a regular, I find a pair of newcomers, young men who poke their heads out of their sleeping bags and say good morning with unusual cheer. They introduce themselves and, over a coffee, I ask them how they've come to bed down on our porch. 'Because God called us,' Adam replies. It turns out that they are theology students and as Lent approaches they have been praying about how to spend this forty days and nights profitably. God answered, and called them to live rough on the streets of London among the down-and-outs who fill up the car parks and doorways and our church porch night by night.

You might wonder, what does it mean to be a minister of Christ in the richest neighbourhood in possibly the richest city in the world? I wondered this often when I was at St Paul's, Knightsbridge, in its tiny parish of staggeringly expensive houses. All the usual things, is the answer, but in their deluxe versions. I had ample resources, great colleagues, a terrific church community and plenty to do; but in a way, it was the hardest place I've ever had to minister, because the rich are so difficult to reach, so amply rewarded by the world that their wealth and prestige is mistaken for a sign of salvation – I must be getting it right, look at my cars! Those rewards can become a sort of barrier between the rich and everyone else (apart from other rich people; though, eventually, even them). Most importantly, it becomes a barrier between them and their deeper needs. We're all going to die, we all worry about our children and our parents, we all nurture deep within us the wounds we can't quite bear to offer for healing. But you can hide them behind a big pile of money and the stuff that money buys; pile it high enough and you might be able to blot out those uncomfortable, disquieting needs entirely.

A commotion in Sainsbury's car park in Kettering. A small group of people are gathered round a tree, looking up at an escaped parrot, one of those unfeasibly brightly coloured ones. No one knows what to do, and then someone shows up with their own parrot, the same breed, in an attempt to coax down the escapee. But the newly arrived parrot isn't interested in coaxing it down. It wants to be like the humans, not like the other parrot, so it perches on the man's arm looking crossly up into the tree. Bizarre.

*

In Peterborough Cathedral, where my bishop has his throne, there's a huge crucifix hanging from the vault over the crossing, an attempt to show Christ's sacrifice on the cross at the centre of the building and its business. It so distressed a pious and important visitor that she had a funny turn and begged the Dean to remove it because it showed a failure rather than a triumph, and the cross is a sign of triumph, is it not? I have no time for this faux squeamishness. The cross is an instrument of torture and death, and Lent reminds us that on it our Saviour suffered and died. We used to be much better at this, with all the elaborate Victorian paraphernalia of death – full-mourning, half-mourning, black bombazine, weeping willows – which endures only faintly now in undertakers' parlours. Even the word 'death' seems to have become unsayable; more and more people prefer the euphemism 'passed away', which always makes me think of flushing the lavatory.

I was in London at the BBC when a partial eclipse happened one morning, for which coverage was so relentless you would think it the greatest solar phenomenon ever to have occurred. Teams of scientists at Jodrell Bank peered up into the heavens as the moon's shadow passed over the face of the sun; news bulletins all led with it, in spite of events around the world which you could be forgiven for thinking more important; and I was summoned to the roof of Broadcasting House to acclaim its significance live on Chris Evans' show on Radio Two.

As it turned out, we didn't bother: the cloud cover was so low and thick that there was no more chance of seeing the eclipse than of seeing the pyramids, and this great wonder passed all but unobserved. It was difficult not to contain a cackle of unworthy satisfaction at seeing all the luminaries peering pointlessly through their special specs at the cloud base while reporters, having to maintain the note of excitement the anticipatory programmes obliged, gushed as they described what might be happening in the heavens if we could only see through the impenetrable barrier of clouds.

In corporate life, I have noticed, it is getting harder and harder to say that things are bad. I have been in meetings recently when our views were solicited about something or another, and when a colleague responded with a critical summary of an initiative that had gone wrong, he was stopped by the person chairing the meeting, who said, 'Positives, positives, I want to hear the positives.' At another meeting, someone asked for critical feedback but insisted it must be framed not in terms of what was bad, but in terms of how we could make things 'even better'.

I like to think I don't need to be protected from bad news, especially when it's news I need to hear. I remember being sent on a 'half-day seminar', as it was ominously called, with a BBC bigwig. A group of us from across the organization spent the morning being told how marvellous everything was, and how exciting were the challenges that faced us, and how amazing the opportunities technological innovation would bring. The seminar concluded with a rather breathless speech from a young apparatchik from Corporate Affairs, intended to raise morale and get us fully on board with the new regime, and make us 'even better' than we already were. Any questions? There was silence until a veteran reporter from the back said, 'Why don't you fuck off, Tinkerbell?'

God is not in the least bit interested in whether we win or lose. Russian soldiers kneel as icons are processed by priests around the ranks massed for battle; footballers cross themselves as they run onto the pitch before a game; athletes point significantly to heaven when they shave half a second from a Personal Best. It makes no difference.

PASSION SUNDAY

One of the perks of being a cleric with a public profile is getting invited to accompany cruises as the on-board God person, to lecture perhaps on the significance to Church history of a port of call, to interpret the Renaissance art encountered there, and to take a 'Holy Communion service' in a pitching lounge repurposed for Eucharistic ends. And so it was I found myself en route to Iceland, through the North Atlantic swell.

I had been a couple of times before to Iceland, falling in love with it unexpectedly on my first visit as a tourist, and returning to make a documentary for Radio Four about the effects of its financial collapse in 2008. I had read and loved the Icelandic Sagas, the vivid adventures of Egil Skallagrímsson and Njal Thorgeirsson, as important to Icelanders as Shakespeare is to us, and I was expecting something commensurate when I arrived: an epic landscape for an epic culture, and if not Ian McKellen in a robe tripping over his false beard, then helmets and horns and halberds. What I found was miles and miles of empty lava fields, a lunar landscape, through which we drove to Reykjavik. It was difficult to see how culture could really get a foothold in such a place, a ragged volcanic rock in the North Atlantic.

Reykjavik back then looked like a whaling station; you couldn't get a drink without passing an act of parliament, its landmark building was a water tank, and it was a thousand miles to the nearest insalata Caprese. Almost as soon as you left the city limits, the road turned to gravel, which we slithered across in our four-wheel drive, going, it seemed, nowhere. I recognised some of the names on the map from the Sagas, which seem as crammed with incident and personalities as Ambridge, but those names turned out to be merely bends in the road. Church, Farm, Parsonage – the almost invariable description of every place in the guidebook.

One of the most notable inhabitants of one parsonage was Hallgrímur Pétursson, who was born in Iceland in 1614.

I had never heard of him until I went there, but he occupies a place in Icelandic literature roughly comparable to George Herbert in ours: the greatest Priest Poet of the Renaissance (discuss). Unlike George Herbert, he was not obvious priestly material. Herbert was well-connected and groomed for great things; Hallgrímur was the son of a bell-ringer. There was a bishop in the family, but bishops in Iceland were not prelates in the way that English bishops were. Practically the only casualty of the Reformation in that country was the Bishop of Skalholt, who held out for Rome when Christian III of Denmark imposed Lutheranism on his subjects in the middle of the sixteenth century. The Bishop got beheaded for his trouble – and not only him but also his two sons, which tells you something about the private lives of the Icelandic bishops at that time. It was a very long way from Iceland to Rome.

Hallgrímur was himself a rough youth, and although he benefited from the beginnings of an education, thanks to his episcopal connections, he ran away from school and ended up in what is now part of Germany but was then part of Denmark. Nothing was heard of him until an Icelandic priest, travelling through Glückstadt, overheard a blacksmith's apprentice cursing his master in his native tongue. It was Hallgrímur. The priest befriended him, and was so struck by the boy he eventually arranged for him to finish his education at the seminary of Our Lady in Copenhagen.

Then events took a rather unusual turn. The southern coast of Iceland in the seventeenth century was vulnerable to attacks from Barbary pirates. They sailed up from what we call Algeria in corsairs to loot and pillage the villages that had once sent their own parties of raiders to loot and pillage during the Viking expansion. One of their favourite destinations was the Westmann Islands, just off Iceland's south-eastern coast, and there on one particularly profitable trip, they kidnapped 250 islanders and took them back to Algeria to be sold into slavery, among them a woman called Gudda Símonardóttir. The Barbary raiders were merciless, killing anyone they thought they wouldn't be able to sell, and this caused such outrage that King Christian IV of Denmark eventually intervened and paid a ransom for their return. Ten years after she and her fellow Westmann Islanders were abducted, in which time Gudda had lived as a slave and a concubine, they arrived in Copenhagen. Hallgrímur's patron, now a bishop, was concerned that after ten years in the Barbary lands they would have lost their Christian faith, so he appointed his bright young student, Hallgrímur, to re-educate them – confirmation classes, really. It was, evidently, a two-way process, for while Hallgrímur instilled the doctrine of justification by faith in Gudda, she (sixteen years his senior) taught him a thing or two and embarrassingly fell pregnant. Hallgrímur offered to do the decent thing, but it turned out that Gudda was already married, which put paid to Hallgrímur's priestly vocation, or so he thought. They returned to Iceland, where she discovered that her husband had died, so they married and he scratched a living as a labourer. Life was hard, they lost a child, then another, but seven years after their return, the priest who had befriended him in Germany, now a bishop, came back into Hallgrímur's life. He was obviously a good talent-spotter, and used his influence to have Hallgrímur ordained and appointed minister to the tiny living of Hvalsnes. Some of his parishioners were surprised that such a man should have been ordained, but he showed himself a skilful preacher; so skilful that in 1651 he was appointed to the rich living of Saurbær, a much sought-after position. It must have seemed like his boat had come in, but life was not to be plain sailing.

Gudda, her contemporaries remembered, was quite a feisty woman, and when she was in one of her moods her husband would be seen sitting patiently outside the parsonage waiting for her temper to blow over. It was also said that she never quite shook off the Islamic faith picked up during her ten years in Algeria (a whore and a heathen, her unkinder neighbours called her). And then disaster struck – Hallgrímur contracted leprosy. He gave up the parish and retired to an isolated farm further up the fjord, and there he died in 1674.

St Mary le Strand, despite its distinction as one of London's finest churches – Gibbs' masterpiece, according to those who know about such things – is little-visited. It stands in one of London's busiest streets, the Strand, slap bang in the middle of two lanes of unyielding traffic, King's College London to the south, the BBC World Service to the north. As an alumnus of both, I suppose it is fitting that it should be me celebrating the Eucharist here today. Most people in churches look east, towards the pulpit and the altar. The priest, however, looks west, at the crowd, and that in itself can be distracting, but at St Mary le Strand you can look out beyond the congregation into the street, and see two files of traffic passing by on either side. Cabs and couriers and trishaws and London buses, Leyland Titans on their way to unfashionable postcodes in South London, Routemasters on the heritage trail, like scarlet dowagers disappearing into the distance.

Standing there, not paying attention to what I am doing, watching the world go by. On Ash Wednesday, I resolved to give certain things up and to take certain things on. In the former category, I've done OK, giving up smoking, apart from a single and, in my view, forgivable lapse outside the Royal Geographical Society on the anniversary of the death of Edward King, saintly Bishop of Lincoln.

I have been less successful in taking things on. In the past I've been diligent, saying more prayers, earlier, and more earnestly, than in the impenitent weeks of Ordinary Time. This year it hasn't really happened. Early in the morning, when I should have been in church and on my knees, I've been in the park walking dogs amid the nodding jonquils and half-eaten KFCs. Instead of the homilies of the Latin fathers, I have been reading Nordic crime fiction; and my surplus, paltry as it is, seems to have been diverted from the rattling poor box into the chiming tills of the Retail Village. My good intentions cannot rise, they are extinguished, they are quenched like a wick. I don't really know why. I'm busier, which makes it harder to find the time to make the effort; and busier with extracurricular activity, which takes me into a world which barely notices, if at all, the Church's calendar. Trying to maintain the disciplines of Lent has left me feeling like St Mary le Strand, stuck in the middle of the road, going nowhere, while everyone else passes by.

On Passion Sunday these anxieties come into sharper focus. The austerities of Lent are more marked, with the veiling of statues and a liturgical paring-down; and as Jesus approaches Jerusalem and the climactic events which are to take place there, our part in his story also begins to take on shape, and body and pattern.

We are not willing participants in this. Jesus, in agony in the garden, is abandoned; Peter, the rock upon which Christ builds his Church, betrays him; and Judas, quibbling over the cost of pure nard, secures a new revenue stream.

Even Jesus himself, in his humanity, is agonised by the approach of his destiny. Take this cup away from me, he pleads, in flesh anticipating the nails, the thorns, the spear, the cross. If you look round churches, you'll often see, painted or carved, an odd collection of hardware – a ladder, a hammer, a sponge, a pair of dice – as peculiar a collection of curios as the thimble, the wheelbarrow and the iron in a Monopoly set. But these are the Instruments of the Passion: the ladder which will stand against the cross, the hammer which will drive in its nails, the sponge, filled with gall, that will be pressed to Jesus' lips, and the dice his executioners will roll to divide up his clothing. The full horror of what is to happen can't be confronted in its totality, not yet, not ever. So we're offered these tokens of Christ's Passion, not as aides-memoires, but as nudges, goads, sending us along the Way of the Cross, towards the New Thing. We are those buses and cabs, indifferent traffic, breaking and reforming around St Mary le Strand in the middle of the road, with places to go, people to see, not even beginning to understand the disruption to our journey.

Many more were to suffer the effects of the Instruments of the Passion for faithfulness to Christ, or to their version of Christ. St Nicholas Owen was a dwarf, born to a devoutly Catholic family in Oxford in 1550, where he worked as a carpenter, an occupation which gave him a debilitating hernia. In spite of this, he became a Jesuit, and united his two callings by becoming the most celebrated builder of priest-holes in England, hired by rich recusant families to make hiding places for the Catholic priests who said masses in their chapels, like the safe rooms installed in the hi-tech mansions of the rich today. Owen worked alone and at night, and so ingenious were his hiding places it is believed some may still be undiscovered. As a Jesuit priest, he was occasionally obliged to use them himself, dodging the search parties sent to round up Catholic clergy. He was eventually caught in one of his own priest-holes at Hindlip Hall in Worcestershire and taken to the Tower. In spite of technically being exempt from torture, having once been squashed by a horse, he was hoisted on the Topcliffe rack and heavy weights were added to his feet until 'his bowels gushed out with his life'. In spite of these agonies, he revealed nothing.

I visit a parishioner in a nursing home. She looks awful after a fall, her face terribly bruised, and she's as frail as glass. A woman who works there says she thought she would die in the night. She has had no sleep but lay in bed holding the care assistant's hand, and wouldn't let go. She can't see me when I come into the room and I have to say who I am. I hold her hand – cold and clawlike – and talk to her a bit, but she keeps on nodding off. I look at her face, grey and shrunken and bruised, and think how terrible to end up like this, especially someone so life-loving. She once showed me a photograph from her childhood in which she sits cross-legged on the lawn with her three sisters, one sitting on a chair behind her, one standing behind her, one standing on a chair behind her, making a tower of girls. They're all in white pinafore dresses and straw hats – a summer's day – and she could not have been more than five, which makes it 1910. I can't see that little girl's face in the one-hundred-and-one-year-old face in front of me.

A nurse comes to see if she'll eat her lunch and I leave her. I doubt I will see her again. And then I feel guilty about not having looked after her well enough, not having given her more time and attention. I cycle home (it is a lovely day) and find myself whistling MacDowell's 'To a Wild Rose', which she wants at her funeral.

Glued to the screen, we watched a glossy black hearse crawl through the heart of London. People thronged the streets, some camping out all night to make sure they got the best view, and they threw flowers onto the hearse as it passed by. As the cortège headed out of town, people of all ages, all backgrounds, came to watch it pass, breaking into spontaneous applause, throwing so many flowers that the driver had to keep stopping to clear the windscreen. A news helicopter hovered overhead, the television studios were full of sombre commentators, and the nation paused for a moment to reflect on the life a young woman cut cruelly short, after adventures and misadventures that had filled the newspapers and news bulletins, who had lived in the limelight and died in the limelight, and, most tragically of all, left two young sons motherless.

Who could forget the funeral of Jade Goody? No coincidence, I'm sure, that her funeral should mirror Princess Diana's, but with a striking asymmetry in the origins of the protagonists. Diana, daughter of an earl, and a member of one of the grandest families in England; Jade, daughter of a man who died of a heroin overdose in the Gents at Kentucky Fried Chicken.

*

Hallgrímur's Passion Psalms consist of fifty hymns, or perhaps metrical meditations is more accurate, which follow Christ along the Way of the Cross, from his agony in the garden to his burial. They take the reader, too, along that journey, accompanying us, step by step, through Lent. In Iceland, for hundreds of years, they were read daily in every household; today they are read, daily, on national radio.

This does not reflect the deep piety of Icelanders; they're as secularised as everyone else in northern Europe today. It reflects more immediately the sheer genius of the poetry. Hallgrímur Pétursson is recognised as one of the greatest of the Icelandic poets, and that's quite a distinction in the most literate country in the world, a country which exists so vividly in its literature.

I don't read or speak Icelandic and know his work only in translation. Nabokov, that great translator, observed that a translation is inevitably a betrayal, and that is particularly the case with poetry. How can you translate the unique music of a language into the unique music of another, quite apart from dealing with issues of meaning and context? This must be especially the case in Icelandic, a language so small that the only other people that can understand it are the Faroese. Finding translators is inevitably difficult, and there are only a couple of English translations of the Passion Psalms (though you can always try the highly recommended translations in Italian and Chinese). The primary question for all of them is whether to try to preserve the rhyme and metre of the original. The two English translations which are current today answer the question differently; the most recent, by Charles Scott, chooses not to, the standard translation, by the slightly unfortunately named Arthur Gook, does, very much so.

I like Gook's. It may sound a bit clunky, like mid-Victorian hymns, but it preserves the powerful pulse and tug of the original. Hallgrímur, a natural poet, wants us to be drawn into the poem, lassoed and hauled in, more like, so dynamic is his word setting.

And Hallgrímur, good Lutheran pastor and preacher, wants us to
be drawn not only into the poem, but into its narrative.

Over the deep, dark, brook of pain
I, too, must pass, and not complain.
My Saviour trod that weary track;
Shall I from troublous paths turn back?

I hear in this an echo of the Scottish metrical psalms of the Free
Church tradition. Like the Passion Psalms, these were products of
both history and location – the expansion of Reformation ideas to
the edge of a civilisation, the Christian Gospel in native tongues
hauling in converts, like fish in a net. The Bible was translated into
Icelandic in 1584 and the next generation of reformers, Hallgrímur
among them, aimed to make it as widely understood as possible
among the people, most of whom were illiterate. In the Middle
Ages, in Catholic Europe, this had really been the job of the artist
and the sculptor, and the image; but in the Reformation, native
tongues were suddenly set free and poets took over.

In Lutheran Germany and the centres of Protestant Europe, this
led eventually to the flowering of the cantata and the oratorio, Bach
and Handel, and we can still experience something of their power
today. Thus Holy Writ gets written into the hearts and minds of
ordinary people, and so with Hallgrímur and the Passion Psalms.
But doesn't retelling the story in this distinctive, local way leave it
stranded? There are fewer than half a million speakers of Icelandic
among the six billion people who currently stride the earth – can
Hallgrímur really have anything to say to those five billion nine
hundred and ninety-nine million five hundred thousand others?

Christ's Passion is embedded in our culture as it was in Hallgrímur's. Embedded in our culture, and shaping – even if few of
us know it – what we think and say and do. When we hear these
poems, we are rediscovering something that is already there. The
Passion Psalms have a purchase that transcends issues of language

and national identity, although, ironically, they work precisely through language and national identity. I suppose Oberammergau does it too, or the Mystery Cycles of Medieval England, or Renaissance polyphony.

Hallgrímur knew this, and the psalms begin not with a *mise en scène* or a list of characters or an overture and 'beginners, please', but with 'Arise, my soul, my heart, my mind'.

Upp, upp mín sál og allt mitt geð,
upp mitt hjarta og rómur með,
hugur og tunga hjálpi til,
Herrans pínu ég minnast vil.

Literally, that's 'Up, up my soul with all my mind, up my heart and with my voice, both thought and tongue may they take part, I would recall our Lord's Passion.'

HOLY WEEK: PALM SUNDAY

Palm Sunday marks the beginning of Holy Week and commemorates Christ's entry into Jerusalem – a triumph, according to the Gospels, with Jesus on a donkey acclaimed by the people with shouts of Hosanna to the Son of David. Their tune would change, and soon. It is an instructive example for a priest about to arrive in a new church for his first incumbency. I think back to my arrival as the new Vicar of Finedon. Or rather, Priest-in-Charge, not vicar, for the living had been suspended, to use a Trollopian phrase, and with the new rules of tenure for clergy the incumbency did not necessarily bring with it the title. It did bring with it, however, the vicarage, and there David and I were settling in as my first Sunday in the parish approached.

It was the first time David and I had set up house together. Since leaving St Paul's, Knightsbridge, I had been living in his house in Wymondham in Norfolk, where he was curate at the abbey, but we were now in a civil partnership and it seemed absurd and somehow faintly indecent to live separately, so we resolved not to. I would live like a student if it were up to me, but David is to parsonages what Capability Brown was to parks, and the decorators were in.

The new vicarage is lovely, built next to the old (1688, twenty-seven rooms) in 2000 to a far higher standard than the equivalents of the sixties and seventies, unsightly boxes standing as incongruously as a squash court next to a Queen Anne gem. It is not only pleasant but practical, with a study separate from the rest of the house, a walled garden at the back and large open garden at the front. It is also insulated and I have not shivered, as the last Vicar of Finedon to live in the old vicarage shivered, by a two-bar electric fire in a room with a noticeable echo.

That first Sunday, parishioners arrived bearing gifts: a welcome box, a bottle of wine, a bottle of whisky. And others walked past, trying not to look like they were looking. Once at a new house I was in the front garden when a lady peered over the fence. 'Are you the new chap?' she asked. I said I was. 'Oh,' she said, 'we thought you were black.' I wondered why. 'We thought you were in the Commodores.' I told her I was actually in the Communards, and then wondered if that information might also elicit some comment in Finedon, for I had arrived not with a wife but a civil partner. If there was any unease about that, I did not notice it. On the contrary, the parish could not have been more welcoming to both of us.

David was in church in his dog collar for the Palm Sunday liturgy, which began with the blessing of palms and a procession around the church (inside, if wet). This procession requires the singing of 'All Glory Laud and Honour to Thee, Redeemer King', one of those endless hymns with a repeated chorus. Inevitably, by the time the front of the procession arrives back at church, the back hasn't yet quite left; by the second verse the hymn is being sung in three different versions, all starting and ending at different times. The priest brings up the rear, nominally in charge of this exercise, which has already begun to fall apart. Leading by following, lightly rearranging chaos, finding a common purpose in our individual enterprises: characteristic of that day they have become characteristic of my ministry, in so many ways.

My first Sunday in the parish and I ended it not in Finedon but at my old church, St Paul's, Knightsbridge, presenting a BBC Singers live concert for Radio Three. I said to the producer it was like having an assignation with your first wife on the evening of your second marriage.

*

Another triumphal entry to a Holy City was signalled on television by long uninterrupted shots of a seagull sitting on a chimney, for a moment the most famous bird in the world. The chimney is the Sistine Chapel's, and from it, at about six in the evening, there issued forth a belch of white smoke, signifying the election of a new Pope. *Habemus Papam*, the deacon of the College of Cardinals announced. A man we had never heard of, dressed in a new white habit, stepped out onto the balcony. Francis I, a significant choice of name, not only because 'the first' follows in the tradition of John Paul I, indicating a new departure; but, more importantly, because St Francis of Assisi rescued the Church from stagnation in the thirteenth century with a life of holiness, gentleness, humility, grace, and resilience.

A new Pope is a paradox, a declaration of business as usual and at the same time a declaration that God is doing a new thing. Anyone expecting dramatic changes in doctrine or practice would most likely be disappointed, although commentators said the same of John XXIII, another unknown outsider, who really did usher in profound change. More likely is a new Pope shifting the emphases. His first words on his appearance on the balcony were '*Buona sera*', an everyday sort of greeting, and he went on '*fratelli e sorelli*', brothers and sisters, the form of address St Francis used for all whom he encountered. So, a Pope who is of the people not just for the people, who takes the bus and cooks his own spaghetti, a man who will, like every other Pope, be eaten by the job.

I saw a piece about Rowan Williams written when he announced his retirement from Canterbury by someone who knew him well, someone who worked closely with him when he was the Archbishop of Wales. The writer was with him the day his appointment to Canterbury was announced, so they had a celebratory cheese sandwich for lunch. The man offered the Archbishop his congratulations. 'Save it,' said he. 'A lot of people are going to be very disappointed.'

Not long after the announcement, I was involved in an event at which Rowan Williams was speaking. I learned a lot; first, that

Lambeth Palace refers to the boss as the ABC, Archbishop of Canterbury; but even better, in the period between his appointment and his enthronement, he's known as the Archbishop of Canterbury Designate Elect – or ABCDE. The real learning came later as he spoke, note-less, to an audience of the great and the good, with such depth and clarity it was like light flooding a dark cave. A few weeks later he was actually enthroned at Canterbury Cathedral. I watched it on telly with a retired Canon of Westminster and two American Jesuit priests. It was indeed a spectacle. The new Archbishop, in a cope and mitre specially made for the occasion, processed to the cathedral and there banged on the door with his staff before the Dean and Chapter let him in as the choir and congregation burst into singing. 'Hosanna,' they sang, like the Jerusalemites greeting Jesus. A lot of people were about to be very disappointed.

He was about to embark on a passion himself, a ten-year passion, caught in the middle of irreconcilable forces, called to hold together an impossible unity, at unimaginable cost to his own standing, his gifts, his friendships. A failure, they say. What would success look like?

I get into a row with a Romanian friend, a priest, about the authorship of the epistles attributed to Paul. He sends me this email:

The base of western human reality is the Humanism which means life without God, the sin understood as a human right. Anglican Church is dying because their believer are dying or are death. They are under sin, they serve the sin. Why outside of these walls is lived a moral life. Because of Romans 2.14. My kind of judgement is linked of that judgement of penance (confession). If I do not judge you (critisise) I will be punished because I was reckless (stolid) with my nieghbour. God is only in books. Good night, boule

PS I want to drink juice or cider. Call me at every time, I am
studying. Now. Do it.

*

I am taking a party of pilgrims to Jerusalem to retrace Jesus' journey
from entering the city in triumph to leaving it in disgrace, so I
have been reading up on pilgrimages generally and got stuck with
Edward Gibbon's encounter with friars singing Vespers in the ancient Temple of Jupiter in Rome. This antique scene made a huge
impression on him and to it he attributed the genesis of *The Decline
and Fall of the Roman Empire*. At Oxford he surprised everyone
by converting to the Roman Catholic Church, but deconverted
on Christmas Day 1754 when his father threatened to disinherit
him. He then wandered Europe, and on his travels came across
those cowed figures chanting the Magnificat among the toppled
columns: 'It was at Rome, on the fifteenth of October 1764, as I sat
musing amidst the ruins of the Capitol, while the barefooted friars
were singing Vespers in the temple of Jupiter, that the idea of writing the decline and fall of the City first started to my mind.' The
work, first published in 1776, is one of the greatest challenges to
those who would seek to live faithfully as members of the Christian
Church, for in it he makes a powerful and elegant case – indeed,
some would say a mortal case – for dismissing the claims of organised religions. The book was an immediate success, and Gibbon
became rich and feted (and served for nine years as Member of Parliament for Liskeard, an office he sought because it brought with it
free postage). He was afflicted by a terrible swelling of the scrotum,
which eventually made it impossible for him to take his place in
society. Desperate, he underwent treatment for this condition but
developed peritonitis and died, aged fifty-six, in 1794.

You cannot know simultaneously where something is and where it
is going – either with precision, but not both: Heisenberg's uncertainty principle, named after the man who worked out the funda-
mental maths of quantum mechanics in Copenhagen in the 1920s.

Palm Sunday is proof of this. We can either know where we are or where we're going – position or momentum – but we cannot know both. Can we really retrace in procession steps taken so long ago, so far away, by someone so unlike us? Isn't there something preposterous or even presumptuous about that? All momentum, and no position? At the church where I was confirmed, the Palm Sunday Procession was taken immensely seriously, so seriously that it was led by a server equipped with a special staff, with which he would point out any dog-mess hazards along the route. At another church, where I was a server, the traditional route took us past Kentucky Fried Chicken, where one year the vicar was hit on the back of the head with a family bucket of coagulating fowl. In another, very different church, all police leave was cancelled to allow our splendid procession, complete with donkey, to leave one magnificent Medieval church, descend the hill, cross the river, and ascend to the other magnificent Medieval church. Momentum, not position, knowing where we're going, but at the expense of knowing what we are.

We're trying to align the here and now to the limitless coordinates of God. We stumble, we take wrong turns, the donkey relieves itself. How can we capture in this moment and in this place the fullness of the mystery of our salvation?

In the 'Agnus Dei' from Byrd's Mass for Five Voices, those five voices make their way towards the end from one chord to another, but not on the same trajectory. If you could slice the sound vertically at a certain point and isolate it, what you would hear would make no sense in itself, would sound random.. But we know where these five voices have come from, and we anticipate where they're going, so it seems that the very tension, the incompleteness of that isolated moment, expresses its own resolution, its own completeness.

Hosannas are already decaying into the dissonance and silence of Good Friday. But the journey doesn't end there – and knowing where we've come from, with a sense of where we're going, we look to that forsaken figure on the cross in all its unimaginable glory.

*

Sometime between Palm Sunday and Maundy Thursday, I go to see a priest to make my confession. It is not the kind that takes place anonymously through a grille, but with someone I know, face to face, and I very often lapse into ranting about the Church, for it gets too much for me sometimes. I used to see an old friend, wise, perceptive, gracious and funny. Once, when I was particularly incensed at something I cannot remember now, as I ranted he mentioned something about his own tribulations, tribulations I knew nothing about. When I had finished ranting and he had given me a blessing, I asked him what had happened. He told me he had developed epilepsy and cataracts, but, worst of all, his relationship with his partner had come to an end, obliging him to move out of their joint retirement home, and then his partner had tried to do him out of some money and refused to speak to him. The bell for the Angelus sounded, so he suggested we break off and say it together, which we did. We stopped on the 'amen', and then he picked up the narrative at the precise point he had left off, with the phrase 'queen's dream', which sounded quite funny coming after 'Be it done unto me according to thy word'.

In the seventies, at the height of the IRA mainland bombing campaign, he was a vicar in central London. His parish was bombed twice; the second time the target was the restaurant next door. He was leading a study group in the vicarage at the time. Hearing a massive explosion, he rushed round to find the place half on fire, glass in the street, police arriving. He went in and asked a policeman if there was anything he could do. Yes, he said, look after that dying man over there. In the corner lay a man in evening clothes and he knelt beside him and comforted him and noticed that blood was seeping, pouring almost, from beneath his clothes, where he'd been cut to ribbons by flying glass. He held the man until he died. When he looked up, he saw the back of the restaurant on fire, but at the front diners were sitting at tables as if nothing had happened. He asked one of the policemen what they were doing and he said they were in shock. It happens a lot in explosions, people carry on as if nothing has happened because they can't take in what has happened.

After the man died – 'Poor chap, just came out for a bite of dinner and never saw East Finchley again' – he returned to the vicarage to find one of his parishioners waiting for him, who helped him change out of his bloodstained cassock and wash the blood from his hands.

You must give people what is good and they will come to like it. So wrote Percy Dearmer, Vicar of St Mary's, Primrose Hill, author of *The Parson's Handbook* and creator of one of the great hymn books of the Anglican tradition, *The English Hymnal.*

He certainly gave, and much of what he gave was good, and many of us came to like it. His admirers have said that Dearmer made the most important contribution in the last hundred years or so to the worship of the Church of England. What I like to do, Sunday by Sunday, owes a great deal to him.

He was born 140 years ago in North London, the son of an artist. He went to Westminster School, and then to Oxford, and was ordained in 1892, arriving as a priest in the Church of England at a time of ferment, with the High Church movement reviving its Catholic traditions. Churchmen had been taken to court for the horrible crimes of mixing water with wine in the chalice and lighting candles on the altar. But the Church of England being the Church of England, the movement had its factions.

On one side, there were the Romanists, wearing birettas, more Roman than Rome, outdoing themselves in devotion to the Pope and the Virgin Mary. They sought to foster in their parishes, often in the poorest slums, popular devotions from Catholic Europe. Curates returning from liturgical field-trips to southern Europe would have the bewildered faithful of Limehouse and Sunderland and Portsmouth scattering rose petals in front of the Blessed Sacrament as the Corpus Christi Procession wound its way down the Commercial Road, or singing 'Ave Maria' in Geordie accents around a clanging shipyard.

On the other side were the Prayer Book Catholics in Canterbury caps, Dearmer's party, which sought to revive distinctively *English* customs of the Church. These followed not the Roman tradition but the Sarum tradition, which originated in the cathedral and diocese of Salisbury, and became standard within the English Church after Henry VIII sacked the Pope. The Sarum tradition was rich and detailed; its customs included the use of red as a liturgical colour for Sundays, blue for Advent, two candles on the altar, the deep bow, the recitation of the first chapter of the Gospel of John at the end of the Mass, numbering the Sundays following Trinity rather than Pentecost, and so on. A number of these customs endure to this day, some very ancient, others of a more recent vintage; for example, the double-breasted cassock, still worn, on pain of death, at my theological college to the irritation of its ordinands. After graduation day you can find dozens of them going cheap on eBay.

Dearmer, to further the English tradition, published an enormous amount, but two titles stand out: *The Parson's Handbook,* 1899, and revised as recently as 1965, and *The English Hymnal,* the green hymn book, which celebrated its centenary a couple of years ago.

The Parson's Handbook is a manual for clergy on how to conduct proper, fitting English worship in proper, fitting English churches, and has had an influence far beyond the High Church circles where it originated. It is full of practical wisdom: *The parish-priest is also ordered to 'say [Evensong] in every church or chapel where he ministereth', having a bell tolled beforehand, if he be at home and be not otherwise reasonably hindered.*

The English Hymnal was a project he undertook with the composer Ralph Vaughan Williams. They wanted to provide a hymn book for this newly enriched liturgy, material which was both 'local and universal' and 'ancient and modern', to pinch a phrase. When it appeared, a hundred years ago, it was immediately denounced

by the Archbishop of Canterbury; there can be no better endorse-
ment, and the green hymn book soon established itself in parishes
and cathedrals across the land. In the opinion of many English
church musicians, it has never been bettered, and this, I think, is
down to its distinctive character, rooted in material drawn from the
ancient Sarum Rite, translated into English and made musically
user-friendly. Having Vaughan Williams as musical editor didn't
hurt either; he gave it body and character by reviving old English
hymn tunes and folk tunes, and providing new tunes, among them
'For All the Saints', which immediately entered the C of E top ten.

I have come to value not only the *Hymnal*'s musical and poetic
qualities, but also its roominess and looseness – how very Anglican!
– in matters where other hymnals have been narrow and sharply defined. Certainly at home in a Catholic world of saints and seasons,
it is also comfortably reformed.

Accommodation is the watchword, I think. Most of what is
good in Anglicanism arises from our efforts to accommodate ideas,
beliefs, practices, people we find uncongenial, not out of some hesi-
tancy about our identity, but because we are secure in strong and
distinctive traditions. Anglican accommodation is not 'let's pretend
we're in this together', it is 'we value you *not* being like us so we
have to be imaginative in working out what our common purpose
might be'. Well, on a good day it is.

Palm Sunday, the beginning of Holy Week, the liturgies and
music that go with it, recovered or rediscovered or sometimes half
made up by Dearmer and his followers, lead into the darkest days
of Lent.

HOLY WEEK

Wednesday in Holy Week is known in some places as Spy Wednesday, anticipating as it does Judas' betrayal of Jesus to the Jewish authorities. Judas, disgusted by Mary Magdalene choosing to anoint Jesus with expensive perfume which could have been sold for the poor, is filled with mounting resentment at Jesus' departure from the plan as he approaches Jerusalem. But the anointing indicates his divinity, which he is about to renounce in order to be sacrificed for the salvation of all things, and as Jesus empties himself, Judas fills his purse with money from the Temple authorities, to whom he has betrayed him – *and it was night*. On this night, *Tenebrae*, from the Latin word for 'darkness', is celebrated. We gather in church to hear a series of readings from Scripture and music, between which the candles on the altar and the Tenebrae Hearse, a large stepped candlestick, are extinguished one by one until only a single candle is left. This too is finally extinguished and we are left in total darkness. Suddenly a great crash rings out, the *strepitus*, symbolising the death of Jesus on the cross, 'and the earth did quake, and the rocks rent' – this is usually achieved by a server slamming the lid of a chest or a door, or in some places by children drumming their heels on the floor to recall thunder. It is followed by an audible snort as members of the congregation wake up.

Off to stay with an old friend from my crazy drug-taking, club-going days on the eve of a friend's funeral. The funeral was for another friend of those times, who died not of the excesses we all enjoyed in the past but of a merciless cancer. We stay up late, too late, looking at photographs, wondering what happened to whom, and eventually I lay sleeplessly in the bottom bunk in my friend's son's bedroom under a *Star Wars* duvet, him unconscious overhead. I think of John Clare's despairing wish, to sleep as I in childhood sweetly slept. Next day we all dress up and go to meet up with some other veterans of the clubs of Ibiza, twenty or so years on, and drive in convoy to his flat, where I walk into a room which looks like that photo album come to life. Faces, some familiar, others whom I half-recognise from the days of Troll, a notorious club we all used to frequent in the Second Summer of Love.

His partner is pale, sleepless, but funny, as ever, and in a party mood we set off walking behind the hearse down the hill to the crematorium. It stops the traffic: dozens of us dressed in everything from suits to tracksuits carrying smart bouquets of lilies and gerberas, and then, East End builders – the departed had been a builder – carrying carnations and chrysanths. At the crematorium, the partner leads the service, which is funny and sentimental. We have 'Seasons in the Sun', 'I Will Always Love You' and 'The Rose' for starters, so much better than the Bach cello suite I'd have for funeral purposes. When we go up to light candles for him, the only child there gets distressed and begins to cry inconsolably, getting even more attention than the coffin. It ends with a House track I vaguely remember from Troll days, and we are just about to leave when his sister decides to make an impromptu speech in which she reveals that he has given her fifteen thousand pounds as a deposit for a house, but she gave it to a cat sanctuary instead.

Holy Week, originally and still best experienced in monasteries, maps imperfectly onto the run-up to the Easter holidays that everyone else is having. I take an assembly, speaking of Passiontide to a floorful of fidgeting de-mob children who half-smile at the gratuitous mentions of Arsenal and *The Apprentice*. Then a haircut, the barber inviting me to laugh with him at the peccadilloes of friends of his from his home village who went on to have distinguished careers in Cosa Nostra, which I mostly manage to resist. When I'm done up in the barber's gown, you can't see my dog collar and it's amusing to see the reactions of other customers when it comes off and they see I'm a vicar. Then to the Council where I give a talk on vocation to the Christian Union, then onwards to take Holy Communion with a lady who looks so terrible I anoint her too. I tell her that the oil I am using is the last of this year's batch, stressing that it is for healing, not wanting to alarm her with anything looking like a last rite, and she says lugubriously, 'Healing? Have you got a pint?' Then I run into a local rascal who cadges a fiver off me for the train fare to Sleaford, then takes a phone call from his ex-girlfriend and lies about his whereabouts. Then Evening Prayer with another regular sitting next to me, shaking with anxiety and smelling a bit. Then home to more desk work, then a talk to a Ladies' Group. I arrive at seven forty-five, as bidden, to find the ladies stuck outside in cars with no one to open the building for them, which is infuriating, because I want to be home by nine. Off we go to someone's house and I tell them about my vocation, twice in a day, edited for each audience. I speak about how odd it feels to find myself doing what I'm doing now, considering where I've come from. I tell them the story about ascending the pulpit at St Mary's Warwick to preach, realising that the first time I visited that church I was a radical Trotskyist. But that's nowhere near as odd as finding myself surrounded by our host's collection of camels (paintings, sculptures, novelties, photographs), talking about the miners' strike to stalwarts of the Conservative Association. From cultural entryism to payment of subs in a sentence. Halfway through I feel uneasy and look behind me to see a cluster of pottery camels looking menacingly over my shoulder. I feel like Tippi Hedren in *The Birds*.

Why do certain events stick in our minds while others fade? What is the significance of these seemingly arbitrary things? Sticking the tines of my fork into salad cream in the dining room at St Peter's

School when I was about six; the flaking blue paint on the fire escape at Wellingborough School; daffodils on the windowsill at Bishop's Avenue in Stratford – why these?

These are not the same as Proustian moments. I realise that the most vividly recalled things for me are moments of anticipation and gratification, which I recall not only in pictures and words but in smell. Not the smell of the things themselves, but a background, slightly metallic yet not unpleasant smell, which I associate with getting what I want. I recall the arrival of my replica Walther PPK in a brown parcel when I was about fourteen, and I remember the smell, or is it a taste, or is it the recollection of a flavour? The flavour of success?

Scene from clerical life: David and I are in our dog collars, walking the dogs in the park, when we come across a group of kids on their way to school. As they draw level, one of them shouts at David, 'Your fucking mother sucks cock in hell.'

When Holy Week coincides with that lovely first burst of spring, I go out on my bike and head into the country. The Hall park is full of wobbly lambs, set dressing for the Lamb of God who is about to take away the sins of the world. I cycle round the park, make for the road that climbs the hill out of the village. It is cold and windy, no one about, and desolate, the promise of daffodils and blossom not redeemed yet by hedgerows and fields and woodland. As I come to the crown of the hill, I see this odd shape on the left, and then realise it is a woman, bent over, with a handsome black Labrador at her side. As I draw level she shouts something. I slow down and ask her what she said. 'I'm not mad,' she replies. I tell her I'm sure she isn't, and she says she's digging up bits of broken glass that have been left lying round and could cut a dog's paws to ribbons . . . and that's your holiday over. I stop and give her a hand. I ask her what the dog is called and she says something that sounds like Martha. Martha? I ask. 'Mollser,' she replies, 'he's a character in an

Irish play.' I ask her which Irish play and she says, '*The Plough and the Stars*.' I say I love Sean O'Casey and it turns out she's a retired university lecturer who lives in Keeper's Cottage. When she asks me how I know Sean O'Casey, I tell her I was Captain Boyle in a production we'd done at Stratford. 'Not with Gordon Vallins?' she asks. Yes, with Gordon Vallins, my old teacher, who was a friend and colleague of hers, and here we are, digging up bits of broken glass beside a lonely little road in the back of beyond. Sounds more like Beckett than O'Casey.

We often gather in 'Del Boy', one of the meeting rooms in New Broadcasting House named after the Corporation's comedy greats, for the *Saturday Live* Friday meeting. We go through what's on the following day's programme, sitting round a boardroom table, while around us, semi-visible through semi-opaque glass walls, other BBC people are in meetings. Once a group of stern-looking managers broke into a chorus of 'Bring Me Sunshine' from *Morecambe and Wise*, and two of them did that funny skip with the hand gestures round the table. On another day, when my attention had begun to wander, I saw a silhouette through the glass that I recognised. It was Jimmy Somerville, my former partner in the Communards, who I hadn't seen for years, back on the promotional circuit with his first new album for a while. Former partners are, I imagine, a bit like former spouses, and goodwill contends with history when we meet. I said hello, a bit nervously, as Jimmy made his way to record *Loose Ends*. I sat with the studio managers while Jimmy sang a new version of 'Smalltown Boy', his first hit with Bronski Beat, which was out thirty years ago. Hearing it was like hearing that brilliant Joni Mitchell album, when she returned to some of her best-loved tracks but decades down the line, experience having overtaken novelty.

Later, we had a chance to talk a little and discovered that we would be meeting the following week on Chris Evans' show on Radio Two, when Jimmy would be singing his new record live and I would be delivering the Pause for Thought, the God slot, for which I am a regular contributor.

On the day, the studio contained not only us, former partners pursuing now our different vocations, but Rupert Everett, whose wonderful autobiography I had been reading. All three of us were veterans of the London gay scene in the eighties and had been in the same notorious place at the same notorious time. I can remember seeing both of them loom out of the strobing haze of the nightclub Heaven, to the sound of Paul Oakenfold and Daz Saund.

Jimmy sang, his voice as beautiful as it was thirty years ago but thickened by the flow of experience, and I could not hear it without feeling a rush of nostalgia for our joint enterprise thirty years before. When my turn came, I spoke about writing my memoir, a lot of it about Jimmy, some of it personal. Before publication I got in touch, offered him a preview, and a right of veto. Not necessary. 'You have every entitlement to write your truth,' he wrote. 'I'm very aware of our history, and some of it I may shudder and cringe at. We also have a powerful, unique and truly wonderful history too. Bring it on.'

Afterwards, I rather gushed at Rupert Everett, saying how much I loved his book. He said he loved mine; I said I really loved his; and we went round this a couple of times, on a carousel of mutual compliment.

On a pre-Easter visit to a parishioner in the nursing home, she tells me that not long after the First World War when she was a little girl, about ten, her uncle took her to the seaside for a holiday. They stayed in Westcliff, the posh end of Southend. They went for a walk along the prom on the morning of their first day there and found dozens of men and women, dead drunk, sprawled out across the benches, staggering along and vomiting in the street. And, she realised later, coupling in the bus shelters and under the pier, though she was too young to understand what was going on as her uncle hurried her past.

Her mother, who lived to be ninety-six, was the first generation to receive the state pension. She remembers her sitting in the drawing room, wearing a velvet choker, saying, 'Goodness gracious, Mr Lloyd George has given me ten shillings . . . for nothing!'

Some American friends are here for Easter, so David and I take them to see Ely Cathedral. The way in is roped off into a one-person-wide funnel, taking you past a lady at a desk with a big sign saying *Entrance fee*. In the small print it asks you to *consider a fee of £4*. I consider it. The whole cathedral, which I love, looks more French than English; the Romanesque ambitions of a Norman Benedictine abbot, I suppose. One of my guests is scared of going up the narrow, steep, spiral staircases to the octagon and the lantern, so I take her in hand and soothe her way up and down. I ask her brother if she's claustrophobic, and he says, 'No, she makes it up.' The night before the phone had gone and she, not being used to English ring tones, thought it was a fire alarm and woke everyone up.

The octagon is extraordinary, made out of seven-hundred-year-old tree trunks still with their maker's marks on them (so much for the 'anonymous' artists and craftsmen of the Middle Ages). The guy showing us around obviously loves his subject; he's a retired engineer, and we're up there for more than an hour as he explains the stresses and the thrusts, and the disasters which have befallen the unstable end of the cathedral, which seems to have been forever falling down. I ask him about the fire risk: ancient timbers inside a huge chimney, directly above a building full of candles and wiring, surrounded by lightning-attracting pinnacles – shouldn't it have burned down centuries ago? But there's never been a fire, not in the lantern. Some kids, a few years ago, started a fire in one of the transepts, which caused a bit of damage, but the fire brigade got there in good time and put it out.

Out on the roof, I look towards King's Lynn (nearly thirty miles away) and spot a strange shape, a few miles distant. Detaching itself from the ground, it comes floating up towards us very slowly. It turns out to be a huge transporter, taking off from the US airbase at Mildenhall. It looks quite surreal, like something from Dante, I realise, standing there among the Medieval pinnacles watching some mysterious flying thing wing its way towards us.

I stay for Evening Prayer. It's quite low-key because the choir is on holiday and a couple of cathedral clergy take it – nice vowels, nicely spoken, very Anglican – for the benefit of me, two or three other civilians and a rascally-looking verger. After the service, as I'm going out, the rascally verger passes me, walking from the north transept to the south transept. As he reaches the crossing, I assume he'll stop and bow to the altar, as I had a minute earlier, but he doesn't. I thought, You can't be arsed; it's six o'clock on a Thursday evening and you're knocking off. But as he reaches the mid-point he slows very slightly and puts his hand up to his face and scratches his nose, in a guilt reflex, I guess.

MAUNDY THURSDAY

Jesus replied, 'You do not realise now what I am doing, but later you will understand.' For me, these are the most reassuring words in the New Testament. Quite a lot of the time I don't know what Jesus is doing, and so his promise that I *will* understand brings relief. Not realising what Jesus is doing comes more sharply into focus once you're ordained and become at that moment officially expert in the mysteries of the Christian religion. How many times in the last decade have I looked out over clumps of enquiring and expectant faces, thinking I have no idea what to say next? In part, this is simply the rabbit-in-the-headlamps feeling we get when we're called upon to hold forth, but, more than that, it is because what Jesus *does* really is beyond us.

He began by astonishing people. At the Epiphany, we heard of wise men coming to the manger and finding in that bundle of dirty hay a truth brighter than the star that led them there; a truth which sent them back to their old lives by another way, and everything was suddenly different.

Then he appears in the Jerusalem Temple, amazing the clergy with his teaching, teaching as one *with authority*. As his reputation grew, so did the rumours about him and the amazing things he did. People who had been blind for years or lame for years suddenly could see and walk, and there were stories of unbelievable things, of water turned into wine, food for thousands produced out of a picnic. And shameless things: he sat down with prostitutes and quislings and thieves, and treated them like family while his own family he left standing at the door. What on earth did he mean by that?

The more we explore, the more we begin to see how ambivalent people felt about Jesus. If this is the Good News, they seem to think, then why do we feel so uncertain about it, so anxious, like those women who discovered his tomb empty on Easter morning and told no one about it because they were afraid?

A paradox: not a puzzle to solve, but a passport, an invitation to step beyond the familiar and to cross the threshold into Jesus' kingdom. This can be extremely disorienting, for his kingdom is not of this world. It's a kingdom in which the king stoops to wash the feet of his followers, like a common slave. It's a kingdom in which we are commanded to love one another. It is a kingdom we can only gain by losing everything. And that greatest paradox of all: the king's victory is his death, the death of a common criminal, death on a cross.

Of course we don't understand it. It's not there to be understood. It's there to claim us.

Some say the job of Christians is to make the gospel intelligible to the world. But sometimes I think that the job of Christians is to make it unintelligible. For in our mission to explain, we divest it of mystery, and so we produce Jesus the philanthropist, or the charismatic historical figure, or the social worker, or politician, or warrior king; someone in our *own* image, someone less than God.

'*You do not realise now what I am doing, but later you will understand.*' 'Later' is a translation of the Greek phrase *meta tauta*, which literally means 'after these things' and is a phrase often used in John's Gospel to move things along; it's a kind of narrative lubricant. So the translators here have taken it simply to indicate a point in the future, like a week on Tuesday. But the case can be made for a translation more faithful to the Greek: *You do not realise now what I am doing, but* after these things *you will understand.* After what things? After his last meal, his agony and arrest and trial and torture and death.

The church we leave on Maundy Thursday is different from on any other night. The altars stripped, the trappings removed, bare and silent as we wait with Jesus for the events which are to follow. Only *after these things* can we begin to understand Maundy Thursday and Good Friday and what lies beyond; what, for now, is quite literally beyond us.

GOOD FRIDAY

In the Wallace Collection I walk through the galleries of armour, unmoved and uninterested, apart from one, where I see perhaps the plainest piece in the collection: a great helm dating from the fifteenth century, Flemish or English, the type used for jousting, with a narrow opening that faces not outwards but upwards, designed to offer not all-round vision but maximum protection from your opponent's lance. There's something brutal about it, bestial even, to do with obscuring the face (like an executioner's hood), the brute character of the material (iron), and its intended use. Imagine meeting this full face on a dark morning and knowing it is your own reflection.

Did Edward Hopper know icons? I'm thinking of that painting by Hopper of a young woman in a petticoat sitting on the edge of a bed in a featureless hotel bedroom reading a railway timetable by the light of a single overhead bulb. It's a scene made desperate not only by the composition and the narrative we may attach to it, but by the use of colour: the not ungentle yellow light and the soft pink of her petticoat look only vulnerable, threatened by the rectangle of black made by the half-raised blind on the window, giving out into the night. The black seems almost to swell, seems set to burst out of its containment and engulf the picture. I wonder if it comes from the Icon of the Anastasis, in which Jesus raises up Adam and Eve from hell. Hell is broken open under his feet, a semicircle of the most intense black that, while subjugated to Christ's triumph, is no less black, no less a fact.

*

April ninth this year falls in Holy Week, and although normal service is suspended in this supremely important week in the Western Church, I nevertheless give thanks on this day for the life of Dietrich Bonhoeffer, one of the greatest Christian witnesses of the twentieth century. He was a Lutheran pastor in Germany, born in Breslau in 1906, the son of a psychiatrist and a teacher and a member of a brilliant family (his brother Karl in 1929 discovered with Paul Hartek the spin isomers of hydrogen). An outstanding student, before he was twenty-four he completed two doctorates in Theology at the University of Berlin; too young to be ordained, he went to the United States, where he taught at New York's Union Theological Seminary. There he was greatly changed by teaching at a black church in Harlem, where, he said, 'phraseology turned into reality' and he became deeply involved in social justice issues. He also fell in love with African-American spirituals, which he took back to Germany. He learned to drive, but so pathetically he passed the notoriously undemanding US driving test only at the fourth attempt. In Berlin he was ordained and became a Theology lecturer at the university, where he became very involved in the ecumenical movement, forging theological and personal friendships with Christians of other churches around the world.

Everything changed after the Nazis came to power in 1933 and sought to remake the German Church in their image. Bonhoeffer refused any accommodation with a regime he immediately understood to be evil, and fought doggedly to preserve the Church from the taint of Hitler's ideology: 'Silence in the face of evil is itself evil. Not to speak is to speak. Not to act is to act.' When the Church acquiesced, Bonhoeffer and Pastor Martin Niemöller helped form the Confessing Church in opposition. Despite an angry call to remain and fight in Germany from his friend, the great theologian Karl Barth, he left for London, partly to strengthen his ecumenical relationships internationally, and was appointed minister of the Lutheran church at Sydenham. In 1935, however, he did return, stung perhaps by Barth's criticism, and founded and ran a number of underground seminaries training ministers for the Confessing Church. It was during this period he published his best-known work, *The Cost of Discipleship*, a study on the Sermon on the Mount. With the outbreak of war he joined the Abwehr, German Military Intelligence, under cover of which he continued to build ecumenical relations, notably with the great Bishop Bell of Chichester. He secured the rescue of Jewish families from Nazi terror, and became involved in plots against Hitler's leadership. For this he was arrested in February 1943 and taken to Tegel prison, where he so charmed the guards that one of them offered to help him escape. But in 1944, after the failure of the bomb plot against Hitler, his connection to the conspirators was discovered and he was sent to Flossenbürg concentration camp. On 9 April 1945, two weeks before US troops liberated the camp, he was stripped naked and hanged at dawn with his fellow conspirators. According to the account of the SS doctor attending, he prayed with great self-composure and died as meekly as a lamb without suffering. It later transpired that the hanged men suffered six hours of agony before giving up the ghost. Bonhoeffer's brother and two brothers-in-law were also executed by the Nazis. His legacy is immense and enduring, especially in Sydenham; his church, bombed in the war, was rebuilt in 1958 and renamed in his honour. He's also one of the twentieth-century martyrs on the west front of Westminster Abbey, alongside Martin Luther King and Oscar Romero.

On Good Friday, St Martin's in Stamford, and at the invitation of the Rector Michael I am taking part in the Liturgy of the Passion. He'd asked me to be one of the Passion Singers – to be Jesus, in fact; a small but, as you will readily understand, critical part. So as dusk fell, after a day of perfect spring weather, I stand in the sacristy in a cassock and drape an amice round my shoulders, don the helmet of salvation, put an alb over my head, to make me white, and a cincture round my waist, as a sign of sacerdotal chastity and spiritual watchfulness (instructions given by a faintly bemused clergyman). The celebrant, who is deaf, stands in his red chasuble in front of the crucifix in deep and silent prayer as we process into the bare church. We move to the sides in the choir to allow the priests and deacons into the sanctuary, then we move back to the centre and all prostrate ourselves in front of the altar. It's deeply moving when you watch it from the pews; when you're actually doing it, it's anything but. You allow yourself to fall onto a cold and dusty floor and lie there in complete silence. The idea, as in any other mode of performance, is to focus the attention of the crowd, and what looks completely natural and unselfconscious from the front often feels awkward and fake on the ground. But it doesn't matter that we lie on the ground stifling a sneeze, or kneel in agony on a cold hard step, or have no idea what happens next; it does matter that the congregation sees something of the mystery of the Passion taking shape in front of them.

And then it's time for the singing of the Passion. The Rector sings the narrator, a pious tenor is Pilate and I am Christ. The Rector moves us into position, him in the centre at the lectern, me to his left, Pilate to his right. He takes something out of his sleeve – a tuning fork – strikes it, holds it to his ear, and intones the beginning. We're performing the shorter version, so I don't have much to sing, but singing the words of Christ on the Cross, in vestments, in church on Good Friday, for the first time, is not something negligible. When I arrived, he asked me if I wanted a rehearsal. I said no; a matter of professional pride.

Not in the calendar, but in my mind on Good Friday is Anne Askew, author, Protestant, self-proclaimed divorcée and the only woman to have been put to torture in the Tower of London. She was born into a landowning family in Lincolnshire in 1521 and was betrothed by her father at fifteen to Thomas Kyme, a neighbour and fellow courtier of Henry VIII. Unfortunately, while she was a devout Protestant, he was a Catholic and a rather unreformed one.

After he'd fathered her two children, she decided to divorce him; in her view, this was permitted by Scripture on the grounds of his adultery. He threw her out for heresy, so she moved to London and became a 'gospeller', a lay preacher. In 1545 her husband had her arrested and brought back to Lincolnshire, but she ran away to London again. She wrote an account of her experiences called *The Examinations*, considered today to give a unique insight into the circumstances of educated Tudor women, and a testament to her intellectual brilliance as she makes the case for her divorce and for her theological convictions. She was rearrested and taken to the Tower and there racked by Thomas Wriothesley and Sir Richard Rich, who demanded she name other women of heretical views, including Henry's inconvenient sixth wife Queen Catherine Parr. She refused and despite the protests of the jailers was racked again by her accusers until her arms and legs were dislocated at the shoulders and hips. She maintained her silence but was convicted of heresy. On 16 July 1546, unable to stand because of the torture she had suffered, she was carried to the stake at Smithfield with three other Protestants, chained there to a seat, and obliged to hear the feeble Bishop Shaxton preach a sermon for their benefit, but she kept shouting, 'There he misseth, and speaketh without the book!' Refusing to recant, she was burned slowly for obstinacy.

On Good Friday I have started posting Stations of the Cross on Twitter, photographs of contemporary events that relate to the fourteen moments from the Passion of Christ which are recalled on this day in a sequence from his trial to his burial. You see them in Catholic churches positioned around the walls; pilgrims move from one to the next singing a hymn and saying a prayer at each station. I have tried to adapt this for social media, and so throughout Good Friday I tweet each station. Throughout the day I put up photographs of contemporary horrors, from an Iraqi Christian crucified by ISIS surrounded by onlookers taking pictures on their phones, to a victim of homophobic Russian vigilantes. Relief too, mirroring

Veronica, who wiped Jesus' face and carried his cross, in the form of a woman from the programme *Benefits Street* looking after her severely disabled son.

I did this for the first time three years ago and every year it gets a bigger following, retweeted not only by Christians but by non-believers too. I do not know why it makes such an impact. Not always a favourable impact. Someone tweeted me back this year to tell me he found what I had done creepy. I suppose he thought I was getting off somehow on the suffering I offered up to general view. But it is not about suffering, it does not stop there. It is about what waits on the far side of suffering, which makes it possible to contemplate horrors no less intense than those of Jesus' day.

HOLY SATURDAY

After the solemnity which falls over us on Good Friday, with typical bathos the Church of England appoints the next day for church cleaning, and people turn up not in grief and silence but with dusters and mops and Brasso. I set to work polishing the crucifix which stands on the altar. As I go over the figure of Christ with a yellow duster, David says, 'Shine, Jesus, shine.'

I leave them to it and head to the nursing home to sing Easter hymns a day early, when strictly speaking we are meant to still be having no fun at all. The ladies and gentlemen are in high spirits, and enjoy singing 'Thine Be the Glory' so much I ask if there are any requests. A lady asks for 'YMCA', and I don't want to spoil the party mood, so we sing it with hand gestures from those who are able.

EASTER DAY

Just before Parish Communion for Easter Day this morning a churchwarden came up and said, 'The Rev's outside.' It was Tom Hollander, arrived out of the blue. He'd been to a baptism at the dawn vigil at St Mary Abbotts and came here en route, circuitously, to his parents. We had got to know each other when I had helped him out during the making of the programme *Rev*, in which he played the vicar of a struggling parish in a poor part of London. He asked me lots of questions, which I tried to answer, but when the programme aired what I noticed most vividly were the things he had got from me which I had not noticed I had given. His character sits in the churchyard having a fag with a down-and-out. When he is summoned back to duty he chews a handful of mints to cover the unpriestly smell of tobacco on his breath. That was me, but I had not noticed I did it until then.

After the service, and the blessing of the Easter Garden, we came back and sat with David in the vicarage garden having a beer – lovely day, blossom falling like pink snow – and talked about the next series of *Rev* in which the trajectory we had just covered, from Jesus' arrest to the Resurrection, would also be covered, and how to try to recapture that in a story about someone now. And then we just sat, in silence, in the sun, as the blossom fell around us, and Daisy ran out of the kitchen door holding in her mouth the sandwich she had stolen from Tom's bag.

*

I am depping in the choir at a neighbouring church for the Easter
Vigil, in which the Paschal Candle is lit and brought into church,
the font is blessed, and we hear the Bible story of our salvation told
and sung. I haven't enjoyed myself singing so much in years: we do
all the usual stuff at mad Anglo-Catholic parish standard, including Nicholson in G for the Gloria, with me on bass, sight-reading
between two stalwarts, both of whom are deaf. If the organist gives
the notes too softly they don't hear it and we begin in three different
keys. The one tenor sings the 'Exsultet', very beautifully, but the
celebrant undertakes the task with obvious impatience, dunking
the Paschal Candle in the font like a sponge finger in a cup of tea.
He races through the prayers, some of the most beautiful in the
whole liturgy, and at one point I think he is going to say, 'In the
name of the Father, the Son and the . . . whatever.' The booklet for
the Easter Vigil concludes with an ALLELUIA! AMEN! in capitals
and exclamation marks and then, in parentheses: *(sorry but there is
no tea tonight)*.

From the car park, they look like football fans heading for an international: fifty clergy, companions and pilgrims, bound for the Holy
Land. Clergy from Peterborough, from Ely, Durham, Oxford and
– rather excitingly – from Montreal in Canada, which is sending
its Bishop, Dean, and Executive Archdeacon (Janet). That's a lot of
socks and sandals.

This is the sight that greets us at Heathrow Airport as we set
out on the journey that all Christians should one day undertake
– to visit the holy sites of Israel and Palestine, where Jesus and the
disciples lived and where he met the climactic events of his life
commemorated this week. Muslims make a pilgrimage to Mecca, if
possible, at some point in their lives. I wish Christians would adopt
the same discipline and make a pilgrimage here.

We fly to Tel Aviv, clear the most rigorous of border controls,
hop onto a bus, and for the next couple of hours we travel through
a landscape that reminds me of a spaghetti Western, and then a

built-up area that looks like Northern Ireland at the height of the Troubles. En route, we are given an introduction to the region by our tour leaders: three clergy and a local guide. He is a Palestinian Christian, a representative of a dwindling minority in the region. The company which has organised our pilgrimage does what it can to sustain the local economy by using their businesses, places to stay, guides, restaurants, even drinking their locally brewed beer, Taybeh, wherever possible.

Eventually we arrive at the most glamorous monastery I've ever visited, run by German monks on the shore of the Sea of Galilee. Tired, I offend the Canadians by asking them if they are very much pestered by bears when they put their rubbish out in winter. We eat our hummus in awkward silence for a moment.

I used to think of Jesus and the disciples walking round deserts under baking sun; but Galilee is as green as Wales and as beautiful as anywhere I've ever been, the hills covered with what look like early buttercups and almond blossom and the silvery green of olives. We head up Mount Tabor, scene of the Transfiguration, and look out across this landscape watched only by the rock badgers, who get a mention in Psalm 104, but not in the Gospels. And they never mention rain either – Jesus never announces the Sermon on the Mount (if fine) – and yet here it rains all the time. We get caught in a downpour as we visit Capernaum, and stand in the streets through which Jesus and the disciples would have walked to the synagogue as rainwater gurgles past us in the gutters.

There's some controversy, of course, over the reliability of who did what and where. Some sites we visit are A-grade, almost certainly the places where Jesus had been, others are a bit sketchier. The Church of the Annunciation in Nazareth, an eye-wateringly bold exercise in late twentieth-century church architecture, is probably not much more than a guess.

But you can stand on the Mount of Olives and see the steps Jesus would have taken to meet his fate before Pilate, and draw water from the well at Sychar (now Nablus) where he met the woman who was no better than she should be.

Wherever, whatever, the inescapable background of political and religious tension recalls us to the present moment. 'Bethlehem, of noblest cities, none can once with thee compare', says one of my least favourite hymns, and my dislike for it intensifies as we pass through the checkpoints and by the watchtowers into Manger Square. Not long ago, tanks were positioned here, and the monks who are custodians of the Church of the Nativity got into a fight. They've lost none of their combativeness, we discover, when a bishop in our party is curtly told to 'stop praying' in the church early one morning; an indoor turf war to complement the big one outdoors, different denominations competing for custody in a depressing tug-of-love.

You can't walk a block in Bethlehem without wondering if the awfulness of religion can really be borne. We visit Hebron, where the madness is at its most intense. Around the tombs of the patriarchs we meet seventeen-year-old kids, the Israelis in fatigues and carrying M16s, the Palestinians in terrible knitwear carrying trinkets. The latter sneak up on us and whisper, 'You are bad people. Do not come here.' The settlers think so too; they threaten our driver and want to throw stones at us. As we backtrack through the souk, I overhear someone say, 'Man's inhumanity to man . . . ooh, cauliflowers!'

And then early on Sunday morning we arrive in Jerusalem and go to the Eucharist at the Anglican cathedral of St George; and amid the deadlocked politics of Palestine and Israel, the fractiousness of the children of Abraham, and monastic fisticuffs, a Canadian bishop and a Palestinian priest stand together and read from the Gospel in Arabic and English, words of reconciliation and peace in the city where Jesus stood powerless before the powers of the world, reconciling us and being our peace. He did so, lest we forget, by hanging on a cross.

*

The trees of the Lord are full of sap
even the cedars of Libanus which he hath planted;
Wherein the birds make their nests
and the fir-trees are a dwelling for the stork.

A passage from my favourite psalm, 104, a passage which unfailingly jumps into my mind at this time of year, as the trees outside my bedroom window begin to unfurl their first leaves in that fizzy green of first growth. In my study, I view the passing scene – or the part of it that goes up and down School Lane – through my Rose of Sharon; some time to go before that brings forth its blowsy yellow flowers. Before long, I expect the bees that live in the gable end will be doing their thing too.

The birds, the bees, the green blade riseth: and we tune ourselves once again not only to nature but to grace . . .

We enter Eastertide and out of the sterile winter new life springs forth. The Christian calendar sits as neatly in nature's year as Christian churches sit neatly on the sites of pre-Christian worship: we point East to the rising sun and the promise that brings, and Easter falls just when the garden is beginning to burst into new life.

But not at Wallingford parish church, location for an Easter edition of *Songs of Praise* filmed not in spring but in winter, at the same time as *Christmas Songs of Praise* to save costs. Pity the poor choristers, shivering in sub-zero temperatures while we edge – very slowly it feels at the moment – to warmer weather. For the outdoor shots with the presenter, a set dresser stuck a few daffs in the ground, trying to suggest the beginning rather than the end of the year. Inside, the congregation, blue with cold in spring fashions, was in bleak midwinter.

Unintended message: This is *not* Easter.

A friend called me one Good Friday to tell me her husband had just died. Forgivably, she wasn't in church on Easter morning. Mick, her husband, was a gardener, and the thought of hearing the story of Mary meeting another gardener who died on Good Friday was intolerable. 'I can't bear to hear that story tripping off the tongue,' she said. 'It sounds so glib.'

Easter holiday weekend, secular prose following religious poetry, and I took Mum and Dad to Deene Park, not open very often so I was curious to see it. So was Mum, who came here to Hunt Balls in the fifties (indeed, to her first ball when, to her irritation, she had to have a chaperone). From the outside it's handsome, haphazard, a mess of Tudor, Georgian and Regency, and on the inside it's even weirder, a mixture of periods and styles, the grand and the not so grand, the aristocratic and the squirearchical, all under one jumble of roofs.

As I was looking at the hammerbeam roof in the great hall, I got into conversation with the guide. We were joined by another man, wearing the tweedy uniform of the country squire, who turned out to be the owner. He asked me where I lived and who I was, and I told him that my great grandmother remembered seeing his great grandfather, Lord Cardigan of the Charge of the Light Brigade, in his carriage outside the George Hotel in Kettering in about 1865. He looked a bit distracted and asked me which house I lived in. I told him and he nodded and sloped off.

Lord Cardigan's second wife, the notorious Countess, lived to be ninety and used to cycle round the lanes during the First World War wearing her long-dead husband's military breeches. Before she landed the belted earl, she was a celebrated beauty called Adeline Horsey de Horsey.

We went to have a look at the garden. 'Have you ever seen a ghost?' I asked Dad as we walked along the parterre. 'Yes,' he answered. 'Just after Father died, I was in the garden at Longmeadow and I looked up and he was standing in front of me, as clear as day.' I was surprised. 'You've never told me that before,' I said. 'Nor me,' added Mum. 'No. I thought you'd think me a bit weird.' I asked him if it might have been a vivid memory, or perhaps he'd seen

somebody else and superimposed Grandpa on him. 'No, it was in
the back garden and there was nobody else there.' I asked him what
he was wearing. 'Plus-fours. So it couldn't have been anyone but
Father.' So was it a ghost? 'I think it was what people call a ghost. I
think it's probably some kind of psychological projection.'

Years later, I was with Dad in hospital. He had been in for weeks
and we had been called out twice when the doctor thought he
would not survive. He was not quite with it, fighting an infection
with a high temperature, but there were periods of lucidity. In one
he asked me, 'Do you think it is possible I saw God?' I said, 'Yes,
I suppose so. What was he like?' 'Oh, I knew he was God. Old
Etonian tie. He said he wanted to keep me on a bit longer. Very
good shoes too.'

Easter this year brings the most glorious weather of the year. I sit
outside listening to *Simon Boccanegra* on headphones and a brim-
stone butterfly flops over the fence and makes an uncertain circuit
of the garden. It feels like June but the magnolia's still out and the
cherry's not yet in flower; the aubretia's out, the tulips are just about
out, the daffs are over. And the swallows are returning. They weren't
in the barn first thing, but as I water the garden, dusk falling, one
flies overhead.

On *Look East* they ask the chairman of the Sandringham Flower
Club to share her most treasured memory of its most famous
member. 'Oh there's one occasion I'll always cherish,' she says. 'It
was just after the Queen Mother's hundredth birthday, so we made
a special presentation to her, and when I handed over the card she
looked at me and said, "Thank you so much." I'll never forget it.'

Why do we believe what we believe? Some things we take on trust,
from people or institutions we find authoritative. Maybe it is wiser
to base our beliefs on evidence? The plain facts in front of us?

But what constitutes evidence? Some say the verifiable, material facts of the universe – gravity, momentum, entropy, those sorts of things. The pictures of Doubting Thomas show someone looking for that sort of evidence, poking his finger into Jesus' wounds, to see if he's really there. But something, we're not exactly told what, eradicates his scepticism, and he gets it – it's Jesus – and he blurts out, almost without thinking, 'My Lord and my God!'

In Luke's version of Easter, a stranger comes alongside the disciples as they walk to the village of Emmaus outside Jerusalem. He has something about him which they find compelling. They ask him to eat with them and it is only when he breaks, blesses and shares the bread that they recognise who he is: the risen Jesus.

This episode parallels the appearance to Thomas, showing that the figure standing in front of the disciples is not a phantom but a real person, Jesus, who is hungry and asks for something to eat. Flesh and blood, like the Jesus Thomas points at.

But Jesus points somewhere else, into the Scriptures. On the road, the mysterious stranger 'interpreted to them in all the Scriptures the things concerning himself', as Luke puts it. That's repeated here, for when he's had his dinner he leads the disciples through some biblical exegesis, showing how the Law and the Prophets are fulfilled in him. The Saviour that Moses and Elijah and the patriarchs longed for, and whom Isaiah and Micah foretold, has arrived – and what's more, he's standing in front of them.

He shows his wounds, he eats a meal – there's the material evidence that he's indeed real – he demonstrates that this is anticipated in Scripture – there's the evidence from authority that it has to be thus. But that doesn't quite cover it.

It is not actually stated that Thomas, in spite of those pictures, really did poke his finger into Jesus' side. Perhaps he did not need to in the end, because something else not only persuaded him but overwhelmed him. 'My Lord and my God' – what could be clearer? – echoing Peter's confession at Caesarea Philippi, as they set out on their final journey to Jerusalem. Jesus asks the disciples who people say he is, and there's disagreement until Peter suddenly declares,

'You are the Christ, the Son of the living God', words which seem to come to his lips before they've been through his brain.

Scripture is elusive too, and ambiguous, and what seems to make perfect sense to you and me may mean something quite different to someone else. Try reading those passages from Isaiah we hear in Advent, foretelling the virgin birth and the Incarnation, with a Rabbi.

I think what Luke is trying to show is that faith in Jesus does not depend on physical evidence alone, nor on the evidence of Scripture alone. I think they're saying that the key to understanding Jesus is the person of Jesus Christ himself. The best interpreter of Jesus is Jesus, and if we encounter him, and find those words rising involuntarily to our lips – My Lord and my God – we speak our way into a new reality. That's why, I think, those who recognise Jesus are so often surprising, even untrustworthy: the woman at the well, the Roman centurion, babes and sucklings. Not authoritative at all.

But what of the disciples' failure to recognise the risen Jesus as they walked with him to Emmaus? This was the man they'd lived with, prayed with, served as Lord since the early days in Galilee. How could they not recognise him? Is their blindness a spiritual blindness, the story a parable, meant for later Christian communities for whom the ascended Christ can be known only through Scripture and in the breaking of bread? I think maybe there's something else here, something to do with the Christian vocation.

It is often said that we are called to be followers of Christ. I don't think that simply means we are to follow his teachings and his example, I think it means that we commit to walk his Way. In the Acts of the Apostles, Jesus' followers are called Christians only once, in Antioch; elsewhere they are called those who belong to the Way. Faithfulness to Jesus means not only experiencing a once and for all conversion – job done – but setting out on a journey with him – we're a work in progress. His own ministry reflects this, a ministry of both set pieces – the feeding of the five thousand, the transfiguration, the crucifixion – and something that happens on the hoof. He is constantly on the move, ministering to the towns and villages of Galilee and Judea, summoning those whom he encounters to leave their settled lives behind and follow him. He is the most footsore of religious leaders and those whom he calls follow him, literally, trailing through Palestine like nomads. Pasolini's film *The Gospel of Matthew* telescopes the two, presenting the Sermon on the Mount as a kind of marathon, Jesus rushing over Galilean hillsides, shouting out the Beatitudes to his followers, who have to run to keep up with him. Christianity is a religion for pedestrians.

So longing to go on pilgrimage is not simply something that comes over us in the spring with the rising of the sap – it expresses the itinerant nature of the faith. This is reflected not only in Grand Tours of the Holy Land, or a rag, tag and bobtail on the Canterbury road in Chaucer's England, but within church buildings themselves. In the Middle Ages, those who couldn't afford to go on pilgrimage would make mini-pilgrimages within the parish church or cathedral, stopping off at points around the building as pilgrims to Jerusalem stopped off at points around the city. In monastic churches you still find this, with side altars dedicated to Calvary, to the Holy Sepulchre, to the Ascension. It is echoed on Good Fridays in Lent in this church when we walk the Via Dolorosa with Christ as we mark the stations of the Cross.

Two radically different perspectives: on the one hand decisive, definitive moments that transform those who witness them; and on the other hand a continuing narrative of exploration and discovery which gradually brings to light truths that would otherwise remain obscure. Sometimes these seem so radically different as models for Christian understanding that choosing one means unchoosing the other. Indeed, there are Christians at both extremes of that spectrum, those who experience God's reality in such a way as to feel utterly and eternally altered by it – and endure agonies of self-doubt when they fail to live up to it – and those whose experience of God is so exploratory, so tentative, that they wonder if they've really encountered his living presence at all. Each extreme finds the other unintelligible, but most of us, I suspect, are a bit of both.

Easter morning, the discovery of the empty tomb. There are four versions of the story, one from each Gospel, and there are some striking differences between them. In Matthew's version the women run to tell the disciples what they've found; in Mark's Gospel they say nothing to anyone because they are afraid. In John it is Mary Magdalene who announces, with notable composure, 'I have seen the Lord'; in Luke's version, too, they move at a more dignified pace.

In Mark's there is no angelic deputation, in John's Jesus appears to Mary Magdalene as a gardener, in Matthew's an angel gallantly rolls back the stone in front of the tomb, and in Luke's two angels appear beside the women and give them a précis of the theology of the Resurrection – very Luke that, too. Some have wondered if these two angels – it's only a single angel in the other accounts – recall the pair of angels that were traditionally said to guard the Ark of the Covenant. But more attractively, perhaps, others have identified the pair of angels with the pair of criminals who were crucified alongside Jesus – Today you will be with me in Paradise, Jesus says to the Good Thief, Dismas; but maybe Luke, who is generous in his scheme of salvation, is saying the bad thief got in too. I hope so.

One of my favourite saints of Eastertide is Toyohiko Kagawa. He was born in Kobe, Japan, in 1888 to a sex-addicted businessman and a concubine. Sent away to school, he was taken in by two American missionaries and converted to Christianity, which provoked his parents to disown him. After studying theology, embryology, genetics, comparative anatomy, and palaeontology at Princeton he became convinced that Christianity in action was the only kind of Christianity he was interested in, so returned to Kobe to live and work in its slums, where he liked to go around holding hands with murderers. This produced a major work, his *Researches in the*

Psychology of the Poor, which did for Japanese society in the 1920s what Mayhew's *London Labour and the London Poor* did for British society in the 1850s. His argument was that the Church, uniting with the cooperative movement and the peace movement, could provide the only workable alternative to capitalism, state socialism, and fascism. This, however, was unattractive to the authorities and he was thrown into prison, so he invented three-dimensional forestry instead, and persuaded farmers to plant walnut trees to protect against soil erosion and to provide nuts to nourish their pigs. He argued tirelessly against Japanese militarism and imperialism, was nominated for Nobel Prizes for both Peace and Literature. After his death on 23 April 1960, he was declared a Sacred Treasure. 'I read in a book that a man called Christ went about doing good,' he said. 'It is very disconcerting to me that I am so easily satisfied with just going about.'

I am ushering a parishioner into my study when I notice the answerphone is beeping to say there's a message waiting. As she sits down, I say, 'Do you mind if I take this?' and press play. 'Hi, Richard, it's Tom Hollander here. I have to be brief because I'm calling from Tom Cruise's plane . . .' I hit pause, but my parishioner looks at me and says, 'Hmm, simple country parson.'

THE ASCENSION

The Mayfair in Boston has been held without interruption every year since 1125. In the Middle Ages it was so important that business and courts in London closed for the duration. By the time I was in Boston as its curate it no longer affected the capital's calendar, but it was still a big day for the town. It is fun, not money, that draws the crowds now, and the Market Place and Wide Bargate and the park were full for the entire week of rides and stalls and kids trying to blag something for nothing.

Because of its ancient origin, it opens with a church service from the gallopers, a gilded and garishly painted roundabout in front of the Assembly Rooms. Revellers sing hymns to a wheezing calliope accompaniment and the Vicar stands, in choir dress, next to the Mayor in his robes and the Chief Inspector in his uniform, leading prayers of penitence. All the local mayors come to join in too, the grand ones from Peterborough and Grimsby, and the less grand ones, from Sleaford and Downham Market (grandest chain by a mile was plucky Wisbech, a clanking golden thing more armour than decoration). In my second year there the Vicar was away and it fell to me to deputise. I ascended the gallopers with the Chairman of Lincolnshire County Council, who stood next to me and sang loudly, with a clear and controlled vibrato, 'The Old Rugged Cross' and 'Onward Christian Soldiers'. A crowd turned out for the service and the proclamation which followed, read not by His Worship the Mayor, but the Chief Executive of Boston Borough Council, a prosaic note among the pageantry. Then the owner of the fairground attractions and the Leader of the Showmen's Guild led the Mayor round the rides and we followed, a free tour, drawing a crowd of kids who all wanted to jump on for nothing too. The rides were manned by fairground lads, cool as cucumbers, slouching nonchalantly as Waltzers whizzed past, jumping from dodgem to dodgem as sure-footed as mountain goats and looking available. Girls doled out candyfloss and toffee apples and the smell of hot grease was everywhere. The most traditional of things, I thought, like a coronation or a street party, although there are signs of the changing times: the garish paintings decorating the rides are of babes in hot pants rather than Veronica Lake lookalikes, and the music, apart from the odd calliope, is pumping drum and bass. It was good fun, people were happy and out and about and joining in. I went on the dodgems with a lad from our youth group and, being a clergyman, I got rammed by everybody else. This is the last time I do this, I thought. I managed to duck out by Wide Bargate and went for a cappuccino in Costa and then back to the Assembly Rooms for lunch.

We sat on a table with some clanking mayors and their consorts. Our Mayor made a speech and the Leader of the Showmen's Guild made a long speech about tradition and the continuing relationship between councils and showmen, and I said grace, which I'd made up specially for the occasion: *Lord who blessed the loaves and fishes, bless this food upon our dishes; and when the Waltzers come to town, pray help us, Lord, to keep it down.* I went back to church and played the organ for an hour while one of our regulars wandered aimlessly around below calling my name and waving until I ignored him and he went and sat down at the back. I walked him home after Evening Prayer. He needed so much attention, and you felt yourself beginning to grit your teeth, and then he suddenly said goodbye and was gone. What a terrible life he leads, I thought, ill and broke and friendless and lonely and tormented, wandering around the only town he knows, a town which is indifferent to his fate if not actively hostile to him, trying to keep his demons at bay.

*

The Ascension, like the Transfiguration, is one of the episodes in the Bible when Jesus is at his most supernatural. Like Elijah, he is taken up to heaven in a cloud, witnessed by the apostles. Fulfilment of prophetic expectation, the writers are making claims about mes- siahship, blah blah blah . . . but a man is whisked up into heaven in a cloud (the little feet disappearing into a fluffy white cloud behind the altar of the Ascension Chapel at the Shrine of Walsingham in Norfolk) like something from *Star Trek*.

On the train heading north, two Dutchmen or Belgians are talk- ing on mobiles. We go through the tunnels between St Pancras and Kentish Town and one keeps saying, *Allo? Allo? Smiggly piggly* tunnel. Tunnel. *Smiggly piggly* tunnel, as his signal fails. And then, after a pause, he says, *Shit bucket.*

In Temple Balsall I meet up with Leslie Houlden, who taught New Testament when I was a student at King's College London. We have supper and then go to a concert at Symphony Hall in Bir- mingham. He did his national service in Germany just after the war and was stationed in Hamburg as part of a chaplaincy team attached to the Ordnance Corps. He brushed up his German by going to hear War Crimes trials, where you got simultaneous trans- lation from German into English. 'You could get a front row seat at the Staatsoper for four cigarettes and hear the NDR Orchestra for three.' I wondered what was it like hearing Wagner, Beethoven and Brahms in a city shattered by bombs, and in a shattered culture, the culture that gave birth to those very composers? 'Oh, I didn't really think about that. I was only eighteen. It just seemed to me to be an extension of hearing Barbirolli and the Hallé in Manchester during the war.'

Leslie had just returned from Copenhagen, where he'd been stay- ing with an old student, an African, now the ambassador of his country to Denmark. He was a student at Trinity, Oxford, when

Leslie was chaplain there in the sixties. 'He gave me one of my more memorable pastoral problems,' Leslie recalled. 'He came to me very agitated one day and I asked him what the matter was and eventually, after much toing and froing, he admitted that it was a problem to do with . . . cattle. He is Xhosa and in that culture you have to make a gift of cattle to the father of your fiancée and suitable cattle were quite hard to come by in Oxford in the middle sixties.' I wondered if Leslie, with customary ingenuity, had managed to find a couple of Friesians and sent them lowing in the cargo hold of a steamer all the way to Port Elizabeth. But no; he convinced the father of the bride to accept cash instead and a hundred quid covered it.

I went to Hamburg too for music, ten days at the opera, and a day off between *Tannhäuser* and *Rosenkavalier* fell on the feast of Pentecost. At the Lutheran Hauptkirche the similarities, rather than differences, between them and us were the more striking. There was a minister, in a black gown and huge white ruff, who smiled a lot. A choir, all men, were in cassocks, funny slit surplices and red woollen collars, which they wore a little too nonchalantly. An earnest young man in specs played the choir organ and some fine Bach on the main organ at the back. We got a plainsong Mass in Latin, a flowing liturgy and the same soft, sing-song modulations of Anglican speech. When we received Communion I crossed myself, and a hawk-eyed member of the choir boldly crossed himself too. The congregation didn't really know what was going on, standing up and sitting down and standing up again, and in the first hymn the choir organist played something different from what we expected to sing and he had to start again (very Anglican that). At the end the – I expect he's called the Hauptgrossesorgelmeisterführer or something – played the voluntary so beautifully I concluded my friend who says there's no such thing as a Protestant cathedral was wrong. Or maybe he wasn't wrong: it was as high a liturgy as a reformed liturgy gets; Anglo-Catholic really.

Then to the Kunsthalle where I spent the rest of the day looking at its fabulous room of Friedrichs, including the *Wanderer above the sea of mist*, that view of Greifswald in the morning with the horses frolicking in the field, and the dark, ink and steel-blue, moonshine over the sea. And there's a collection of expressionist painting, including Nolde's funny triptych *Im Hafen von Alexandria* and Kirchner's *Self-Portrait with Model*. Lots of stuff by the Nazarenes, which I could live without; although tucked away in a back room (with the Alma-Tademas), I found a small picture by Gerome of Muslims at prayer to a background spiky with minarets.

I called in, too, at the new gallery of contemporary art, which was built, with much fanfare, on the northern side of the Kunsthalle. I saw there a series of photographs of state death chambers, from Virginia to New Mexico. They were empty, off-duty, spick and span, photographed in a neutral bluish cibachrome, and utterly utterly grim. Some were white and clinical – a stainless steel toilet and basin and a neat bed in the holding cell, a state-of-the-art gurney, cruciform, with smart velcro straps – one was obviously a conversion job, the steel airtight door of what was once a gas chamber giving on to a gurney instead of a chair, thoughtfully husbanding the hard-earned tax dollars of the barbarian citizens of wherever – one, Nebraska I think, was done out, desperately, in vinyl wood-effect panelling, to make it look more homely – another was battered and low-rent, the gurney like something from *Dr Kildare*. But most disturbing was shot after shot of electric chairs, antiquated now, with fabric-covered cables and *Doctor Who*-ish dials and levers. Cruel and unusual punishment.

Later, at *Rosenkavalier* at the Staatsoper, I suppose I should have been forewarned by the poster, which showed an elegantly manicured hand stretched out on a white linen sheet, barbiturates scattered all around. I got into the auditorium and gasped when I looked at the stage and saw in the middle of it a huge round bed surrounded by music desks. For some reason in Act One (and only Act One) the orchestra was on stage, dressed in powdered periwigs and tights, the action cramped and confined on the big bed in the middle. The conductor, in eighteenth-century court dress, was led on stage by the Marschallin and Oktavian, both dressed in knickers and bodices, doubly arresting in the case of Oktavian, a travesti role; a woman impersonating a man dressed as a woman. The overture struck up and they started frolicking on the bed (all those horns). Soon the bed filled up with a fine Baron Ochs played by Kurt Moll (who played Ochs twenty-five years ago in this same theatre) and some daft blackamoors. Act One concluded with the Marschallin upending a pill bottle all over the bed, which made me involuntarily groan.

In Simon Winchester's history of the Oxford English Dictionary we read about Sir James Murray's two predecessors in the editor's chair, Herbert Coleridge and Frederick Furnivall. Coleridge, a brilliant young scholar, was the first editor and designer of the pigeonholes that were eventually to contain millions of slips sent in from correspondents all over the world. His tenure was short, alas. On the way to a meeting of the Philological Society in the London Library in April 1861 he was caught in a spring shower, which gave him a chill. The chill turned into consumption and on St George's Day, 23 April, he died at the age of thirty-one. His last words were, rather sweetly, 'I must begin Sanskrit tomorrow.'

Furnivall was a more robust character, the model for Water Rat in *Wind in the Willows*. He was a fanatical rower and used to recruit waitresses from the Aerated Bread Company's teashop in Hammersmith to teach them how to scull. One of them, Blanche Huckle, remembered 'Furney' as 'one of the kindest gentlemen I ever met'. He would invite the girls to picnics up the river and give them presents of two pairs of stockings each. He married his lady's maid, Lizzy Dalziel, and then abandoned her when he was fifty-eight for his secretary, Teena Rochfort-Smith, thirty-seven years his junior. Two months later she burned to death in Goole after an accident striking a match. He spent the rest of his life feuding with

Swinburne, whom he called Pigsbrook, about the metrical properties of a play attributed to Shakespeare.

At Mirfield we climbed the Tower at six thirty to ring in Ascension Day. After a crash course in handbell-ringing we did a few ragged circuits of rounds, tittums and queens, and I thought how Ascension Day was once – not so long ago – an observance almost as familiar as Christmas and Easter, but has now become something so arcane its practically cultic. Where once we would have caught the general mood we now appear eccentric, anti-social, peculiar.

One of the Romanians came to see me when I was writing a sermon. I didn't want him to come in but resistance was futile and he hung around annoying me for half an hour. Eventually he asked me if I thought he had offended a parishioner by asking her if her husband 'had another woman'. I gently suggested that he hadn't been kind to ask such a question, but he demurred. Then he said, 'Why you no tell your wives and mothers about the sacraments? I talked to this woman in the town and all she wants is sausages. Sausages and drinks. And travel.'

Prayer on the board:

Jesus, I will not take no for an answer. Get me a PIN so I can get a job.

*

Johnny, our most faithful attendee at Evening Prayer in Boston, now knows most of the words off by heart. He is in such a fog of medication and bewilderment that he goes for the responses in a slightly over-dramatic way, intoning 'Hear my prayer' with a plangent rising note. At first you think he's taking the piss, and maybe he is a bit, living in a world which he knows to be savage and indifferent, but I think it is him trying to find a way in. He has another irritating habit; every time the word Alleluia is said, he interjects, 'Alleluia, Richard!' and repeats it anxiously until I acknowledge him. He cannot read well but he has a good memory and an acute ear and when he joins in the words of the Magnificat he does so in my accent rather than his own, long As rather than short, because he's mimicking what he hears. And now he keeps saying 'on the contrary' to me, not knowing what it means, but knowing it is somehow a joke, a joke he wants to share.

I talk to a Canadian woman, on a cycling tour of this part of England with her husband. She is retired but fit, sixties I guess, and looks like an academic on holiday. We chat for a couple of minutes about this and that, and then she says, 'You're a handsome man. Are all the women of the parish after you?' I must have looked a bit nonplussed. 'Don't Catholic priests get chased by women? Something to do with being unavailable?' Most people just ask about the strainer arch.

In Finland with my friend Kev for a Ring Cycle at the new opera house and on a day off went to see HJK Helsinki play FC Jokerit at the new Finnair Stadium. Jokerit won 3–0. After the match, I sat on a rocky outcrop at the top of a hill overlooking a park. I thought of Brunnhilde on top of her rocky crag surrounded by a circle of fire and started singing the 'Ride of the Valkyries' to myself. Only it wasn't to myself; there was a man sitting behind me who I hadn't noticed. I turned round and saw him and said Hi, but he just looked at me and gave me a grudging hey hey, the Finnish greeting, and looked away.

Later Kev and I went to a bar and met two blokes, a bankrupt biodynamic herb gardener and his boyfriend, a sex therapist. They'd decided to give up all they had in Helsinki and go to live miles from anywhere growing herbs biodynamically on the strength of a Tarot reading. They took us to a Finnish Tango Club, a gay Finnish Tango Club, in a poky suite of rooms in a block just by the Hotel Torni. Here a mixed crowd of young, old, gay, straight and undecided dance tangos (and the Finnish version of the tango) to records made by Olavi Virta, their pre-eminent home-grown tango star, a man with an unbelievably beautiful voice who died, forgotten, of drink in the sixties. We loved it there; it was so strange and oddly enchanting, with portly fifty-year-olds dancing beautifully to this passionately Latin music and mad Finnish words.

In the morning we went to the Lutheran Cathedral for Pentecost. Bach Prelude and Fugue on arrival, a good choir singing Sibelius, and a service which made me want to be a Lutheran. Plain, unfussy liturgy with the reading from Acts in English by a Roman Catholic priest, supported by an Orthodox priest and the cathedral clergy. Good to have a reading about the Holy Spirit making foreign languages intelligible in English instead of Finnish. I left early and went back to the hotel to get Kev up and we caught the twelve o'clock hydrofoil to Tallinn. On board, we met a party of older women who turned out to be from the Scottish Wagner Society. They were all fascinated by Kevin's Keith Haring tattoos and came up to ask him shyly if they could see them. Tallinn is unbelievably beautiful; a Hansa port and it looks like one, Stockholm more than anything, but untouched by development, at least until independence in 1991.

It is the 217th anniversary of the death of Casanova. Born in Venice in 1725, the son of a dancer and an actress, he was afflicted by nosebleeds which his mother sought to heal through the intercession of a witch. This was unsuccessful and his parents tired of him, sending him away at the age of nine to a boarding house in Padua. He never forgave them, and moved in with a priest who taught him the fiddle – and he fiddled around too with the priest's sister; his romantic career had begun at the age of eleven. He was a brilliant scholar and studied law at university but got into debt gambling and had to run away to Venice, where he became a canon lawyer. He was constantly getting into trouble for dallying with his powerful patrons' daughters and nieces and servant girls, and kept having to scarper. A short spell in a seminary ended when he dallied with a cardinal's nieces, though not before he sought (unsuccessfully) in an audience with the Pope a dispensation from eating fish, which he found unappetising. He then became a soldier, but had to pack that in when he lost all his money playing cards; then a professional gambler, but kept losing; then a violinist, but that did not last either. Eventually, he had some success as a sort of occult physician, having saved the life of a senator poisoned by mercury; for a while he enjoyed the senator's grateful patronage – until he blew it all again through gambling and sexual extravagance and had to flee after an accusation of rape was made against him.

He lived abroad for some years, in Paris and in Dresden (where he bumped into his mother) and Prague and Vienna, but on his return to Venice was arrested for heresy and moral turpitude and sentenced by the Doge to five years in the infamous and impregnable prison known as The Leads, from which he promptly escaped, leaving behind a note quoting Psalm 118: 'I shall not die, but live, and declare the works of the Lord.' He ended up in Paris where he became a famous mountebank, until he met his match in the notorious impostor the Count de Saint-Germain, who claimed to be three hundred years old and had the power to create diamonds. On the run again, pursued by debtors, worn out with lechery, he visited the monastery of Einsiedeln in Switzerland and was about to enter the novitiate when he met a girl and all that was forgotten. Further misadventures occurred; in Paris, where he fell out with a powerful marquise having told her he could turn her into a young man; in England, where he was much enervated by venereal disease; and then on, ever on, to St Petersburg and Belgium and back to Paris, where he met Benjamin Franklin at a balloon demonstration.

By now rather haggard and broken as a consequence of his enormities, he surrendered to the undying love of a seamstress called Francesca who moved in and took care of him and they ended up in Prague, where he met Mozart and became a librarian before dying at the age of seventy-four. Reconciled to the Church and fortified by her sacraments, his last words were, 'I have lived as a philosopher and I die as a Christian.' Prince Charles de Ligne, who thought him the most interesting man he had ever met, said in summary:

> The only things about which he knows nothing are those which he believes himself to be expert: the rules of the dance, the French language, good taste, the way of the world, savoir vivre. He is sensitive and generous, but displease him in the slightest and he is unpleasant, vindictive, and detestable. He believes in nothing except what is most incredible, being super-stitious about everything. He loves and lusts after everything.

*

I am in early to do Pause for Thought on the Chris Evans show on Radio Two. I make my way over from the *Saturday Live* office in New Broadcasting House to Western House round the corner, where Chris's studio is on the top floor. You can always tell the star wattage on the show by the number of autograph collectors gathered round the door, and today they are so many the security guard on duty has put up a couple of crash barriers, to which they flock like swallows to a telephone line, even though there is plenty of room to either side. Perhaps it feels polite to form a crush. I stop and say hello to a few I have known now for thirty years, since I first started appearing on *Loose Ends* when Ned Sherrin was the presenter. Inside, I take the uncomfortably small lift to the sixth floor and the studio, where Chris is sitting behind the desk talking to a man with an improbably gravelly voice. Another man, looking like he had got up for this too early, was sitting in his hat and coat, and I slid into the seat between them. I thought I recognised the man with the gravelly voice as the actor and director Harvey Fierstein, but actually it was the Hollywood film producer Harvey Weinstein, a very different proposition. As I sat down, I said hello to the man in the hat and coat and he said 'Hello, sir' in reply. It was only at the end, after I had done my piece, that I realised it was George Clooney.

'Who's on the show tomorrow?' one of the autograph collectors asked as I left and, embarrassingly, I could not remember. But they were there next day, fewer than turned out for George Clooney, but every Saturday morning when I leave to get my train home I stop and talk. One of them, whose name I have never managed to catch, has a Super-8 camera, rarest of devices now, for which he bought as much film stock as he could when the format began to disappear into history. 'Why stick with Super-8?' I once asked, and he told me that he had been filming celebrities on it since the fifties, and has footage of everyone from Frank Sinatra to Adele. His favourite film he took years ago in the gardens next to the Savoy Hotel, where Warner Brothers were putting up their most famous stars on a publicity trip to London. He has sixty seconds of Fred Astaire, Cyd Charisse and Cary Grant sitting winsomely on a bench.

Driving back at about five, I chose to go up Willoughby Road and over the Maud Foster Drain at Rawsons Lane to avoid town-centre traffic. So did a lot of other people and we had to queue to get onto the little bridge. I got over it and was waiting at the junction with Horncastle Road, cars behind, cars coming from Horncastle turning left and cars coming from Boston turning right, so nobody was going anywhere. Then I noticed the lady in the car at the head of the queue waiting to turn right, gesticulating. I thought at first she was singing along to the radio but realised that she was absolutely screaming with anger. I then realised she was screaming with anger at me. She was middle-aged and well dressed and in a red hatchback, but she looked deranged with fury. It threw me: I couldn't see what I'd done wrong and if I had done anything wrong it was out of proportion to her reaction. I looked puzzled and pointed dead ahead, indicating that I wanted to cross over Horncastle Road and that was why I was where I was, on my side of the road, not trespassing in her space. She completely lost it in a way which was both annoying – what's your problem? – and ridiculous: I couldn't hear what she was shouting, so her criticism was lost on me. I crossly gestured back and turned left to get out of the way and everything moved on. But it stayed with me for the rest of the evening.

It is the anniversary of the Wardsend Cemetery Riot in Sheffield. The cemetery at Wardsend (originally World's End and believed by locals to be the scene where Christ's triumphant return in glory would take place) was consecrated by the Archbishop of York in 1859 on land bought by the Reverend John Livesey, vicar of the parish of St Philip, to provide more burial space for the rapidly expanding population of the parish as the Industrial Revolution transformed the city. They built a chapel, and a house for the sexton, and it was the only cemetery to have a railway line running through it. First to be buried there was a little girl called Ann Marie Marsden, who is, in keeping with tradition, the 'Guardian of the Cemetery'. Unfortunately, she seems to have rather failed in her duties, as accusations were made that the vicar and his sexton, Isaac Howard, were not burying bodies but selling them to the city's medical school for use in anatomical dissections, a common anxiety during the expansion of Victorian cities as demand for graves outstripped supply.

Disquiet grew, and on the evening of 3 June 1862 a crowd gathered at the cemetery and there was a tremendous riot. The sexton's house was burned down, the Howards only just escaping with their lives, and graves were opened by families to see that their loved ones were actually buried there, before order was restored. Obliged to stand down, the vicar and Mr Howard were eventually found to be innocent of the charge of bodysnatching but guilty of reusing graves; they were convicted and fined by York Assizes, and sent to prison. Both men were later pardoned by Queen Victoria and paid compensation. Mr Livesey was reinstated as the Vicar of St Philip's and is commemorated by Livesey Street, which affords access to the back of the greyhound racing track at Owlerton. The cemetery was closed for burials in the 1960s and sadly, despite the sterling efforts of a preservation society, is now neglected and greatly threatened by Japanese knotweed.

*

Our preacher this morning at Solemn Mass for Pentecost began thus: 'I think I was about three years old when I first encountered the friends of Dorothy . . .' He went on to compare the gifts of courage, intelligence and heart to the incomparable gift of the Spirit, Our Lord, but the organist played an improvisation on 'Somewhere Over the Rainbow' during the offertory. In our coded world this got a few laughs, although I sometimes think it is participating in the game of our enemies. It seems a retrograde step after twenty years in what began as gay liberation and became gay normalisation; although not in the Church, where to be gay continues to be a complex matter of concealment and disguise. 'Do you have to be so in-your-face about it?' someone asked me a while ago, which really means 'I don't want to know about it.' I am not sure if this is a visceral reaction to the things that gay men are believed to do, or an example of the Church being unable to cope with things it cannot control. Sometimes I think it is just a dislike of anything slightly upsetting – which obliges a rethink of the vicar, a questioning of one's own assumptions and attitudes – a very Church of England distaste for anything, in my father's disapproving words, 'a bit weird'.

PENTECOST

Pentecost, known also as Whit in English tradition, completes the movement begun on Ascension Day. Jesus goes up, the Holy Spirit comes down, to provide us with the necessary gifts for salvation and the assurance of God's continuing presence. Among those gifts, traditionally, is glossolalia – the gift of tongues. On a YouTube clip a young man, praying in the spirit, suddenly switches from American English to another tongue, a language given by God, yet unrecognisable to man. *Sarrividikidorra badedurkonoshofee . . .* If you're not used to glossolalia, it can be disconcerting, but it is a very common feature of Christian discipleship. At the end of the Gospel of Mark, Jesus appears to the disciples and tells them that his followers will speak with new tongues; in the first letter to the Corinthians Paul discusses speaking in 'various kinds of tongues'; and, most famously, in the second chapter of the Acts of the Apostles, the Holy Spirit descends on the disciples at Pentecost and they begin to speak in other languages, as the Spirit gives them the ability.

A friend of mine, a recovering evangelical (in his words), remembers being invited to pray in the Spirit, and receiving the gift of tongues. After a hesitant and self-conscious start, he found himself suddenly carried away, eloquent in a language he'd never heard before, an experience which left him elated, ecstatic. It was electrifying, it transformed his life.

Today, looking back from a position of sympathetic scepticism, he regards speaking in tongues not simply as a youthful excess of zeal but as a technique for firing up emotional circuits that the more staid forms of worship cannot reach. It is exciting, it is momentous, it carries one away.

However, the Spirit's gifts are not only for young men prophesying and seeing visions, as Acts has it, but for old men dreaming their dreams too.

Like most monastic communities, Mirfield has become, in the past thirty years or so, a place of old men, and there are not enough novices coming in to sustain its life in its present form. Fifty years ago the novitiate was full, the monastery was full, and so were its daughter houses in London and South Africa and its Retreat House in Cambridgeshire and its hostel in Leeds. Today there's only the community and the college, and the future for both is uncertain.

All futures are uncertain; visiting, I was not struck by a sense of gathering crisis, rather by an atmosphere of business as usual. The great monastic church was closed, for reordering, so services were happening in the refectory, with polystyrene tiles overhead and, beneath the pungent top notes of incense, an ineradicable odour of cabbage. But the plainchant went on, the daily offering of God's praises, not *sarrividikidorra*, but the bus come round again, picking us up and dropping us off, sticking to the timetable.

No tongues of fire, no rushing winds, no exaltation. Another evangelical friend took me to a charismatic do and grew impatient with what he took to be aloofness on my part. 'Why can't you just join in?' he asked. Because if I did, I'd be faking it, I thought; but I said nothing and to show willing when he burst into tongues, I silently mouthed 'Pugh, Pugh, Barney McGrew, Cuthbert, Dibble and Grub', which was all I could think of in the ecstasy of the moment.

Monks, cloistered creatures, don't do cocktail parties. The art of small talk withers in monasteries, so the launch of a fundraising appeal was not looked forward to with great anticipation by many of the brethren. I was wondering if there'd be much in the way of progress to report when I went up. I called in on the Superior, just back from the United States on a fundraising trip. I couldn't think of anyone less likely to relish the prospect of standing in a room full of strangers, far from home, in the middle of an economic crisis, rattling the poor box. So how did it go?

He had really enjoyed it. I must have looked surprised, for he went on to tell me that the whole community was enjoying the fundraising process because it had obliged them to think about what they're for, to make sense of themselves. They were rediscovering a sense of purpose, and renewal. Something was again at work among them.

At church today, during the recessional hymn, the boat boy stuck out his tongue at a woman in a pew as he went by.

When guests arrive for *Saturday Live*, at an unusually early hour for a weekend, they are met at Main Reception and brought up to the fifth floor of New Broadcasting House, a reverse curve in glass and steel in answer to the Portland stone prow of Old Broadcasting House. There they are taken to the Green Room, really a sort of guest parking bay where parsimonious hospitality provides some limp pastries and the kind of coffee that comes out of a vacuum flask with a pump handle. There is sometimes an interesting dimension to these pre-programme encounters, because of the mix of the well known and the all but unknown. A household name, wearily practised in the art of media promotion, may spend half an hour sitting next to someone who volunteers at a peculiar library, or went scuba diving with a Soviet-era dictator, or tickles trout. The rapport that almost invariably follows is what makes for a good programme. That unevenness of experience may require a little management; Aasmah Mir, my co-presenter, and I make a point of going to see the guests before they are led into the studio, as a way of making the shift from coffee and croissants to a live studio a little less unnerving for those who have not done it before. Not all are unnerved, but we forget sometimes, being familiar with radio studios, how unusual an environment it is for those who are not.

And there is something ritualised about the shift, the crocodile that forms up as the hour approaches, the procession down a corridor, then through a heavy door, controlled by someone with a pass, and then into the studio, where you are seated in a chair, and connected to pieces of equipment, while being observed by a stranger behind a thick glass window. Dead man walking! I sometimes think as the guests troop in, and I see someone's eyes widen slightly at the sight of these sinister instruments and the thought of the ordeal ahead. Most people, of course, are fine, but some guests are daunted when the green light goes on and it hits them that two million people await the sound of their voice. Once or twice I have seen people fall apart at that moment, unable to form a sentence, or even to speak. Once someone fell asleep while we were on air and when I turned to him to ask a question I saw that he was not really with us and had to kick him under the table.

The readings appointed for Pentecost are from Acts of the Apostles, when the apostles receive the Holy Spirit, and from Genesis, the story of the Tower of Babel; a twofold story, old and new testaments, about communications. The first reading presents language as monolithic, which produces, in turn, a monolith, the Tower. God, in his anger at our imperfection, destroys it and we are scattered across the earth in a Babel of tongues, misunderstanding and misunderstood by each other. The Holy Spirit returns at Pentecost to heal us; tongues of fire dance over the apostles' heads and they suddenly, miraculously, understand each other. But God doesn't restore us to the one original language; he makes us intelligible to each other in our own tongues; human understanding, not perfect regulation, is given. Human understanding is a consequence of perfect regulation; God makes the creation and then retreats from it sufficiently for us to be us in it.

We set off for the Cotswolds and our friend's party straight after church on Pentecost Sunday. Traffic was terrible as usual round

Oxford and I got so impatient at the A40 roundabout I moved forward, looking right, without actually checking to see that the car in front had pulled away. Crunch. I got out and the driver of the car I had hit got out, a young man, but not an angry young man, fortunately. There was no damage, so I gave him my number in case anything came up and we went our separate ways. David said that was like giving someone a slate at their local garage.

Got to our friend's house, so pretty on a perfect early summer day, it was almost unreal. Followed the slow-moving queue of cars into a field where a youth in a tabard directed us, then walked up the road to the house, which is stunningly pretty. It's Tudor, in Cotswold stone and tiles, with a lovely garden, a guest cottage and a tennis court. A band was playing, tables were set for lunch outside, and the garden was already half-full. I sat the whole afternoon eating paella and gossiping.

Later I went for a walk with David, round the back of the garden which gave onto a field. Behind, tennis was happening; in front a village cricket match was half-done. I stood there, Pimm's in hand, thinking 'Aaah, England,' and just then an RAF Hercules took off from Brize Norton and flew low and slow over the scene. I said in a Spart voice, 'And thus we see this whole sickening spectacle is in fact totally a function of the military industrial complex . . . '

Listening to Butterworth's *A Shropshire Lad*, I am struck by how much it sounds like a Bernard Hermann score for an Alfred Hitchcock film, although it was composed in 1912. It's very beautiful, and I've been playing it quite a bit while I work and it's crept into my consciousness so I find I'm anticipating the tune accurately, but the dynamics inaccurately (paying half attention instead of full attention), so when I hum along I suddenly burst out too loud, thinking brass when in fact it's flutes.

Mass for Ascension Day, me as thurifer, and I managed to cense the faithful in so violently flamboyant a way they flinch.

After Mass, David and I went to supper with a retired priest who shot down the often retold story that the former Archbishop of Canterbury, Lord Carey, got the job by mistake. The story has it that the Crown Appointments Committee sent Number 10 the traditional list of two names in the understanding that Mrs Thatcher, like her predecessors, would accept the first name on the list without demur as a matter of convention; just to make sure, they added Carey's name at number two in the knowledge that no one could ever choose him. She did. 'It's a good story, but it's not true,' said my friend. I asked how he knows. 'Because I made it up.' The real reason for Carey's appointment was skilful politics on the part of his supporters.

The politics of Church appointments had shaped his own life too. When he was vicar of a famous parish, a friend who had just been made a dean told him that he'd been informed of his good fortune, not by letter, but by two letters in the same envelope, one from the PM, the other from the PM's Private Secretary; when you get those two letters you know your life is going to change. One Saturday morning, not long after, my friend returned from church and noticed a pile of letters on his secretary's desk. As he flicked through them, he discovered a thick envelope. He opened it, and two more thick envelopes fell out, both embossed on the back: Number 10, Downing Street. At that very moment, as he was holding both envelopes in a trembling hand, one of his curates came in for a chat and he had to stand there making small talk with his future in his hands. 'And I stood there,' he told us, 'listening to this curate going on and on, and the only thing going through my mind was BUGGER OFF! I felt so guilty about it I had to go to chapel and open the letters in front of the Blessed Sacrament.'

Thanks to the looting of Italy by eighteenth-century English aristocrats, at the National Gallery in London we have a depiction of Pentecost by Giotto, a single panel from a predella. It is a small painting showing the disciples, seated in a kind of loggia, tongues of flame over their heads, a dove hovering above. Outside, passers-by listen in. It is the story of the giving of the Holy Spirit.

Not only the episode but the artist, too, is immediately recognisable. Before Giotto, painters were not really thought of as deserving cultural immortality. They were workmen, anonymous, and rather than create in their own image, they did so in what looks like the Byzantine tradition of the East, the tradition of icon painting. Figures were shown in highly formal ways, against stylised backgrounds of buildings and hills and trees. We can see the influence of that tradition in this picture: the architectural setting, formal and centred, the stately composure of the disciples, their heads picked out in golden haloes and surmounted by tongues of red flame; the symmetry of those two passers-by. But there's something radically new and different in Giotto's work. His figures have a liveliness and realism about them that sets them apart from the formal figures familiar in painting up to that time.

He was a Florentine, a contemporary of the great poet Dante, and, like Dante, endlessly fascinated by how human beings behave. There could be few better places or times for such people to live and work than fourteenth-century Florence. It was lively with factionalism and infighting and intrigue and politics and gossip and scandal. In such a place, the formalities of Byzantine painting were transformed, pre-eminently in the work of Giotto, and we see for the first time figures drawn from life, animated and characterful, dressed in clothes that move and yield as they do, and, above, all with faces just as expressive as any you see in the street today.

The bible account merely tells us that the passers-by were amazed to hear those within speaking in different languages so that they could be understood by all; but I don't think these two look amazed, I think they look shifty. They are not overhearing but eavesdropping, ducking down beneath the wall and craning their necks to hear what's going on, like characters in a film. In Dante's *Divine Comedy* the famous and infamous Florentines he encounters would have been known by the poem's readers. Were these figures too recognisable to their contemporaries? Were they two notorious gossips of the day?

The eavesdroppers draw us in, inviting us to be complicit with them, earwigging on what's going on inside. And that for me opens up an absorbing question: what does it mean that the Holy Spirit made everyone suddenly intelligible to one another? I think Giotto finds that question absorbing too and perhaps that's why these two figures, the eavesdroppers, are so arresting, more arresting than the disciples themselves in their dignified polyglot conversation. We, the spectators, don't quite get that far, we're not plugged into a simultaneous translation like representatives at the United Nations. I think we stand with the eavesdroppers on the outside looking in, struggling to understand what's going on.

Is Giotto saying that this is the way the Holy Spirit works, not necessarily by transforming us into something radically new, tuned into a frequency never before heard, lit with unearthly fire and speaking in foreign tongues, but by revealing God's presence and power to us, gossipy, curious, shifty creatures that we are, in our real-life limitations and confusions and self-interest?

EMMAUS

Our last full day in the Holy Land and the attractions of the pilgrim way are beginning to pall slightly. Yesterday's itinerary took us along the Via Dolorosa; stopping for ice creams after Jesus fell the third time, we reached the Church of the Holy Sepulchre, scene of the Crucifixion, by a back entrance that took us around an unvisited edge of this all but edgeless cathedral, so ancient, so organically sited within the maze of the Old City that you cannot tell where the profane ends and the sacred begins. Today, in a concession to our venal natures, we are going shopping, and concluding with a visit to Abu Ghosh, known in the Christian world as Emmaus, about seven miles from Jerusalem, the place to which the disciples were walking in the days after the Crucifixion when they fell in with that mysterious stranger who opened their minds to the Scriptures and was suddenly revealed as Jesus when they broke bread together at supper.

It turns out that we might as well have walked to Emmaus ourselves, because we hit the worst traffic jam I have ever seen in Jerusalem and our tour bus sits unmoving as the minutes tick by, which seems not to bother our demob-happy guide too much, but it bothers me because I really want the pilgrimage to finish here.

Here is an ancient church built on the site where these events are believed to have taken place, now the abbey church for a monastery, a community of French Benedictines in what is nowadays an Arab and Muslim district. Perhaps that experience makes them generous and hospitable; they have given us permission to use their

church for our final Eucharist – not some ramshackle altar round
the back for our unorthodox rite, but the high altar. We are late,
and being Benedictines their hospitality, a charism of the Order,
contends with their regularity, another charism of their Order.
When we arrive, the gate is shut and we stand in the car park outside, wondering what to do. David rings the bell and rings it again
until a monk arrives, wearing white suitable for the climate rather
than the black more often worn by followers of St Benedict, which
sets off the rising red of his face. Irritation or shortness of breath?
After a brief conversation in which David uses his hilarious French,
the monk admits us, goes to speak to the Abbot, and we are invited
to join the community for Solemn Vespers, the principal service
of the evening – Solemn, marked by the highest degree of ceremony, because it is the Eve of the Annunciation, one of the great
festivals of the Church. After that, we may celebrate our Eucharist.
We wait outside in the monastery's beautiful garden and someone
announces that one of our number is not feeling well, though she
does not complain, so maybe we should go home? I ignore this.

We are let in to the church, built by the Crusaders in a different
age, with a stone throne for the Abbot behind the altar and then
the choir stalls where the community sits and stands and sings and
prays. There are ancient frescoes on the walls, one of them a Crucifixion, with Jesus on the cross at its centre, and then on either side
the two thieves, Cosmas and Dismas. The fresco is so damaged you
cannot see their faces, only the outline where they would have been.
We sit in the aisles in silence, detuning from the traffic jam and one
another, and tuning in to the silence, which is rich and deep, and
then broken by the tiny swishing sound of the community arriving in procession, led by nuns, the Benedictine sisters with whom
they share this place, in a different habit and veiled, with black
African faces among the white European faces. The monks follow
and finally the Abbot in a cope and mitre. Instead of an organ,
the accompaniment to the chant is played on a sort of cimbalom;
it's a fragile, very beautiful sound, transparent and open-textured,

through which the chant flows like water. The psalms are followed by readings from Scripture, given in the measured, quiet, slow way of this tradition, so different from the hectoring dramas we often hear in churches now, as if the stories need everything you have got in order to penetrate. There is a period in the service when prayers of intercession are offered, addressed to God and carrying the concerns of the community and its individual members. This is led by a monk, who says out loud a series of short petitions to which there is a sung response.

And then they do something completely unexpected. Each member of the community offers his or her own prayers, for people, for things, but does so by singing them rather than saying them. It begins as a sort of jumble of sounds, neither in time nor in tune; but then come together and form harmonies, then peel away and reform in different harmonies, rising and falling in volume and in different rhythms, which cross and re-cross but find each other again in the incense-thickened air, coiling up to the vault and out into the street, noisy with traffic, and the call to prayer, and the throng.

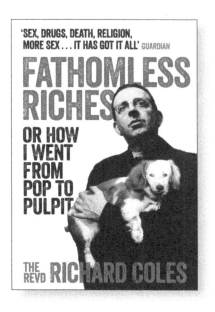

'He's the best vicar ever' Caitlin Moran

Fathomless Riches is the Reverend Richard Coles's warm, witty and wise memoir in which he divulges with searing honesty his pilgrimage from a rock-and-roll life in the Communards to one devoted to God and Christianity. The result is one of the most unusual and readable life stories of recent times, and has the power to shock as well as to console.

'Beautifully written, disarmingly frank and utterly charming'
Mail on Sunday